HIGH TECH START UP

The Complete How-To Handbook for Creating Successful New High Tech Companies

JOHN L. NESHEIM

Saratoga, CA

High Tech Startup: The Complete How-To Handbook for Creating Successful New High Tech Companies

Production Coordination: Fritz/Brett Associates
Typography and Page Layout: Nicholas J. Vitale
Jacket and Cover Design: Dan Andersen
Editing: Elaine Brett
Proofreading: Karla Zee
Indexing: Elaine Brett

Library of Congress Cataloging-in-Publication Data

Nesheim, John L., 1942-
    High tech startup / John L. Nesheim.
        p.   cm.
    Includes bibliographical references and index.
    ISBN 0-914405-71-3
    1. New business enterprises. 2. High technology industries.
  3. Venture capital. I. Title.
  HD62.5.N47 1992
  620'.0068—dc 20   91-29695
                                                 CIP

4 5 6 7 8 9   97 98 99 00 01

ISBN 0-914405-71-3

CONTENTS

Preface

Why bother trying to help more entrepreneurs succeed?

Too many new businesses fail to become successful, including high tech startups. If we could improve the proportion of successes, the economic benefits stagger the mind.

In *The Winning Performance*, Clifford and Cavanaugh (1985) say that "If just 1% of the companies in existence today had had the will and the skill to reach midsize—$25 million in sales—the American economy would be more than double its current size."

The typical venture-backed high tech startup has a 60 percent likelihood of going bankrupt. What are the areas in which startups need help, and what are the payoffs for helping them?

- *High cost of capital.* Venture capital investors are experienced at taking high risks and require high returns. Most founders are not.

- *Scarce management.* Competent startup managements are scarcer than good ideas. Most qualified managers are naïve about raising venture capital.

- *Business plans are poor.* Venture capitalists said they were neck-deep in new business plans, very few of which were well written—let alone worth being read, and fewer still deserved to be financed.

- *Financial rewards can be very large.* A CEO of a successful startup can become worth $6 million in five years.

- *Increased competition between more numerous, similar startups.* With billions of dollars at work in venture capital pools, there is increased competition between startups in any given business sector.

- *Big companies react more quickly.* Billion-dollar companies detect and act on business opportunities faster, competing with startups.

This book is intended to help the leader of a high tech startup improve his or her odds of success. It also aims to help the corporate venture capitalist evaluate startup candidates for acquisition, as well as the new "internal startups" that are emerging.

We will analyze successful and unsuccessful high tech startups and the techniques their managements use to start, finance, value, and launch a new business from seed financing through initial public offering, and we will provide data on the financial rewards of equity ownership and dilution by venture capitalists of famous high tech startups.

This book has six goals:

1. *To prepare the CEO for the surprises yet to come.*
2. *To prepare the CEO for negotiations.* "How much is my company worth, and why?"

3. *To make clear the personal cost of leading a startup.*

4. *To improve the CEO's odds of success.*

5. *To help corporate development managers work with new ventures.*

6. *To help new venture capitalist partners and associates get off to a running start.*

Conventions and Practices Used in This Book

Most case studies use disguised names. Each case is based on actual events. Research for this book was conducted over a period of six years, during which more than 300 interviews were done with over 180 individuals in more than 120 companies in the United States.

Preface 2: The Internet Era

How different is the Internet era for entrepreneurs? Our recent research shows some significant differences:

- *Things happen a lot faster.* Internet time is in months. It used to be in years. Projects must be completed in a few months and be profitable very quickly.

- *Things happen a lot slower.* Venture investors, burned by rushing and their excesses in the past, have tripled the time they take to investigate startups ("due diligence"). Nine months is common. This is frustrating to founders. It is often fatal to naïve startup leaders.

- *Initial public offering valuations for "pure play" Internet stocks are astronomical.* Story stocks are back in. Speculative fever has moved to Internet stocks. The historically high valuation ratios are keeping investors sitting very close to the exits.

- *Big corporations have gotten very good at creating competitive new enterprises.* Whether spun out ("spin-outs") or retained ("spin-ins"), the new ventures are growing, many of them successfully. Phantom stock has returned. Dreams of riches are stalking the halls of Fortune 100 companies once again.

- *Everyone has many strategic partners, quickly aligned, and a business model that requires them.*

Otherwise, all the prior lessons still apply. The following tables are examples of two famous Internet era startups on the day of their initial public offering. More can be found at the end of this book and at www.startupweb.com.

SARATOGA VENTURE FINANCE EQUITY TABLE
WAGES AND STOCK OWNERSHIP AT INITIAL PUBLIC OFFERING

Netscape Communications Corporation

Internet software		State of Incorporation: Delaware
Mountain View, California	Initial Public Offering (IPO) date: August 5, 1995	Date of Inception: April 1994
Price per Share $28.00	Company Value: $1,068,520,432	Years from inception to IPO: 1.3
Stock symbol NSCP	Internet URL: http://home.netscape.com	

f = Founder / D=Director		(4) Est 12 Mos Comp	(3B) Officers' Ownership	(3),(6),(7) Mgt & Emps Ownership	(1) Pre IPO Ownership	(2) Post IPO Ownership	(3B) Officers' Ownership	(3),(6),(7) Mgt & Emps Ownership	(1) Pre IPO Ownership	(2) Post IPO Ownership	IPO Value Per Share $28.00
fD Chairman	James H. Clark	$0	56.1%	41.2%	30.0%	25.5%	9,720,000	9,720,000	9,720,000	9,720,000	$272,160,000
D Pres, CEO	James L. Barksdale	$0	23.1%	17.0%	12.3%	10.5%	4,000,000	4,000,000	4,000,000	4,000,000	$112,000,000
fD VP Technology	Marc L. Andreessen		5.8%	4.2%	3.1%	2.6%	1,000,000	1,000,000	1,000,000	1,000,000	$28,000,000
VP Engineering	Richard M. Schell	$80,000	2.3%	1.7%	1.2%	1.0%	400,000	400,000	400,000	400,000	$11,200,000
VP Marketing	Michael J. Homer	$215,000	1.7%	1.3%	0.9%	0.8%	300,000	300,000	300,000	300,000	$8,400,000
VP Sales & Field Ops	Conway Rulon-Miller	$225,000	2.3%	1.7%	1.2%	1.0%	400,000	400,000	400,000	400,000	$11,200,000
VP GM Integrated Apps	James C.J. Sha	$200,000	3.5%	2.5%	1.9%	1.6%	600,000	600,000	600,000	600,000	$16,800,000
VP CFO	Peter L. S. Currie		1.7%	1.3%	0.9%	0.8%	300,000	300,000	300,000	300,000	$8,400,000
VP Gen Counsel & Sec	Roberta R. Katz		1.7%	1.3%	0.9%	0.8%	300,000	300,000	300,000	300,000	$8,400,000
VP Human Resources	Kandis Malefyt		1.7%	1.3%	0.9%	0.8%	300,000	300,000	300,000	300,000	$8,400,000
OFFICERS & EXECUTIVES			100.0%	73.4%	53.4%	45.4%	17,320,000	17,320,000	17,320,000	17,320,000	$484,960,000
ALL OTHER COMMON				21.1%	15.4%	13.0%		4,976,328	4,976,328	4,976,328	$139,337,184
TOTAL COMMON BEFORE OPTIONS				94.5%	68.8%	58.4%		22,296,328	22,296,328	22,296,328	$624,297,184
OPTIONS-Outstanding				3.6%	2.6%	2.2%		855,000	855,000	855,000	$23,940,000
OPTIONS-Available				1.9%	1.4%	1.2%		443,672	443,672	443,672	$12,422,816
OPTIONS-Total				5.5%	4.0%	3.4%		1,298,672	1,298,672	1,298,672	$36,362,816
TOTAL-Executives and employees				100.0%	72.8%	61.8%		23,595,000	23,595,000	23,595,000	$660,660,000
Investors (includes major venture capital; excludes management as investors)					27.2%	23.1%			8,816,444	8,816,444	$246,860,432
Other Investors					0.0%	0.0%			0	0	$0
TOTAL-Investors Preferred & Other (shares, options & warrants)					27.2%	23.1%			8,816,444	8,816,444	$246,860,432
PRE-IPO: sum of all stock					100.0%	84.9%			32,411,444	32,411,444	$907,520,432
Initial Public Offering-New shares sold						13.1%				5,000,000	$140,000,000
Option to underwriters						2.0%				750,000	$21,000,000
TOTAL OUTSTANDING including Options & warrants						100.0%				38,161,444	$1,068,520,432

Vesting for Incentive Stock Option Plans is usually over 50 months after 10 month wait period.

CPA firm	Ernst & Young
Lead Underwriters	Morgan Stanley / Hambrecht & Quist
Counsel for Company	Wilson Sonsini
Counsel for Underwriters	Morrison & Foerster
Outside Directors	Kleiner Perkins - John Doerr; Adobe - John E. Warnock

IPO Total cash raised before fees and expenses		$140,000,000	
Paid to underwriters	Less:	$9,800,000	7.0%
CPA and other related expenses	Less:	$900,000	0.6%
	Net:	$129,300,000	92.4%
Shares sold by company		5,000,000	100%
Shares sold by selling shareholders		0	0%
Total shares sold in this offering		5,000,000	100%
Option to underwriters		750,000	15%

REVENUE $M Last 6 Months	REVENUE $M Prior Quarter
$16.6	$11.9
Growth/Year NM	Growth/Year NM
Nr employees: 257	

SARATOGA VENTURE FINANCE EQUITY TABLE
WAGES AND STOCK OWNERSHIP AT INITIAL PUBLIC OFFERING

Internet software
Sunnyvale, California
Price per Share $13.00
Stock symbol: YHOO

Yahoo! Inc.
Initial Public Offering (IPO) date: April 12, 1996
Company value $481,458,874
Internet URL: http://www.yahoo.com

State of Incorporation: California
Date of Inception: March 1995
Years from Inception to IPO: 1.1

f = Founder / D=Director		(4) Comp	(3B) Officers' Ownership	(3),(6),(7) Mgt & Emps Ownership	(1) Pre IPO Ownership	(2) Post IPO Ownership	(3B) Officers' Ownership	(3),(6),(7) Mgt & Emps Ownership	(1) Pre IPO Ownership	(2) Post IPO Ownership	IPO Value $13.00 Per Share
D Pres. CEO	Timothy Koogle	$68,750	11.4%	5.5%	3.0%	2.8%	1,025,510	1,025,510	1,025,510	1,025,510	$13,331,630
fD Chief Yahoo	Jerry Yang	$65,000	44.3%	21.3%	11.8%	10.8%	4,003,750	4,003,750	4,003,750	4,003,750	$52,048,750
f Chief Yahoo	David Filo	$65,000	44.3%	21.3%	11.8%	10.8%	4,003,750	4,003,750	4,003,750	4,003,750	$52,048,750
Sr VP Business Ops	Jeff Mallett		NA	NA	NA	NA	NA	NA	NA	NA	NA
Sr VP, CFO	Gary Valenzuela		NA	NA	NA	NA	NA	NA	NA	NA	NA
Sr VP Product Devel	Farzad Nazem		NA	NA	NA	NA	NA	NA	NA	NA	NA
OFFICERS & EXECUTIVES		100.0%	48.1%	26.5%	24.4%		9,033,010	9,033,010	9,033,010	9,033,010	$117,429,130
ALL OTHER COMMON				6.6%	3.6%	3.3%		1,231,716	1,231,716	1,231,716	$16,012,308
TOTAL COMMON BEFORE OPTIONS				54.7%	30.2%	27.7%		10,264,726	10,264,726	10,264,726	$133,441,438
OPTIONS-Outstanding				25.8%	14.2%	13.1%		4,834,868	4,834,868	4,834,868	$62,853,284
OPTIONS-Available				19.5%	10.8%	9.9%		3,665,132	3,665,132	3,665,132	$47,646,716
OPTIONS-Total				45.3%	25.0%	23.0%		8,500,000	8,500,000	8,500,000	$110,500,000
TOTAL-Executives and employees				100.0%	55.1%	50.7%		18,764,726	18,764,726	18,764,726	$243,941,438
Investors (includes major venture capital; excludes management as investors)					15.9%	14.6%			5,415,344	5,415,344	$70,399,472
Other Investors					29.0%	26.6%			9,865,228	9,865,228	$128,247,964
TOTAL-Investors Preferred & Other (shares, options & warrants)					44.9%	41.3%			15,280,572	15,280,572	$198,647,436
PRE-IPO: sum of all stock					100.0%	91.9%			34,045,298	34,045,298	$442,588,874
Initial Public Offering-New shares sold						7.0%				2,600,000	$33,800,000
Option to underwriters						1.1%				390,000	$5,070,000
TOTAL OUTSTANDING including Options & warrants						100.0%				37,035,298	$481,458,874

Vesting for Incentive Stock Option Plans is usually over four years.

IPO Total cash raised before fees and expenses		$33,800,000	100%
Paid to underwriters	Less:	$2,366,000	7.0%
CPA and other related expenses	Less:	$700,000	2.1%
	Net:	$30,734,000	90.9%
Shares sold by company		2,600,000	100%
Shares sold by selling shareholders		0	0%
Total shares sold in this offering		2,600,000	100%
Option to underwriters		390,000	15%

CPA firm	Lead Underwriters
Price Waterhouse	Goldman Sachs
	Donaldson Lufkin
	Montgomery

Counsel for Company	Counsel for Underwriters
Venture Law Group	Wilson Sonsini

Outside Directors
Sequoia Capital, Michael Moritz; Ziff-Davis, Eric Hippeau; American Media, Arthur Kern

Source: Saratoga Venture Finance © All rights reserved. See prospectus for data. The above contain certain estimates.

REVENUE $M Last 6 Months $1.4	REVENUE $M Prior Quarter $1.1
Growth/Year NM	Growth/Year NM
Nr employees: 49	

1

Introduction to Startups and Their Funding

The research on which this book is based provided a lot of data about startups, their probability of success, and how they are typically organized. Let's begin with 31 facts about typical high tech startups—many of them contrary to popular stereotypes.

1. The chances are 6 in 1,000,000 that an idea for a high tech business eventually becomes a successful company that goes public.

2. Fewer than 10 percent of the funded startups go public.

3. Founder CEOs own less than 4 percent of their high tech companies after the initial public offering.

4. Founder CEOs can expect their stock to be worth about $6,500,000 if the company succeeds in going public.

5. Successful venture capitalists expect to personally earn about $7,000,000 (in addition to cash wages) over five years for each $50,000,000 pool of capital they share in managing.

6. Business plans are typically poor and are not well received by venture capitalists.

7. "Unfair advantage" and "sustainable competitive advantage" are missing in most business plans—but are considered by investors to be critical if the high tech startup is to have an acceptable chance of succeeding. Plans lacking such an advantage rarely receive venture funding from experienced, successful venture capitalists.

8. On the average, a venture capitalist finances only 6 out of every 1000 business plans received each year.

9. Venture capital investors own 70 percent of the startup just before it goes public.

10. The personal costs of doing a startup are high, affecting families and friends as well as individuals. Fear and burnout are common. However, those costs must be balanced with the rewards of personal and professional satisfaction and the potential financial paybacks, which can be more gratifying than the rewards of working for a large corporation.

11. Bankruptcies occur for 60 percent of the high tech companies that succeed in getting venture capital.

12. Mergers or liquidations occur in 30 percent of startup companies.

13. A vice president's stock is worth about $2,000,000 at the time of the initial public offering.

14. The average worth of the stock for all employees (not including vice presidents and other top managers) on the date of the initial public offering is about $100,000.

15. Investors in venture capital pools aim to earn in excess of 22 percent each year on their money, about 8 percent more than if they had invested in all the stocks of the companies making up the Standard and Poors 500 company index.

16. The 10 percent of the startups that succeed compensate for the other 90 percent of the companies in the venture capitalist's investment portfolio. In essence, the successful founders are paying for the substandard performance or bankruptcies of the bad investments.

17. Cash compensation for U.S. startup managements remains below levels offered by larger corporations in spite of the scarcity of startup talent and tax law reductions in the United States.

18. The median starting salary for a founder CEO in 1990 was about $120,000. Cash bonuses based on the company exceeding its business plan increase that to $155,000 by the time the company goes public.

19. The vice president of sales in a startup often earns more cash compensation than the CEO. This occurs when incentive compensation plans are linked to sales that exceed those of the business plan.

20. Of the startups that get to an initial public offering, the median company takes at least three and typically five years to get to the public offering stage. That is an increase of more than a year over the waiting period experienced during the 1980s decade of startups.

21. Equipment lease financing and leasing of facilities and leasehold improvements have proven to be reliable and competitively priced sources of capital to augment equity raised to finance a startup.

22. Having a talented CEO as a founder greatly increases the chances of getting a startup funded. A close second is having a complete management team ready to go to work, with experienced people for each of the key functions.

23. Over $40 billion was committed to pools of venture capital in 1990. It was managed by more than 2000 actively venturing individuals in over 500 firms.

24. Competition between venture capital firms has increased sharply since 1983, causing the pendulum to begin to swing back in favor of the entrepreneur. Since 1987, the venture pool has produced underperforming portfolios, resulting in a survival-of-the-fittest mentality as general partners leave the venture business. However, whatever the trend, venture capitalists still end up owning the vast majority of the stock of a startup, typically in excess of two-thirds of the company.

25. Mergers and acquisitions of startups increase when the market for initial public offerings cools off.

26. Investors' interest in new issues rises and falls depending on the interest of institutional investors in the stocks of public companies traded over the counter, as well as in blue chip stocks traded on the New York Stock Exchange. In general, windows for IPOs open and close, based on whether there is a hot market for stocks in general.

27. Pricing of private rounds of venture capital by investors follows the same financial guidelines and measurements used to price securities of publicly traded companies. Investors translate risks and rewards into acceptable levels of expected return on investment, which becomes the basis for the dilution of founders' shares.

28. Competition for the shares of a startup is the best way to increase its valuation and to reduce dilution for founders. Competition is enhanced by careful planning of the strategy for the capital-raising

campaign. However, such deliberate planning was noticeably absent among founders of high tech companies, especially those started by engineers.

29. The boom venture decade of the 1980s has ended. Gone are portfolios yielding an easy 60 percent compounded return on investment. Venture capitalists cannot count on finding home runs or "wild ones"— which returned 100 percent in three years for monies invested in a Lotus or Apple startup. Portfolios started in 1983 and later are yielding less than 4 or 5 percent. People are exiting the venture business.

30. Mixed sources of venture funding are a way of life. As the number of classical venture firms eager to fund high tech startups shrank, a need and opportunity was created for funds from other sources. An increasing proportion of the share of the financial market for venture funds is being taken over by corporate funds, foreign sources, wealthy individuals called "angels" and "49ers," as well as by family funding and bootstrap deals.

31. Internal startups within established corporations are an emerging phenomena; they have allowed emerging growth companies to sponsor an entrepreneurial spirit while retaining an uninterrupted focus on the parent company's bread-and-butter business. For internal startups to be successful, special attention must be paid to the unique characteristics of such new enterprises.

Critical Issues

There are a number of key economic forces driving the venture capital funding of high tech business.

- *ROI—return on investment—drives the startup business.* It is measured in two ways: (1) A crude measure is that of how many times the value of one share invested rises by the time the initial public offering is over. This is called the "multiple." (2) A more sophisticated measure—the only number that really counts—is the annual compounded return, or percent per annum (p.a.), that the general partners in the venture capital firm return to the limited partners, pension funds, university endowments, and so on. To put it another way, how long the limited partners had to wait for the multiple to be returned determines the true percent annual ROI.

- *Cash flow is what is managed.* All the accounting in the world does not matter to the founder who is struggling to meet payroll while launching the startup's first products into a very competitive jungle.

- *The IPO (initial product offering) is the holy grail.* Everyone has their eyes on that final goal. Mergers stand a poor second in attraction, because venture investors can generally negotiate higher valuations for a public issue.
- *Liquidity is everything for the VCs (venture capitalists).* Anyone inhibiting attainment of liquidity quickly learns why VCs have earned a reputation as "vulture capitalists." A business plan must have an acceptable "exit strategy" that converts the investors' shares into cash.

Those are the economic laws that govern a startup. The CEO who understands them will win more often and will survive to savor the grand IPO day.

Venture Competition

Venture capitalists are driven by competing venture firms to maximize their return on investment. The general partners share in about 20 percent of the profits of a pool of money provided primarily by huge institutional funds, such as pension plans for Fortune 100 megagiants and billion-dollar university endowment pools.

If VCs earn a high enough ROI on their first pool of institutional funds, they will have a chance to bid for more. They are competing against the alternatives—such as the stock and bond markets—that are open to institutions. The economic and business factors that drive stocks and bonds also drive the VCs, and therefore must drive the startup CEO.

Venture Money Surge Leads to Problems

Venture capital projects have been a successful way of investing institutional money over long periods of time (10 to 12 years). But with success, more money has followed. This in turn has led to serious competition between pools of venture capital. Since the surge of funds began in 1984, there has been a dramatic alteration of the risk-reward ratio for high tech startups.

The *Venture Capital Journal* reported that during the ten years since 1977, the total of annual additions to venture capital partnership pools rose 15 times, from a rate of about $200 million per year to more than $3 billion annually. This was especially noticeable over the four years from 1983 to 1987. This surge of money looking for investments has in turn sharply increased the number of new business plans created in a given year by people proposing startups.

The surge in business plans has increased the competition among startups that aim their technology at the same new perceived market opportunities. One example is the personal computer disk drive business, which boomed in 1984 and then went bust along with many startups. Another example is the minisupercomputer market; Convex and Alliant made it to IPO, but veteran venture capitalist partners say that another dozen companies or so were floating around at the same time the managers of those two founding groups were knocking on doors seeking seed rounds of venture capital. File server companies started in the late 1980s may be the next wave.

Another effect of the success of venture capital investing is that big corporations have vastly improved their ability to see, decide, and act on new market opportunities. The giants have begun to invest their own "corporate venture capital." Since 1981, the number of acquisitions of venture-backed companies has more than tripled. And pioneering managements of established high tech companies have invented a new form of internal venture capitalism dubbed "internal startups." These have attracted top managers and proven to be successful in competing for already scarce high tech talent.

Result: Dilution, More Risk, Less Stock, Lots of Work

All of the forces just mentioned have increased the risk of failure of a high tech startup. Perhaps the cutbacks during the early 1990s in fresh funds fueling venture capital pools will alter this situation. Few if any other trends have emerged to offset this increased risk. Accordingly, investors have been following a trend of requiring higher and higher returns on the monies they have invested on behalf of their institutional clients. This means that less wealth is available to be shared by the founder and employees.

In modern portfolio terms, these trends have sharply raised the cost of capital for the startup. In more ordinary parlance, the founders have to give up a lot more of their companies today than they used to, particularly since the boom days of 1983 when startups such as Altos, Ashton-Tate, Microsoft, and Televideo went into business and retained 80 percent or more of their stock for employees and founders.

The amount of stock given up by founders is spelled out in Chapter 7 in detailed tables for a number of famous startups. Research of Securities and Exchange Commission (SEC) documents by Saratoga Venture Finance revealed that CEO founders should expect to get to IPO owning not much more than 3 percent of their companies. That share of stock will be worth about $6.5 million at that time. They will have to work very hard for four to five years and must have a lot of good fortune and big breaks to be able to cash all their chips in within two years after the IPO. Three years to IPO is rare, five is common.

FIGURE 1-1. Chances of Success for a High Tech Startup

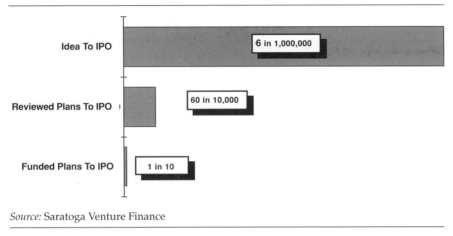

Source: Saratoga Venture Finance

Is a startup worth the personal cost required? That is among the key issues for the CEO considering a startup. Before a would-be founder can answer the personal questions, he or she must focus on another question: "How should I plan and control the venture capital formation process, from seed through multiround financing to IPO so that I have an unfair advantage in getting the funds I need in order to succeed?"

The Everlasting Process of Raising Capital and Other Stresses

The entrepreneur must realize that the process of raising venture capital never ends. From the first to the last of the 14 stages of the venture capital formation process described in detail in Chapter 3, the CEO is continuously occupied with problems of how to raise needed capital. Experienced startup staff members of both successful and unsuccessful companies said the same thing: "You never have enough money, things always take twice as long to do as you think, and there is never enough time to stop raising capital while you focus on running the company."

Analysis of more than 80 successful startups from 1981 to 1987 revealed the extra strains put on a CEO. Stress begins with the wide range of outside professionals—20 categories can be cited—with whom the CEO must be in continuous contact, beginning almost immediately upon launch of the new enterprise. This puts a new kind of pressure on managers whose careers have typically been strictly as "inside" executives. Such managers are usually not experienced at dealing with lawyers, board members, bankers, leasing companies, landlords, Wall Street, and shareholders.

Sources of Capital

The sources of venture capital are varied and often colorful and creative. For example:

- "Bootstraps" like Sigma Designs, Inc. of Fremont, California, get funds from personal savings and friends and relatives.
- "Classics" like Linear Technology of Milpitas, California, raise their monies from the usual VC gang at 3000 Sand Hill Road in Menlo Park, California, and other centers of venture capital such as those in Boston, New York, Dallas, Minneapolis, and Los Angeles.
- "Creative" startups like Chips and Technologies and Worlds of Wonder get money from suppliers, landlords, and business partners who are acquainted with their skills as managers.

There are other unconventional sources of funding. Equipment lease firms like Meier & Mitchell of San Francisco provide substantial funds to augment equity capital of high tech startups, and wealthy individuals continue to emerge as supporters of startups. Megabuck luminaries like Ross Perot are called "angels," and independently wealthy founders of startups are dubbed "49ers"—a term harking back to the gold rush successes in California in the 1849 era. Both represent unofficial pools of funds that go to work backing startups.

And the creative list goes on and on. Later in this book we will provide lists of venture capital sources.

More important than lists are techniques for planning and negotiating with money managers who are responsible for investing venture capital. Details are provided in case studies in later chapters.

Some Findings About Rewards and Risks

Saratoga Venture Finance has carefully dissected the prospectuses of IPOs to extract the facts on the ownership, ROI, and sharing of the wealth among famous high tech startups.

We found that CEO wages ranged widely, from $65,000 per year to $230,000. The median was about $125,000 prior to IPO. The trend in the past few years is for cash compensation to rise as the number of startups has continued to make good management scarce; additional factors affecting this trend are that the 1986 Tax Reform Act has made wages more valuable and equity capital gains less so, and the percentage of ownership by founders has dropped.

Investors dominate ownership; their proportion usually exceeded 70 percent just before the IPO. There was no correlation between percent sold to investors versus the amount of capital raised.

Return on investment of famous VC firms has been slashed since the high point of 50 percent annually that was a "slam dunk" in the boom days of 1978-1983. Kleiner Perkins managed one partnership pool in those days that returned nearly 65 percent p.a. Other funds exceeded even that. In the 1990s, returns like that are just a dream for investors.

In 1987 a portfolio return in excess of 25 percent p.a. would be among the top performers, according to private sources we polled, and average returns were around 17 percent p.a. By 1990, we found that most portfolios had single-digit returns. "The turkeys hatched since 1983 have come home to roost," said one venture capitalist. Some pundits, major VC players themselves, have said that there will be some VC pools that will have lost all the investors' money by the time the partnerships are liquidated.

Over the past two decades, VCs have formed a vision of a "typical" portfolio of investments. About 60 percent of the startups funded by VCs can be expected to go bankrupt. Fewer than 15 percent even get to IPO, and less than 10 percent is typical. Our database shows that 9.7 percent reach IPO. The remainder are either merged into large companies, sold off as "fire sales," or go on eternally as "zombies"—companies too small to get to IPO.

These and many other details about the companies studied are shown in the Saratoga Venture Tables in Appendix A; the tables include wages, options, founders' shares, venture capitalists' multiples earned, and how much the Wall Street firms got in fees to take the startup public.

The Personal Costs

Coping with political power plays is just one of the factors that contribute to the psychological and emotional costs of leading a startup. There are many more, including the effects on the CEO's physical health and family. Some CEOs said they loved it anyway, while others said they hated every minute of it and would never do it again.

Some of our research in this area sharply contradicts popular myths. Here are highlights of what we found:

- *Hours worked per day for startup CEOs are long, but are no more than those worked by an aggressive manager in a growing division of a much larger company.* This surprised us, as it did most of the people we interviewed and analyzed. No one said that a startup was *less* work than their last job as an employee.

- *Terror is a constant companion.* Forbes magazine often says that "Entrepreneurs should run scared." Based on our surveys, they do!

Inc. magazine surveys and testimonials support the belief that fear of failure is a constant companion.

- *Founder CEOs seldom last as employees for more than three years.* This is universally lamented by all parties, including the VCs. We will discuss the reasons and cures later in this book. Silicon Valley psychologists report that few founders make it to the IPO without personal emotional trauma.

- *Burnout and heart attacks, marriage problems and divorces are no more frequent than in other high tech jobs.* Employees of startups may actually be a bit less prone to such problems if the CEO sets a good example of regular exercise, enough sleep, and proper diet, along with a balanced personal life.

- *Honesty and integrity (or a lack of them) are as common as in bigger companies.* Contrary to the expectations of some observers, no evidence could be found that the stress of a startup produced a pattern of especially immoral, or moral, behavior.

Future Trends

Based on the research done by Saratoga Venture Finance, we are willing to make a number of predictions of future trends:

- A shakeout of venture fund managers will continue to occur, leveling out by the mid-1990s.

- The trends of the 1980s indicate a significant slowing of the flow of fresh funds into earliest stages of new ventures. This will continue as surviving VCs spread their investments across all rounds of funding for new enterprises.

- $2 to $3 billion of new venture capital will become available each year, sustaining the $40 billion pool at work in 1990.

- Some funds will never return. Others will diversify more, into low tech and leveraged buyout investments. Offshore investing will be done by several, attempting to get away from intense U.S. venture competition. The remaining VC leaders will converge and dominate.

- Specialization of venture sources will continue: biotech, electronics, and other segments of industry and technology.

- Merger and acquisition activity will rise and fall in cycles that are the reverse of those of the U.S. stock market.

- Business plan screening by VCs will remain generally quite tight. Those that best articulate the unfair advantage of the proposed business will get funded.

- Extra caution by VCs will require CEOs to be better prepared for their launch strategies. A candidate with successful prior experience as a CEO will be sought after first by investors.

- More favor will be placed on deals with complete, first-class, experienced management teams with a long-run or "marketable" CEO in place. Inexperienced teams will find it very difficult to get money.

- Attracting as complete a startup core team as possible will be even more essential to success.

- Corporate venturing will continue, mostly for secondary stage funding. And the corporations will use more "internal venturing" structures.

- Foreign venturing, especially from Europe and Asia, will continue and even accelerate.

- The U.S. IPO market will continue its cyclical strength, subject to ups and downs resulting from excesses and from trends in the broader equity market.

- New overseas markets for IPOs, like London in the 1980s and Taiwan in the 1990s, will emerge and be tested during the remainder of the decade.

- Intense pressures will continue from investors for an exit strategy that gets them liquid within five years of investing.

- VCs will be delighted to invest in deals whose prospects can get investors ten times their money in five years. VCs will compete even more aggressively for cream-of-the-crop deals.

- Investment banking desires for high tech IPOs will not abate, but will result in reshuffling the rankings of the leaders in that intensely competitive business.

- Employers and giant corporations will be more predatory in legal action aimed at preserving company proprietary intellectual property and key employees.

- Tax uncertainties and trends toward more changes in accounting rules make the careful choice of a CPA firm more important in the 1990s.

- A greater percent of ownership will be retained by founders who deliberately plan a capital-raising campaign complete with strategy and alternate sources of venture capital.

- The proportion owned by the CEO will decline a bit over the next decade as intra-VC competition wanes.

- Venture equipment lease firms will continue to bid for financing of the better deals done by the top VC firms.
- CEOs will have more of an opportunity to set an example of a balanced personal life for the startup culture, as the scarcity of qualified CEOs adds to their power.

Strategies and Implementation

This book presents a classic strategy for starting a high tech company and securing multiround financing. The case studies provided in each section were carefully chosen to reveal how the classic strategy can be modified to fit the special objectives of the founding team.

The focus of the book is on how to use ROI as an anchor in developing a startup strategy, especially for pricing each round of venture financing.

The author hopes that the information provided here will allow the CEO to spend more time doing strategic thinking, and finding and improving a sustainable competitive advantage for the company's long-term well being.

If there are fewer failures, more jobs, and better lives as a result, the author will be very satisfied.

Historical Overview

What High Tech Entrepreneurial Capital Formation Is

Startup high tech capital formation is the process that results in sufficient cash to fund the growth of a new enterprise. The entrepreneur should obtain this funding at a price low enough to continue to motivate the personnel talent that is needed to get the work done on time.

- Capital formation is a process.
- The process is ongoing for the startup; it never ends.
- The process must be deliberately planned and managed.
- One measure of whether it is being successfully managed is the financial flexibility or adequacy of funds that the startup survives on during the process.
- Another measure of success is how motivated key employees remain after they learn how much their holdings have been diluted by the latest round of funding.
- A final measure is how much the process has strengthened the company's "sustainable competitive advantage," also known as its "unfair advantage."

How Entrepreneurial Capital Formation Has Evolved

In the twenty years up to the 1950s, venture capital was almost a hobby for the genteel rich: a game for those with inherited wealth, a small portion of which was invested in the revolutionary ideas of a few entrepreneurs. ROI was long in coming; seven to ten years was common. IPOs were rare and seldom reported in the *Wall Street Journal*.

During the 1960s, a few observant individuals talked some holders of wealth into pooling their funds in the form of limited partnerships for the specific purpose of regular investment in new companies, particularly those claiming to have made a technology breakthrough. This decade spawned Digital Equipment Corporation, Data General, and people like Arthur Rock, Tommy Davis, and Fred Adler, as well as Hambrecht & Quist . . . and a few dozen defunct companies in businesses like keyboard data entry, video records, custom mainframe software services, hang-on-the-wall TV, and undersea farming. Investors made money. And the name "venture capital" was launched.

The favorable results of the 1960s, particularly the high tech boom of 1964 to 1969, led to a venture capital spurt in the early 1970s. It was short-lived and entrepreneurs soon saw the slowdown become rampant: Congress made changes that boosted the tax on capital gains; the U.S. culture went through the painful years of Viet Nam; soaring inflation shot ROI (and dilution) requirements up to record levels. The result: not enough new funds were attracted to replenish the fully invested venture pools.

By 1979, the additions to the limited partnerships under the management of independent private venture capital firms had sunk to less than $179 million, according to *Venture Capital Journal*. But good times were ready to stage a comeback. Political lobbying by electronic company alliances of venture capitalists and the CEOs of their startups were successful in attaining changes in tax laws. The changes favored high tech companies engaging in intense amounts of R&D. And the capital gains tax was lowered significantly.

In 1980, the new funds rose to $681 million, and by 1983, they had soared to more than $3.4 billion for one year alone. Some economists told us that the inflows were simply a result of lower ROI hurdles attributable to reduced inflation and the end of domestic turmoil over Viet Nam. Others were adamant that the tax changes were critical in getting the new-funds faucet turned on again.

By the end of 1986, a total of $24 billion had been placed in the hands of general partners whose private venture capital firms filled a one-inch thick directory of sources of venture capital. There were two major U.S. venture capital industry associations, complete with staffs who lobbied Congress and the White House.

Names like Microsoft and Lotus had become familiar to the general public, along with Gates and Jobs, Sand Hill Road, Silicon Valley, and Route I-128. IPO was a set of initials known to most college graduates, and the word *entrepreneur* hit the covers of books on the *New York Times* best-seller list. And people had invested and lost in companies like Eagle and Visicorp.

Wall Street firms that had become contenders for high tech IPOs included smaller, specialized firms such as Robertson, Colman & Stephens and large, widely diversified firms such as Goldman Sachs. The massive influx of competing money caused a scramble (some called it a shark-infested feeding frenzy). Venture firms began actively positioning themselves to be differentiated from the crowd. Some began to specialize. Fresh monies had already spawned the first generation of medical and biotech startups. The Genentech blockbuster IPO made it official: it was now legitimate to include the initials M.D. in the title of a CEO of a high tech startup. Electronic sectors like telecommunications were now large enough to attract venture firms committed to focusing most investments in a single sector. And a venture fund of funds called Crossroads was successfully started by Hal Bigler to invest in the best of the best venture partnerships.

Corporate Venture Capital

Meanwhile, back at corporate headquarters, the CEOs of the giants began to become more active in the high tech startup business. Venture investors had learned of the high prices that pharmaceutical giants were willing to pay for medical, biological, and genetic engineering firms. Now they saw companies like Analog Devices, Apple Computer, Kodak, and Raytheon begin to invest directly in startups.

The corporate investors said they were mainly seeking access to new technology—that it was faster and cheaper to buy it than to invent it internally. Even IBM made forays in venture investing in the 1980s, using its own brand of investment. Its deals included the acquisition of Rolm.

Acquisitions accelerated during the late 1980s as corporations committed more funds to acquire startups, particularly before the new companies got past the IPO stage. Venture Economics reported that the number of such acquisitions of venture-backed companies rose from 32 in 1981 to 101 in 1985. Venture capitalists said the rate of deals continued high in 1986 and was even higher after the October 19, 1987 Wall Street crash.

Venture firms welcomed this additional channel for liquidity. The many floundering startups of the boom years of 1982-1983 were on the auction block for whatever they could fetch. The glory days of easy 50 percent annually compounded returns year after year were gone.

Good and bad acquisitions were made. As one investment banker said, "Every company is worth something at some price."

Wall Street and Investment Bankers

In the early days of venture capital, a few Wall Street firms made good money focusing some of their efforts on underwriting the few initial public offerings available in the 1950s and 1960s. They were dubbed "The Four Horsemen." Why is not clear, although during our interviews the reference was often made to a recasting of the biblical Four Horsemen of the Apocalypse. Investors and CEOs beware? Anyway, the industry has always had a sense of humor.

The four firms were, in the approximate order of their power and influence in the decade of the 1970s:

> Hambrecht & Quist, San Francisco, CA
> Alex Brown, Baltimore, MD
> L. F. Rothschild, Unterberg, Towbin, New York, NY
> Robertson, Colman & Stephens, San Francisco, CA

These firms specialized in emerging high tech growth companies and became well positioned to make a great deal of money in the boom of IPOs in the 1980s.

Until the PC boom legitimatized the high tech venture capital and new issues industry as a place for serious investors to put part of their funds, high tech stocks were left for the more unusual investors and were shunned by conservative equity investors from giant institutions, who control the trillions of dollars invested daily on the stock exchanges of the United States.

Consequently, their main-line investment bankers, firms like Goldman Sachs and Morgan Stanley, also stayed on the sidelines, leaving the Four Horsemen to do most of the IPOs.

The PC boom of 1981-1984 changed all that.

By 1986, *Forbes* mixed into the "IPO Top 20" investment banking names like Goldman Sachs, Merrill Lynch, Kidder Peabody, and Morgan Stanley. Aggressive sales personnel from these firms, known as "new business managers," could be counted on to knock on any startup's doors within weeks of its Round 1 funding. The competition had grown so fierce that, of the Four Horsemen, only Robertson, Colman & Stephens (renamed Robertson Stephens & Company) was ranked in the top ten that year. Rothschild was virtually out of the IPO business.

The Wall Street trends have reduced the cost of capital to startup companies (competition to fund a startup is said to be an entrepreneur's best friend) and are keeping the wealthy, powerful investment banking firms on their toes. It has not been uncommon for CEOs to drop a leading firm

TABLE 2-1. Trend in Years to IPO for Startup Companies

IPO Year	Median Age of Companies at IPO
1978	9
1979	9
1980	6
1981	5
1982	3
1983	4
1984	5
1985	3

and pick a different one after their company's most recent financing was poorly handled.

A noticeable new-issues trend during the 1980s was the sharp drop in the number of years a startup was in existence before it went public. Pressures for liquidity are always intense for all parties—venture capitalists, limited partners, founders, and employees. Venture Economics generated the comparative data on the number of years to IPO for startup companies shown in Table 2-1.

According to several seasoned investors, premature offerings can kill companies and fool investors. The SEC knows this all too well. Each year a large number of opportunists attempt to bilk investors by offering securities of shaky startups. The well-known VCs and investment bankers shun such deals.

The classic venture-backed firms have maintained good reputations. Most have yet to be involved with a major scandal on Wall Street. An exception was the legal harangue over Osborne Computer. Nonetheless, *Fortune* and *Forbes* constantly warn investors that IPOs represent dangerous waters for the naïve investor.

The 1990s

So where has the capital formation process brought the venture capital business? For one thing, to a new stage in its maturity. That is a certainty. The implications of this new stage are very important for the budding startup CEO to be aware of. Details follow in the next chapters. Here are a few items to keep in mind as you begin to form your startup plans:

1. *Venture capital portfolios are returning single-digit rewards to their investors.* By the time the feeding frenzy of the 1980s ended, the turkeys came

home to roost. This means the 1990s is a decade of survival-of-the-fittest venture firms. Less competition for a deal will mean a higher cost of capital to the startup.

2. *Complete management core teams are eagerly sought out by investors.* The lack of adequate managers for startups has become the number-one lament of the investor. Startups beginning with a single electrical engineer and an idea are very unlikely to get any funding.

3. *A validated market is an intense requirement to attract capital.* The "cross your fingers and hope" days are over; now investors demand a measurable, validatible market.

It all boils down to a fresh need for a well-planned, carefully prepared campaign for raising capital. That is the primary responsibility of the founder CEO. This book is written to help you create and succeed with such a plan. The decade of the 1990s represents a time when the surviving venture pools are full of capital looking for homes in exciting, promising startups. It is your job to tell the venture capital sources why your team should be funded next—at the price per share you are asking for. Chapter 3 will get you started with that process.

3

The Process
of Forming
the Company

The founders can dramatically increase their chances for successfully raising the capital they need to start a new high tech company if they understand the venture capital formation process. This chapter examines in detail the 14 stages of this process, which is summarized in Figure 3-1.

Each of the 14 key stages has a main focus activity that must be adhered to. We will talk about the most likely amount of time required for each stage.

We will identify typical participants, along with the motivations of each, and suggest tactics for negotiating with them. We will describe what kind of help is needed to succeed at each stage.

Major costs are given for each activity of a key stage. Those numbers can be used to plan budgets. We will analyze the risks at each stage and make suggestions for reducing potential problems to manageable tasks.

For all 14 stages, we will present the output and the related ROI. Two case studies are included in the discussion of the stages. The first,

FIGURE 3-1. The Startup Capital Formation Process →   →   →

Key Stages:	1 → Idea	2 → Kitchen Table	3 → Founder's Commitment	4 → Pullout from Employer	5 → Business Plan Creation
Main Focus Activity	• Secure a vision	• Solidify a dream	• Get firm commitments from key people	• Leave current employer; "stay clean"	• Write fresh business plan
Elapsed Time Required	Months to years	2-6 Months	1-2 Months	1 Month	2-6 Months
Typical Time Schedule: Cumulative		6 Months	Month 7	Month 8	Month 14
Typical Participants	• Yourself	• Friends and founders	• Founders only	• Founders • Lawyer	• Founders • Consultants • Lawyer • CPA firm • Patent lawyer
Help Needed	• Creativity	• Confidentiality • Business judgment • Technology • Marketing • Strategic thinking	• Commitment of 1 to 3 founders	• Good legal counsel: intellectual property and labor law	• Wise business judgment, especially marketing and financing • Sustainable ("unfair") advantage
Major Costs	• Own time	• Time of several people	• Nerves to commit	• Nerves to start to live on own savings	• Time • Personal computer • Spreadsheet • Word processor • Copy machine
Main Risks	• Lacks commercial realism	• Secrets leak out	• Cold feet of founders	• Counter offers or threat of legal action by former employers	• Plan is not worthy of being funded • Plan lacks distinctive competence
Results: ROI & Output	• Inspiration and vision	• Crisp view of risks-reward tradeoffs	• Yes or no from founder candidates	• Clean, legal separation from former employers	• Inspired document • Sustainable advantage • Clever strategy

© *Saratoga Venture Finance, 1991.*   *continued*

FIGURE 3-1.   The Startup Capital Formation Process   (continued)   →

6 →	7 →	8 →	9 →	10 →	11 →
Filling Management Team	**Raising Seed Capital**	**Closing Capital & Incorporation**	**Finding a Home**	**Startup**	**Secondary Capital Rounds**
• Attract vital talent	• Get $ cash commitment from lead venture investor	• Get $ cash into bank account	• Rent working quarters	• Hire people • Get started building first product	• Raise more $ cash • Leverage expensive equity
2-9 Months	2-12 Months	1-2 Months	1 Month	6-18 Months	2-6 Months each round
Month 18	Month 27	Month 28	Month 29	Starts Month 30	In Years 2-4 after Seed Round closes
• Friends • Consultants • Media • CPA firm • Recruiters	• Venture capitalists • Consultants • Founders	• Lawyer • Venture capitalists • Founders • Commercial banker	• CEO • Real estate broker	• Board of directors • Investors • Employees • Suppliers • Strategic partners	• Venture capitalists • CEO • Equipment lessors
• Candidates • Compensation plan • Wise people selection	• Whom to contact • Coaching on presentations • Judgment on pricing and valuation	• Good negotiating tactics • Financial counsel • Legal advice	• Real estate broker • Faculties consultant	• Startup experience	• Venture capital leads • Equipment lessors
• Lots of time for interviewing	• Time • Patience • Copies • Deliveries • Phone & fax • Travel	• Legal fees	• Time • Rental deposits	• Burn rate: $ per month	• Time of top management
• Compromise • No money, no hire • Leaks of secrets • Distractions from business plan	• No lead venture capitalist • Get shopworn	• No cash, so must start over	• Bad choice: size, location, $ per month, wrong length of lease	• Short of good people • Product completion slips • Competition starts too soon	• Lack of management focus • Run out of cash, miss payroll • Bankruptcy
• Recruitment of top notch managers	• Firm commitments of seed venture capitalists	• $ Cash in the bank	• Place to work for a year	• Live company in action	• Sufficient $ cash in bank • Price per round higher than last round

© *Saratoga Venture Finance, 1991.*   *continued*

FIGURE 3-1.   The Startup Capital Formation Process   (continued)

Key Stages: (continued)	12 → Launch First Product	13 → Raising Working Capital	14 !!! Initial Public Offering (IPO)	✔ Overall
Main Focus Activity	• Get customers	• Leverage equity	• Get shares liquid • Cash in some chips • Celebrate	• Create and grow a viable, exciting, successful high tech company
Elapsed Time Required	1-2 Years from start on work	3 Months for each banking or leasing round	4 Months including road show	4-8 Years from start to IPO
Typical Time Schedule: Cumulative	24-36 Months	After first quarter of profitability	Goal: IPO at end of year 5	Aim at 5 years start to finish
Typical Participants	• Customers • Whole company • PR firm	• CEO • CFO • Commercial banker	• Investment banker • Securities lawyers • Wall Street analysts • Industry media • General public	• Many risk takers
Help Needed	• Strong marketing skills • Positioning of company and first product • Cash reserves • Quality of execution of plan	• Profitability • Savvy banking and leasing contacts	• Timing • Pricing of shares	• Lots of effort • Several big breaks
Major Costs	• Burn rate: $ per month	• Time of CFO and CEO	• Underwriters' fees • Legal fees • CPA fees • Printer fees • Travel costs • Road show slides	• $3-$50 million of investors' capital
Main Risks	• Lack of focus • Product slips • Product underperforms • Poor market acceptance • Big competitor counter-punch	• Have to use precious equity instead of cheaper loans	• Bad price per share • Market window closes • Business sours	• Company survives but is too small, not able to get public
Results: ROI & Output	• Finish first product • Begin first sales to customers	• Funding for growth in working capital needs	• Venture capitalists: x5 to x10 • Founders: $millions each • Employees: x months of wages • Image as successful company	• Viable company • Great place to work • Created $100 million of wealth • Growing, high ROI business

Sigma Designs, Inc, provides a good illustration of bootstrapping; and the second, Compaq Computer Corporation, illustrates Stage 5, Creating the Business Plan.

The initial stage is getting the idea for the company, while the last stages include the IPO and new relationships with Wall Street investors. The stages in between are equally important, each with its unique characteristics.

Stage 1: Getting the Idea

One question that people often ask us is, "Where do I get a good idea from?" Research shows that the sources are as varied as the activities of the human mind. Hobbies and personal pastimes rank high in the most-often-cited category. The personal passions of Steve Wozniak and Steve Jobs, and Bill Gates and Paul Allen resulted in two new companies, Apple and Microsoft. Other founders simply decided to leave a current employer and walk across the street to start a new company in the same business, as was the case with SEEQ and Linear Technology. Bad eyesight started a new printing technology, and an entrepreneur's personal physical similarity to Benjamin Franklin launched a personal service business.

The ideas are described monthly in a vast variety of magazines such as *Inc.* In addition to being fascinating reading, the articles are provocative and can stimulate the entrepreneur looking for a good idea.

One thing is certain: Creative minds keep coming up with lots of fresh thinking. "There is no shortage of ideas!" exclaimed Regis McKenna, the public relations pioneer of high tech, speaking to a newspaper reporter who had speculated that after the boom of 1982 to 1983 the gold vein had run out.

One other thing is certain: The VCs said they will continue to be willing to listen to fresh ideas of enthusiastic people. There are more than $40 billion in funds gathered by venture firms that are committed to financing new enterprises. Venture capitalists want to find good companies to invest it in.

Main Focus Activity.   In Stage 1, the founder-to-be with an idea should focus on this: *Secure a vision for a company.* The soul of a new company is born at this time. Without sufficient belief in the vision, the new idea for a business usually ends up as just a discarded dream. This vision becomes especially important later, in the formation of the company culture. And it shapes the sustainable competitive advantage.

Time Required.   We have found that Stage 1 usually takes shape slowly, over a period of at least a year, and commonly more. However, ideas that

**TABLE 3-1. Participants in the Capital Formation Process
in Typical Order of Involvement**

1.	The Person with the Idea The Leader	11.	Commercial Banker
2.	Key Followers Buddies Founders	12.	Real Estate Broker Landlord
3.	Family Wife Children Mom and Dad Relatives	13.	Key Suppliers Furniture Telephone Utilities Insurance Benefits
4.	Friends Personal Business	14.	Recruiters Buddy System Contingent & Fee
5.	Business Consultant Startup	15.	PR Firm
6.	Lawyers General Counsel Patent	16.	Media Local National Industry
7.	CPA Firm Accounting Taxes	17.	Customers
8.	Venture Capitalists	18.	Wall Street Securities and Exchange Commission Wall Street Analysis Investment Speaking Forums
9.	Board of Directors		
10.	Equipment Leasing Company	19.	General Public

are formed quickly can also be successful. Bill Gates and Paul Allen were in college when a computer they saw on the cover of *Popular Mechanics* magazine set their juices boiling and led to the Microsoft success story.

Typical Participants.   Stage 1 is the lonely stage, with the entrepreneur sitting alone contemplating the alternatives until they are either discarded or built into a structure ready to be discussed in secret with a trusted friend. This loneliness will not last—many other people in many roles will become involved as the process continues. Table 3-1 outlines who will be involved as the 14 stages proceed, and in what order.

Help Needed. The most help needed during Stage 1 is in the area of emotions. Psychologists tell us that this is a delicate time in one's personal life, when an individual does an immense amount of soul searching. Emotions stored for years surface in surprising and often awkward ways. And one asks deep questions of oneself: "What do I want to do with my life? Do I want fame or financial success? Can I cope with the stress of leading a startup? Will my spouse be willing to support me if I try to do a startup?" Dealing with these questions at this time will increase the odds of success later. Stage 1 is a profound decision point, equivalent to deciding whether to have a first child or not, and why, and when, and at what cost; it has the same importance as deciding to become a parent.

Major Costs. The major cost at Stage 1 is time—the founder's time. We found few if any out-of-pocket costs at this stage. Good thinking time was the major requirement for doing a good job at Stage 1.

Main Risks. There is one major risk in Stage 1: lack of realism. Realism is a must, if only to help the founder focus on obstacles and create out of them a sustainable competitive advantage. This is the time when the would-be entrepreneur must quickly get away from dreaming and into the realm of possibilities.

However, a vision is necessary, if only to sustain an individual who is up against seemingly impossible odds. Here is how one veteran of the personal computer era put it to Paul Zachary of the *San Jose Mercury News* in 1987: "'We were damn fools,' says [Lee] Felsenstein, who designed the pioneering Sol computer in 1976 and later the Osborne 1. 'We just ignored the dire predictions that it couldn't be done.'"

Output and ROI. The founder's main output and return on investment in Stage 1 will be these:

- *Enjoyment*. At the very least, there is the fun of dreaming.
- *Inspiration*. One's creativity will have been stretched.
- *Personal profile*. Would-be entrepreneurs will know much better who they are and what their source of purpose and fulfillment in life is.

And the individual who decides to go on to Stage 2 will have constructed that precious "Vision for My Own New Company."

Stage 2: Meeting Around the Kitchen Table

Now the excitement starts to rise. The founder thinks he or she has a good idea and must take the vision to the next step. Stage 2 is the first testing ground and involves a brief, intense burst of private activity.

Main Focus Activity.   The main focus in Stage 2 should be: *Solidify a dream*. This is the time to start refining the vision into the stuff that successful new enterprises are made of. It takes dedicated blocks of time to do it and requires openly sharing the vision with a few trusted friends, in familiar circumstances. Our interviews revealed that *it was true*—most of these meetings took place around kitchen tables!

Time Required.   Stage 2 took most startups from two to six weeks to complete. The discussions varied in intensity; some of the CEOs we spoke with had only a couple of meetings; others went to four- and eight-hour sessions on weekends.

Typical Participants.   At Stage 2, entrepreneurs first share their vision with a trusted friend or two. In our interviews we found that this person often became an active participant later in the life of the startup, often as a cofounder. Stage 2 also included contact with a respected new businessman, former startup leader, lawyer, or startup consultant experienced in doing venture capital deals. As Mike Phillips of the Palo Alto law firm of Morrison & Foerster put it, "My firm and others with venture experience in Silicon Valley see all kinds of people in a week who are trying out a new idea. The person is understandably quite cautious and needs to talk confidentially with someone connected to the venture capital world, someone who can help steer the founder's vision, usually toward more realistic thinking about what makes a successful startup, the kind of thinking that can increase the likelihood of the founding team getting their seed round of venture capital."

Help Needed.   Stage 2 requires help in maintaining confidentiality and getting good business judgment. The only way to have confidentiality is through personal trust and discipline. We found no one who used nondisclosure documents in Stage 2.

Good business judgment came from the quality of the professionals and veterans that the founders talked to.

Major Costs.   Like the prior stage, Stage 2 costs time—of at least one more participant. Some lawyers will work for brief periods of time without charging a fee. It is important for the founders to ask how the attorney will charge them. (See Chapter 4 for details on how to select the best legal counsel.)

Main Risks.   The top danger in Stage 2 is that the secret could leak out. It is dangerous if one's current employer gets word that an employee is forming a new company—before the employees have prepared for departure (see "Ethical Departure from an Employer" in Chapter 4). It is even worse if the idea gets snatched up by someone else, including another startup group or even that same current employer. Founders told us of extraordinary efforts they used to conceal the proprietary nature of their ideas. And we heard a few sad stories of people who lost their ideas and never got started at all. Others got started but were stopped by lawsuits disputing rights to intellectual property and people.

Output and ROI.   When Stage 2 is done, the founders will have sorted out the risk-reward trade-offs. Paperwork was rare at this stage, probably because of the intense need to keep ideas confidential.

Stage 3: Getting the Founders' Commitments

Stage 3 is next, and the excitement grows. This is a delicate phase in the life of the startup, one that begins to separate the doers from the dreamers.

Main Focus Activity.   In Stage 3, the successful startup CEOs should focus on this: *Get firm commitments from key people.* That sounded easy to us, but the CEOs said this was hard. Even worse, however, several said they got into trouble because they skipped over this step.

This was the problem: When the pressure rises, the core team quits. It is difficult to stand up to rough personal negotiations and nerve-racking waiting time. Employers fight to retain good people. The CEO who has not obtained *firm* commitments from the core team is very likely to find his company melting before his eyes like butter in summer heat.

A sense of reality is crucial. It is better to find trusted friends dropping out at this early stage than see them quit later, when keeping the core team intact affects capital funding. Such last-minute dropouts can kill a venture capital deal before it is funded.

Time Required.   We found that startups spent one to two months getting personal commitments from the core team. This was often done in parallel with the Stage 2 kitchen-table talks, but successful CEOs preferred not to proceed to Stage 4, pullout from employer, until Stage 3 was completed.

Typical Participants.   In Stage 3 the work is concentrated on the founders. Other key personnel, such as good circuit designers and software programmers, are put on hold for a while. This is done to solidify the core of the team, the core that would be presented to the venture capitalists as competent, qualified, and able. It is also the team that will share the most in the financial spoils and be directly involved with presentations and negotiations.

Help Needed. The original founders will need help from additional founders, typically one to three other people. Each will be needed to help assess the others, particularly the likelihood of their actually joining the startup when the CEO tells them that "now is the time."

Major Costs. The major cost in Stage 3 is to the nerves. The entrepreneur must confront people and get them to either commit or drop out. There may be key people whom the founder senses may drop out if they get cold feet after their employer threatens legal action. The founder must now be able to count on the core team that is so necessary to get the company off the ground.

Main Risks. The major risk is not doing this step and finding out later in a critical moment that the team consists of a bunch of people that are only half-committed to the founder's vision of a startup.

Cold feet on the part of cofounders is dangerous; it can sink an enterprise later on, just when raising seed capital seems to be going well. We heard several sad tales of exactly that happening.

Output and ROI. Go/no-go decisions and firm handshakes are the precious outputs in Stage 3. That sets the foundation for a shared vision, one that has a core of committed, enthusiastic founders to lead it.

Stage 4: Pullout from Employer

Now the test of nerves begins as pressures mount. It is time for the founders to break away from current employers and begin working full-time on the new enterprise. Here is where a lot of different approaches to startups appeared in our research.

Venture capitalists were overwhelmingly consistent here; all said, "Leave your current employer before you write your business plan." Venture capitalists hate investing in a startup that gets bogged down in lawsuits that drain precious time and cash resources. The case histories of the SEEQ and Linear Technology lawsuits between former employers and the founders are classics that formed this rule of venture capitalists.

Some venture capital firms will actually lend the core team a room, telephone, and computer to support them in writing the business plan.

However, the founders of one class of startup, called "bootstraps," argue against leaving employers until later on in the life of a startup, in order to continue earning wages until the last possible minute. This breed of startups is exemplified in the following case study.

Case Study: Sigma Designs, Inc.

Sigma Designs is a good example of a bootstrap. Here is how the founders did Stage 4, as reported by Steve Kaufman of the San Jose Mercury News.

The Sigma story started in February 1982, when several engineers at Amdahl Corp. tinkered with an add-on, PC memory board in one of their homes in Sunnyvale. The venture started out as a hobby, but the thing worked, and they realized it might generate a lot of business. They displayed it at the annual PC Fair in San Francisco, advertised a little in a personal computing magazine and added a so-called multi-function board to their product line.

A year later, they were selling 100 boards a month at $500 to $600 a shot, and Jimmy Chan, the vice president of product development, became the first to leave Amdahl to work in the business full-time. Tran, the president, followed him eight months later, at which point the company was producing $125,000 in monthly sales. When Jason Chen, the vice president of manufacturing, joined the company in June 1984, monthly sales had skyrocketed to $800,000.

Sigma went public on May 15, 1986.

Most well-known startups are not bootstraps, but follow the more classical process outlined in this report.

Main Focus Activity.   In Stage 4, the focus is this: *Stay clean*. The objective is to avoid being sued by a former employer. And the goal is to leave with a "win-win" solution. When Sierra Semiconductor founders left National Semiconductor, they left with a cordial relationship, and contracts were soon signed that gave both parties access to technology, products, and production. Jim Diller and his core team took Sierra public in 1991. That was quite different from the lawsuits that transpired between Linear Technology and National in the early days of Linear. Linear's Bob Swanson and his core team were pioneering, and legal precedence was set by the outcome of this core team's departure from National. Linear went public in 1986.

Time Required.   It took about one month on the average for founders to clear out of their employment situations. Anticipation of this event can speed up the departure time, especially for engineers and other personnel who can get tied up in longer projects that they feel obliged to complete before joining the startup. Jerry Anderson, founder of the computer-aided engineering startup Valid Logic of San Jose, California, said he lost six precious months to hardcharging competitors Mentor Graphics and Daisy Systems because the technical founders were tied up in completing work at Lawrence Livermore Laboratories and finishing their Ph.D.s.

Typical Participants.   The main concern is to get the founders away from their employers and on the job with the next stage of the startup. CEOs advised against becoming distracted at this time by attempts to also get the next wave of employees out of their jobs.

Help Needed.   Founders should be getting top legal help at this stage. We studied several startups that simultaneously engaged two law firms: one for general legal counsel and the other for intellectual property. This reflects the growing importance of creating and protecting companies' intellectual property.

Major Costs.   It is at this stage that the first cash costs start. If founders leave their employers before the seed round is raised, they must live off of their savings or do some part-time work such as consulting.

Some law firms ask for a small retainer; $1000 per month was often cited. Many others, particularly the veteran firms familiar with startups, did work on contingency in this stage.

Main Risks.   The number one risk is a lawsuit by a founder's former employer.

The number two risk is losing a founder to an employer's counteroffer.

The number three risk is a lawsuit by a company for which a founder is doing part-time consulting.

Output and ROI.   The gold medal in Stage 4 is that the members of the founding team achieve a clean pullout from all their employers.

Stage 5: Creating the Business Plan

Stage 5 is the time when the founder's vision goes on paper in the form of a business plan. This is where hard decisions are made, ideas discarded, and fresh breakthrough strategies documented. It is hard work.

Main Focus Activity. The focus at this stage is on *writing a well-con-ceived business plan*. It is more than words or a financial forecast that shows yet another $100 million startup in five years. Rather, it is a writ-ten plan that tells how the founders plan to turn their vision into a sus-tainable competitive advantage. Tips from the pros are presented in Chapter 5, "Preparing the Business Plan."

Time Required. Founders reported that they needed a lot more time than they thought to prepare their business plan. Two to nine months must be allowed. Most startup personnel underestimate the time require-ment of this phase by a factor of two. The following case study reveals how that happened to one of America's most successful startups.

Case Study: Compaq Computer Corporation

Here is how Business Week *reported Compaq's experience with the Stage 5 pro-cess in its cover story of June 29, 1987.*

> *But after 13 years, Canion [Joseph R. "Rod" Canion, president of Compaq] tired of [Texas Instrument's] bureaucratic style and its emphasis on tech-nical excellence at the expense of marketing. The turning point came in 1980. After he set up a disk drive manufacturing unit, Canion was abruptly transferred to another business unit because management considered his job finished. The job just begins when you start selling product, he contends. You need to continue the marketing focus. The last straw was his assign-ment to the group designing TI's first office microcomputer. Canion quit within 18 months because he felt management misunderstood personal com-puters. His biggest gripe, ironic in light of Compaq's present market battle: TI wouldn't accept the importance of IBM's products.*
>
> *Canion and TI buddies William H. Murto and James M. Harris set up Compaq—and promptly got off to a slow start. Contrary to its early adver-tising, the company did not spring to life one afternoon when the founders sketched the idea for a portable PC on a napkin at a Houston pie shop. According to L. J. Sevin, Rosen's partner in Sevin Rosen Management, Canion called with a plan for building circuit cards to expand the storage capacity of IBM PCs. Sevin was underwhelmed. He felt that the product was "a little too easy to do. We made him go back to the drawing board."*
>
> *Canion's fourth or fifth idea clicked. It was for an IBM-compatible por-table. With $1.5 million in seed money, Canion and his crew began design-ing Compaq's first PC in February 1982. By early 1983, when Compaq began shipping its portables, the company had raised $30 million. In late 1983 it raised $66 million more in a public offering, then finished the year with sales of $111 million.*

Typical Participants. Now enters the "herd of helpers." They are used by all the CEOs of successful startups to prepare a better business plan. This list includes:

- *Founders.* The founders meet as a group to talk, write, and edit.
- *Consultants.* Saratoga Venture Finance is an example. These local consultants specialize in work for a fee in the risky, preseed round stages of a startup. Several also stand in as CFO, or even CEO or VP Marketing.
- *Lawyers.* Both general and intellectual property counsel can make important contributions.
- *CPA firm.* CPAs help with the numbers, but a quality firm will act as a great business advisor as well. (See Chapter 5's section on "The Role of a CPA Firm" for advice on how to pick a good firm.)

Help Needed. The most help the founders will need will be in the strategic thinking area, principally in marketing and financing. And no matter what skills exist in the founding technology team, observers were firm in their insistence that there were never enough effective results in the area of working out a sustainable or unfair competitive advantage. (For tips on how to solve this thorny, critical problem, see Chapter 5's section on "The Importance of Unfair Advantage.")

Major Costs. Major costs will be kept low if the founders can convince the herd of helpers mentioned above to work for free for a while longer. If not, the CEO must start adding up the hours per helper and multiplying by hourly billing dollars. Top venture capital law firms in Silicon Valley bill senior partners at $150 to $250 per hour. Top CPA partners are billed at slightly lower rates. For contrast, New York lawyers cost at least $100 more per hour, frequently $300 more per hour, and higher.

Most veteran legal and CPA firms will work out a custom arrangement. An introduction through a close friend or consultant can be very helpful.

Other costs to be covered are typing and copying, secretarial, and supplies. The fledgling group will need a personal computer and spreadsheet software. Saratoga Venture Finance has created a special software package called StartUp™, which forecasts financial statements running on Lotus 1-2-3 or Excel. It includes a handy set of tools to get the CEO of a startup off to a flying start with a complete set of financial projections. (See Appendix B for details on what StartUp contains, how it works, and how to obtain a copy.) The purpose of the software is to encourage the entrepreneur to do more strategic thinking and less time-consuming modeling and financial forecasting.

Main Risks. The number one risk is that the founder will produce a plan not worthy of pursuing, and that the hard work up to this point will appear to have been for naught. That has happened to the best of the startups, as Compaq's founders learned.

The number two risk is that the plan will not be worthy of being financed but will be funded anyway. This strange phenomenon was encountered in several of the startups we interviewed. VCs often said they bet on a team of experienced managers much more than on their business plan. The risk in this situation is that no one is very sure what is going to happen.

Output and ROI. The gold medal is for a business plan that is an inspired version of the founder's vision, built on a foundation of a well-thought-through sustainable competitive advantage.

Stage 6: Filling the Management Team

By this stage there is a business plan in which the founders have confidence. There is also a set of projections showing the headcounts needed to set the new company in motion. Now comes the task of filling out the rest of the team, particularly key managers. Who, when, and for how much stock?

Chapter 6, "The Team," discusses in detail what venture capitalists look for in the people involved in a startup.

Main Focus Activity. Focus in Stage 6 is this: *Attract the vital talent.*

Some investors will bet almost solely on the people leading a startup. They argue that if all else goes wrong, top people can recover and at least make something of what otherwise would be a wipeout. The key to success here is understanding what vital talent is all about.

Time Required. This is a very time-consuming step. Our interviews revealed that from two to nine months can be expected to elapse before the CEO assembles a complete team of talented leaders who will pass the tough scrutiny of the best venture capitalists' secret checkouts of chosen personnel.

Typical Participants. Startup CEOs used about every conceivable means to find and attract top personnel. Interviews showed that the primary method was the buddy system. Through word of mouth, friends pass along the news that someone is forming a startup and needs certain talent.

Second was the use of the "herd of helpers" from Stage 5. The CPA firms were surprisingly helpful in finding marketing and sales candidates as well as accountants. They are careful to avoid recruiting from among their clients. The top high tech CPA firms consist of very well-connected businessmen.

The third method was use of the media, either in the form of "leaked" PR or in recruiting advertisements. Some startups received a great deal of response to an ad that announced that a startup was in formation. More common, however, was an interview with the business editor of the local newspaper, who was given an exclusive on the story of the entrepreneur leaving a famous employer to start his own company. The published articles attracted a lot of attention, including that from venture capitalists.

The fourth method was engaging recruiters. This method was used almost exclusively after the seed round, and especially when the founders needed a strong CEO. Not all founders want to be the CEO of a startup; instead they prefer to become chairman *and* CEO, leaving daily tasks to chief operating officers (COOs) and presidents. Needless to say, recruiters are very expensive for a startup, with or without seed capital in the bank. (See Chapter 6 on more pros and cons on the use of this and other methods of hiring needed talent.)

Help Needed. Help in making wise judgments is what is needed most in this stage. It is worth more than gold.

Finding scarce talent is the second area in which help will be much needed. Founders should remember that A-quality players will attract A-quality players.

Also needed will be a thorough compensation plan, prepared in advance of actual recruiting. Wages, bonuses, and stock (founders shares and incentive stock options) must be ready in writing, in terms of dollars, formulas, and number of shares. Sadly, plans for distribution of shares beyond the core team are typically nonexistent.

Major Costs. Everyone agreed here: recruiting takes enormous amounts of time. This will be the entrepreneur's greatest cost at this stage. Plus the costs of business meals.

Only rarely did startups recruit from out of town and thus incur the related high cost of such travel expenses. Relocations of families did occur, though rarely.

Main Risks. Here are the major risks, listed in the rank order mentioned in our interviews, starting with the most significant and most likely:

1. *Compromise.* CEO after CEO said "Do not, under any circumstances, compromise your high standards in order to attract a warm body to complete your team."

2. *No dough, no deal*. If your company is not funded, candidates often say no. Yet such people are needed to help attract funding. This Catch 22 was commonly the lament of founders in this stage. Chapter 6 details techniques used by CEOs to deal with it.

3. *Leaks of secrets*. CEOs told horror stories about marketing and technical candidates who said no to offers of employment, then returned to their employers and disclosed a great idea that they had discovered during interviews at a startup.

4. *Distraction*. Not only does recruiting not advance any product development work or market research, but it can even threaten a business plan if a series of experienced candidates tell the CEO they think it will fail for very plausible reasons, some of which the CEO had not yet thought of.

Output and ROI.   At the end of this stage, the CEO will have all vital talent committed to joining the startup, at various agreed-upon dates.

Stage 7: Raising Seed Capital

The founders must have a strategy for attracting investors. They must decide which VC firms to contact, how to get ahead of all the other hungry business plans on the VCs' desks, and how to demonstrate convincingly that they have an unfair advantage.

Main Focus Activity.   Here the focus is: *Get a firm commitment from a strong lead venture capital firm*. Once the lead firm provides backing, other investors will follow.

Time Required.   According to our research, this phase typically takes a long time, much longer than the founders anticipated. Anything from two to twelve months can be expected, with nine months the median.

Typical Participants.   There are three categories of participants at Stage 7:

1. Venture capital partners and their technology and market consultants.

2. The entrepreneur's own coaching consultant, if one can be engaged.

3. The startup's core managers, whether or not they've left their employers.

Help Needed.   The founders will need help in three main areas:

■ *Who to contact*. See Chapter 9 for help here.

■ *Coaching on presentations*. Founders need to understand the ways and wiles of venture capitalists. See Chapter 9.

- *Valuation, dilution, and deal pricing judgment.* Here is where millions of dollars of potential wealth are negotiated. Chapter 9 provides special case studies of two startup deals. Saratoga Venture Finance has researched how much of the company the startups had to sell, at what prices, and for what percentage of the startup. Every share is accounted for and presented later in this book in the form of the Saratoga Venture Tables™ to assist the CEO in negotiations with experienced venture capitalists.

Major Costs.   Major costs at Stage 7 will be these:

1. *Time,* to pitch to a lot of venture firms, some several times.
2. *Emotional stress,* particularly trials of patience and fear of failure as personal cash dwindles, as a spouse doubts the company will ever get started, and as the founder goes through the first rollercoaster ride of a venture deal.
3. *Cash expenses for travel to VCs* (rarely have VCs paid for a founder's travel to see them), copying expenses for reproduction of business plans (100 copies were common), heavy Federal Express charges (everyone seemed to send every business plan by overnight mail), and high telephone bills. At least $1000 must be reserved for these expenses.

Main Risks.   The number one risk cited was *getting no lead VC.* Someone must step up to take the lead.

The number two risk is *getting shopworn.* This is tricky to avoid and quite important. (See Chapter 9 for help.)

The third risk is *selling stock too cheaply.* Valuation work was typically done naively, without adequate facts or detailed calculations. Chapter 9 will help the CEO plan this strategy.

Output and ROI.   The founders want four things at the end of this step:

1. A committed lead venture capital firm backing the startup.
2. Firm dollar commitments for a percentage of the startup company.
3. A fairly priced deal.
4. A timetable for getting to the closing date, with cash in the bank.

Stage 8: Incorporation and Cash in the Bank

This is the stage at which the founders must select an attorney to close the deal with the funding sources and to incorporate the company.

A commercial bank must be selected so that the funding sources' money can be deposited. When the stage is complete, money is finally available to do the work that until now had been just a powerful vision.

Main Focus Activity. In this step, there is one and only one focus: *Get the money in the bank account.* Salespeople call it "closing the deal."

It is insufficient to get a venture capital firm to say it will do the deal. The founders must get cash in the bank. As the ancient proverb puts it, "There is many a slip 'twixt the cup and the lip."

Time Required. It always takes longer than anyone believed likely. One should expect one and sometimes two months for the lawyers for the startup company and those for the venture capitalists to do their work—that's how long it will take until the negotiating work results in a deposit slip in the new company's bank account.

Typical Participants. The people the CEO and other founders will work most closely with at this stage are:

- *Lawyer.* A good attorney is needed for incorporating the company, distributing founders' shares, and the considerable other legal work. (See Chapter 4 for more details.)
- *Commercial banker.* A good bank—one whose focus is servicing business accounts—is needed for a place to park the cash, invest it, set up a checking account, and do company payroll. (See Chapter 11, "Commercial Bankers," for the services of a banker in this phase of a startup's life.)
- *Founders.* Founders will participate in negotiations. For the first time, founders will see one another behaving as a group around the negotiating table. We were warned to expect anything from such participants in this phase, especially in discussions on how much of the company to sell to the venture capitalists.
- *Venture capitalists.* VCs will be the heavies at this stage, for obvious reasons. Chapter 9 reveals how successful CEOs negotiated with the VCs and got good deals.

Help Needed. Most of all in this stage, the founders will need good negotiating skills, street-smart tactics, and strategy.

Major Costs. The major cost will be for legal services. It can be hard to get a law firm to do the work on a contingency basis, but several CEOs succeeded in doing so because the likelihood of funding appeared so good. The founder should plan to incur at least $1,000 to $3,000 in legal and related expenses by the time the seed round deal is successfully completed.

Main Risks. The main risk is *getting no cash*. This happens to successful startups, however. Compaq was mentioned earlier. Another example is Gordon Campbell, who, after getting no venture funds, changed strategy. He raised funds for the amazingly successful Chips and Technologies, Inc. of San Jose, California without a dime from the classic venture capital firms.

The next biggest risk is investors dropping out of the funding. We were told of many, many cases in which the lead venture firm suddenly bowed out without any warning. Chapter 9 discusses why CEOs believe this happens and how to handle it.

The final major risk is the notorious *creeping close*. This is a dread disease that all CEOs feared the most. It happens when everything is done, but the money is not yet in the bank. Everything seems to take "just a few more days" and the requests for information seem endless. A CEO of a minisupercomputer startup in southern California told us, in gripping detail, how his team finally got their seed round and celebrated at the president's beachfront home. People resigned from their employers the next day. And the following Monday afternoon the lead VC firm called to announce its pullout from the deal due to unforeseen internal problems of the firm. (See Chapter 9 for more stories of intrigue.)

Output and ROI. Getting the cash in the bank. After it is counted— then, and only then, should the founders and managers celebrate.

Stage 9: Finding a Home

Now there is money in the bank! The time has come to spend some of it and get a place to work, other than around the founder's kitchen table.

Main Focus Activity. In Stage 9, the focus is simple: Get *appropriate working quarters*.

Time Required. This usually takes one month or two—the time to look for working quarters, sign the thick lease documents, and get the place cleaned up before you move in.

Getting a facility for heavy manufacturing can take longer, although most CEOs said one month was all it took for them to make up their minds. The paperwork can take a few weeks to finish. The landlord may have to paint and clean up before you can move in.

Typical Participants.   The lead participant at this stage is a real estate broker. However, going direct may be better and can produce some surprisingly favorable benefits. Chapter 10, "Leasing as a Source of Capital," presents a fascinating case study involving the landlord as venture capitalist. And the founders at one manufacturing-intensive startup hired a financial consultant to help them attract venture leasing funding because of the large amount of capital equipment that the factory would tie up.

Help Needed.   A real estate broker experienced in the special needs of startups was very helpful, according to several CEOs. A founder benefits most from a broker's hands-on experience with a startup in this phase. CEOs told us about lots of tricks to save on capital and cash flow. These included complex terms and conditions in the lease with respect to flexibility in future moves to other quarters.

Furniture, cubicles, phones, and computers eat up about $3000 to $4000 per employee, more for engineers with workstations. Leasehold improvements used up large, unplanned chunks of the budgets of several startups that we spoke with. Unused rented space is a terrible waste of capital. And the CEO must decide how long a lease to sign, for how many square feet, of what kind of space.

Major Costs.   The major cost will be the CEO's time to find the home. The broker's fee is passed back to the startup but is buried in the monthly lease of the facility.

Some startup CEOs deliberately rented facilities and furniture on a month-to-month basis until Round 1 funding was completed. Their strategy was to buy time and cash savings until the full-time startup team could refine the business plan to a greater degree.

Main Risks.   Your biggest risk is: *Picking a bad facility.* There are a number of things that could make your new quarters a bad investment:

- *Bad location.* You can't attract the new hires. It could be a poor commute, for example.
- *Wrong image.* Again, you can't attract new hires if your quarters project a cheap appearance.
- *Wrong size.* Too small is as bad as too large.

- *Monthly rent too high.* This wastes precious cash.
- *Too long a lease.* Yes, it is tough to predict the speed of the startup's growth, but someone must pick a number.

Output and ROI. The result is simple: The startup now has a good home. A great home will increase the ease of attracting fine employees and impressing good customers.

Stage 10: Starting Up

With a home of its own (for the next three to five years), the new company is now ready to *officially* get started.

Main Focus Activity. Our CEOs were about equally split on priorities at this stage, so we list both of them as equally important:

1. Hire the necessary people.
2. Get started building the first product.

Some CEOs remembered getting burned by starting work too soon or by losing many months in launching the first product because they put off hiring extra people until much later. Hiring almost always falls behind plan.

Time Required. It takes from 6 to 18 months to get the first product ready to ship to the first customer. CEOs said that six months meant that either (1) they had done some of the product development with their former employer's support (Sierra Semiconductor is a good version of this arrangement), or (2) they had built the prototypes in their garage before leaving their employer (see Case Study: Sigma Design Systems).

CEOs also said that VCs get very nervous if the first product takes much longer than 18 months to get to market. Closing of market windows is a constant threat. Chapters 6 and 10 discuss this problem in more detail. Medical, bio, and genetic engineering startups have taken the longest time to develop their first products, while software is expected to take the shortest time to get to market. Electronic hardware-based systems fall between those two categories.

Typical Participants. At this stage the CEO is confronted with a new—often frighteningly new—set of participants. These include the new boss: the board of directors.

Others include investors not on the board, all the new employees the CEO is responsible for managing, and a bevy of suppliers of services and hard goods, not to mention industry media, technology newsletter writers, and local press, as well as neighbors who never before spoke to the CEO, and doting parents and relatives.

Help Needed.   The best help is prior startup experience. No two ways about it. Perhaps that is why VCs told us that they are about as happy to have a CEO on his second startup (even though the first one failed) as they are to have Mr. Eversuccessful in Every Situation who has never done a startup before.

Major Costs.   The CEO's mind will now begin to focus night and day on a single financial number: the *burn rate*. This is the amount of cash used each month to pay for anything and everything.

The company now has employees. Who are expensive. And who can spend a great deal of money in a day. Soon the CEO grows rather more miserly in salary offers than he or she used to be at the old Fortune 500 employer.

Costs per month mount up quickly as telephones, voice mail, lobby furniture, plant service, security service, and so on are added. It is easy to spend $400 to $500 per person per month, just to open the doors for work each morning.

And then the engineers start submitting their purchase orders for computer-aided design equipment, and the manufacturing people present their budgets for test gear, etc. This is when the CEO must start adding zeros to all numbers forecast for cash expenditures.

The smart CEO should think about all of this when preparing the business plan financial forecasts. The value of such forethought is obvious.

Main Risks.   The successful VCs and their startup companies said that these were the main risks in this phase of the fledgling company's life:

1. *Slips in product completion schedules.* More than anything, this made everyone the most nervous. The Kleiner Perkins venture capital firm calls this the risk of "repeatable technology."

2. *Insufficient market and too much competition.* As a mindboggler, a famous university study showed that 69 disk drive startup companies got rolling during the heyday of the personal computer, around 1983, each predicting a 5 percent share of the market for itself. Customer acceptance can be lackluster for many reasons. Competition can come from unexpected sources—either from a giant company that sets the industry standard, or, more frequently these days, from other startups.

3. *Shortage of good people.* This was a lament by everyone, from entrepreneur to entrepreneur.

Output and ROI. The end result is a hustling, bustling company of enthusiastic people eager to transform the founding vision into a commercial reality.

A company with a heart.

And a high burn rate.

Stage 11: Raising Secondary Rounds of Capital

The joys of operating a new company last for a brief moment, until the reality sinks in that there is no way for the founders to complete the first product and get sales started with the cash that remains in the bank.

Main Focus Activity. In Stage 11, the main focus should be this: *Raise enough cash and leverage precious equity.*

Time Required. About 25 percent of the CEO's time and 20 percent of the time of those reporting directly to the CEO will be consumed just by raising needed capital during the next one to four years. A major regret of numerous first-timers was that they did not realize this axiom of startup companies. It is especially a problem if the CEO is also the chief technology manager.

Typical Participants. Each round of financing will be very closely managed by the startup's lead venture capital firm. The reasons are explained in Chapter 9. The CEO and the CEO's key communicators will be deeply involved.

And a new participant will appear on the scene: the equipment venture lessor whose role is explained in Chapter 10.

Help Needed. The CEO will need the most help from the lead VC. But note carefully: *CEOs said that they felt the fund-raising leadership HAD to come mainly from the CEO to avoid disasters such as missed payrolls.* CEOs warned never to count on anyone except the CEO to raise the money.

Equipment lessors as middlemen can help raise millions of additional dollars of capital for startups. And experienced consultants can save time, effort, and shares for the company's management and employees.

Major Costs. Time is the major cost. Lots of it. Personal stress levels also rise in this stage.

Main Risks.   There are three main risks at this stage:

1. *Running out of cash.* A surprising number of CEOs missed payrolls before secondary rounds of capital were in the bank.
2. *Lack of management focus.* This was the lament of every operations person we talked to, particularly those with little prior "outside" experience (with Wall Street, PR, news media, or treasury operations such as banking, financing investments).
3. *Bankruptcy.* Yes, Virginia, it can happen to even the best of them, for both good and bad reasons. That *is* one of the risks of doing a startup. According to our research in 1987, about six in ten startups went bankrupt. Not all startups survive to the second round of financing.

Output and ROI.   A successful Stage 11 results in two vital signs of startup health:

1. Sufficient cash in the bank.
2. Equity at a significantly higher price per share than in the last round.

   For guidelines on pricing the successive rounds of venture capital, see Chapter 9 and the Case Studies in the chapters that follow.

Stage 12: Launching the First Product

By now the CEO and managers have built up a head of steam and are racing to meet deadlines. The cash is burning rapidly, and the first product is nearing its alpha test milestone.

Main Focus Activity.   Here is the most important activity: *Focus.* Focus is Number 1 to most of the successful entrepreneurs we spoke to. It is a mistake to spread out into other products, technologies, or customer segments. The important thing is to uncover the big market opportunity and stick to the original business plan in order to exploit that opening and be the best at doing it.

A close number two priority is: *Find customers.*

Customers spell relief and hope. Most of all, they spell cash *inflow.* To find good customers, one needs good products, starting with the first one. Some startups never get more than one chance to try with other than their first product. Therefore, it must be the best the company's people know how to make, consistent with what the targeted customers say they want.

Time Required.   The launch of the first product takes place in a rollout, usually from one to two years.

Typical Participants.   There are three major players at this stage:

1. Customers
2. PR firm
3. The whole company

Help Needed.   This is the time to flex your marketing muscle. All that you've got. You will need wisdom in positioning the company and its first product, consistent with the founder's plan for sustaining the company's competitive, unfair advantage.

Major Costs.   The major cost is the boost in marketing and sales expenses needed to roll out the first product. Meanwhile, the burn rate is growing as new hires come on board each month. And the cash balance drops daily.

This stage requires amazing human fortitude. The CEO's emotional highs and lows will increase in amplitude. Entrepreneurs who doubt our findings can check it out when they get to this stage by asking their spouses or closest friends for a description and evaluation of their recent behavior, before and after this stage gets under way.

Main Risks.   Here are the major risks at this stage, listed in rank order:

1. *Lack of focus.* Everyone must concentrate on getting the first product launched ASAP.
2. *Product schedule slips.* Every management and personal behavioral technique available must be used to keep on schedule for the launch date—without burning out employees and their supervisors.
3. *Underperformance.* The worry of every entrepreneur is that the product will not perform up to initial design specifications. *Overperformance*, also known as "creeping elegance" is a close cousin to this risk. Tight coupling of marketing and engineering will help reduce such problems.
4. *Poor market acceptance.* It is a common worry of CEOs who aim at a new, unestablished market. Just ask IBM's PC Jr folks.
5. *Jaws, or Big Company Counterpunch.* This is becoming more common as the world giants learn to react faster. And they can always use their muscle for changing standards and sending lawyers to slow down a delicately poised, vulnerable startup.

Output and ROI.   The first fruits of the CEO's labor will be the first product and a very excited, confident company of hardworking, competent employee-owners. The CEO's boss, the board, will be handing out pats on the back, and the industry media representatives will be lining up to do stories on how the founders and the company got so successful so soon.

Stage 13: Raising Working Capital

The founder CEO might think that by now all the capital-raising days are over. But in fact, they never end. Like teenage boys at dinner, startups are amazing in how much they can consume.

One very successful startup showed us its original business plan. The company had grown twice as fast as predicted and reached its public offering two years earlier than planned. The one shocking oversight in the underlying assumptions was that the company required *double* the originally predicted capital base per dollar of revenue. The founders (and their first-tier venture capital backers) had failed to realize that the engineering staff alone would tie up as much capital as total inventory. The R&D and customer support staffs used the company's own manufactured systems to do their work, but in much larger quantities than anticipated. Success breeds its own brand of capital problems.

Main Focus Activity.   During this phase of life, the company's financial focus should be this: *Leverage equity.*

Time Required.   Starting in the first profitable quarter, the CEO will be continuously involved with raising working capital. This will supplement the prior rounds of venture capital.

Typical Participants.   At the stage, the lending officer of the company's commercial bank will visit the office for the first time. And the company's chief financial officer will get much more involved with leading this phase of capital raising.

Help Needed.   The most help will come having from the company's *first profitable quarter.* Banking savvy and experience will be required.

Major Costs.   The major cost—other than the cost of the actual loans—is the CEO's *time.*

Debt is a lot cheaper than equity and is worth millions in value to the founders because it does not further dilute equity.

Main Risks.   The main risk is that the loan may have to be repaid at the worst time—that is, when the company is waiting for large collections from customers but is short of cash for the next payroll.

Output and ROI.   The test of success at Stage 13 is how much extra cash the company has in the bank at the end of the effort. Financial flexibility is the main objective.

Stage 14: Initial Public Offering

At last The Day has arrived: The founders have decided to go public!

Main Focus Activity.   Here are the priorities: (1) *get the shares liquid (registered)*, (2) *cash in a few chips*, and (3) *celebrate!*

Time Required.   Startups usually take three to five years to get to this point. However, the median number of years required has dropped noticeably, from an average of nine years for IPOs in 1979, to three years in 1985, and back to about five years in 1990.

Chips and Technologies set a record, going public in seven quarters from date of inception.

Typical Participants.   Enter the Wall Street clan: investment bankers and security analysts, and their lawyers. Joining them will be the securities law expert from the startup's law firm and the startup's CPA firm.

And now the CEO gets to deal directly with institutional investors who will come to hear the company's story during the CEO's road show.

Finally, the CEO gets to cope with all those members of the general public who now know his phone number and who feel they are owed a personal explanation for the company's $1.25 stock price drop yesterday.

Help Needed.   The CEO needs help from experts in investment banking, Wall Street, and securities law. Each expert will get a share of the money that is raised.

Major Costs.   An IPO is the most expensive cost measured in both absolute and percentage terms. The company can count on spending $500,000 on lawyers, printing, etc. And the underwriting syndicate gets about 7 percent of the total capital raised (in other words, millions of dollars).

And not a nickel of these expenses is tax deductible.

All the details are spelled out in Chapter 13, "Wall Street and the Initial Public Offering." This information will help the CEO's negotiations with the investment banker.

The amount of time required of the company's finance staff is high, as is the time required of top management for due diligence and road shows.

Main Risks.   The main risk is *missing the window*. CEOs warned us of coming out too early—or too late. This is discussed in detail in Chapter 13.

Related risks include a stock price that is too high—or too low; selling into a souring stock market; hitting an unpredicted quarter of soft sales.

The ultimate risk is that the offering may have to be pulled off the market and offered another time . . . or never at all.

Output and ROI. Successful IPOs produce all of these things:

- Image of success in the high tech industry. This can help salespeople sell credibility more easily.
- Investors increase their invested monies from 5 times to 200 times or more.
- Founders become multimillionaires (on paper).
- Employees increase their net worth by a nice multiple of monthly wages.

Managing the Post-IPO Stage

Most of this is covered in detail in Chapter 13; suffice it to say here that this is territory calling for experience. It is a dangerous stage to tackle without good advice and much experience.

Dealing with skilled Wall Street security analysts and little old lady investors on the same day calls for an experienced, dedicated expert. The specialized securities laws must be understood and carefully adhered to.

And the CEO and founder must remember to work out a personal strategy for dealing with Rule 144 and other regulations that greatly limit the amount of stock that they can sell during the years immediately following the initial public offering.

Overview of the Entire Process

In summary: The entrepreneur chose to focus on converting an idea to a vision that became a commercial success. It took somewhere between four to eight years to get to the IPO.

The entrepreneur learned to deal with a vast array of participants, all of whom earn something because of their dealings with the startup.

The help the founders needed was half effort and skill, and half taking advantage of the big breaks, good and bad.

The founder got strangers to believe in his or her vision to the tune of $3 to $50 million, and spent it all.

The core team worked very hard, and incurred a significant personal cost for such success. And so did many other fine employees.

The founder took a chance—on becoming a small, going-nowhere company, on going bankrupt.

The rewards are a cornucopia of satisfaction: seeing a viable company alive and doing business well; working in a great place with terrific people; earning investors $30 million to $500 million; becoming personally worth millions; gaining more self-knowledge about one's identity and motivation; drawing closer to one's spouse and family; learning to balance one's life and still be the leader of a very successful high tech startup.

4

Getting Started Legally

It is critical for startups to have good legal assistance from a very early stage. There are two general categories of legal help that the entrepreneur needs to get started: (1) legal assistance with intellectual property issues—which means assuring that the core team members depart from their employers in an ethical and legal manner, and protection of the startup's own intellectual property; and (2) general legal work, including incorporation.

The attorneys you hire can help you more effectively if you understand what their job is and how to select the best ones for your needs.

Kinds of Legal Help Required

First of all, prospective entrepreneurs need a careful plan to avoid trouble when departing from their employers. Changes in the U.S. Patent Court since 1983 have increased the value of fighting to protect proprietary intellectual property. Established companies have changed from passive to aggressive protectors of their intellectual property. Furthermore, the now-classic cases of SEEQ versus Intel and Linear Technology versus National Semiconductor have taught the legal community where the lines of battle are to be drawn.

Experienced legal counsel will help the entrepreneur sidestep potential problems and greatly reduce the chances of a court battle. In addition, the startup company's intellectual property also needs protection.

The startup's law firm must be skilled at patent work and the many specialized tasks associated with managing intellectual property. For example:

- Business contracts for specialized startups such as genetic engineering joint ventures and computer software companies require special experience not possessed by all law firms' staffs.

- Licenses to and from other companies require customizing and understanding of the business purpose behind the deal being negotiated.

- Nondisclosure agreements require advice on how to incorporate them into company policy.

- Engineering notebooks and the procedures for administering them should all be part of a deliberate strategy worked out with counsel.

Incorporating the company involves administrative tasks that are more effectively done by a law firm than by a lay person. The founders need guidance on the number of shares to issue, the class of shares, and the number of shares to assign to each person in the core group. Good counsel is knowledgeable in these areas and provides guidance based on experience with similar undertakings. Stock options require state government approval, and counsel will help the founders avoid the pitfalls in the rules attached to this important area.

Experienced and savvy attorneys can be of immense assistance when the time comes to negotiate each round of financing. They will look out for the best interests of the founders.

Finally, U.S. securities law is a specialized area that requires wisdom and intimate familiarity with the procedures and practices of Wall Street.

Here is advice from a veteran of Silicon Valley, Mike Phillips of Morrison & Foerster of Palo Alto, California:

> In selecting general counsel for a startup, the entrepreneur is essentially taking on a business partner who will play a key role in many of the company's important milestones. The entrepreneur should focus on the following factors in the selection process: competency, integrity, personal fit, and availability. Besides the obvious, competency requires substantial experience in connection with high technology and startup businesses. As to personal fit, make sure you pick a lawyer that you are comfortable with at a personal level, someone with whom you can communicate and who listens to you. Availability is also important because you want the lawyer you pick to be the one that actually does the work and not one that disappears after the selection process.

And Robert Latta of Wilson, Sonsini, Goodrich & Rosati of Palo Alto, California, advises:

> A startup CEO is well advised to be especially sensitive to the special kind of law and business issues that affect a high tech startup. Few law firms have significant experience practicing such law. This is especially true in cities outside of high technology pockets, whereas it is the strength of some firms in Silicon Valley, Southern California and Boston. There is a good solution to this problem: several startups have chosen local legal counsel for general legal work such as real estate leases and litigation, and then use high tech counsel from law firms steeped in the special work required in startup securities law, strategic partner agreements, international contracts, intellectual property, stock options, and venture capital deals. Notwithstanding geographical separation, this has proven to work well in the world of fax machines and telecommunications. And it seems to save money in the long run. One final suggestion: Be sure to meet the lawyer who will provide the sharing of minds needed by the CEO of the fledgling company—that is rarely the prominent partner with whom the CEO meets the first time.

For starters, the CEO could contact the firms reviewed by *Inc.* magazine (1990) in the article entitled "10 Top Lawyers in High Tech."

Choosing General Legal Counsel

Law firms that are experienced with startups handle both general legal work and intellectual property matters. However, we found that two different attorneys are often engaged, one for special patent work, and one for regular legal work. Here is what our research revealed an entrepreneur should look for in a good attorney.

Look for firms that are experienced with startups. Particularly valuable is the law firm that has lived with a startup from seed-round days through IPO.

Avoid using a law firm that does more work for venture capital firms than for startups. The problems are different and the startup's needs are different. There is also the possibility of mixed loyalties if the attorney continues to provide representation for the entrepreneur's investor group.

A friend who will have to subcontract most of the work is a poor choice. VCs want to deal with experienced personnel from a single firm.

Avoid automatically using the largest firm in town. Bigness is not necessarily goodness.

The law firm to choose is an experienced firm that is smart enough to provide a workable solution rather than the ultimate, costly solution, and that provides nuts and bolts how-to advice instead of lots of theory.

After selecting the right law firm, the entrepreneur should select an individual attorney or group of attorneys after determining who he or she is most comfortable with. The relationship with the particular counsel who will handle the legal work is more important than the size of a law firm or any nuances in community reputation.

Fellow CEOs, venture capitalists, and investment bankers are good sources for referrals to attorneys with relevant experience.

The entrepreneur should think of the long term and pick a firm that can go all the way to IPO with the startup. Changing firms along the way is difficult and expensive.

Choosing Patent Counsel

Competent patent counsel is not easy to find. The work is specialized and requires both technical and legal skills. Recent shifts in patent law and the sudden increase in the number of lawsuits mean that even more attention must be paid to issues of intellectual property law. Trademark skills and a knowledge of copyright law are also required.

Your candidates should be familiar with such landmark cases as Texas Instruments versus NEC, Polaroid versus Kodak (instant cameras), Lotus versus 1-2-3 clones (software). Close ties to even more specialized counsel in Washington, D.C., can also be important.

Ethical Departure from an Employer

Driven by threats to their success in setting an industry standard, established companies have recently added legal strategy to their corporate long-range plan.

For instance, Apple and Intel regularly use PR to deliberately rattle legal swords, threatening any upstart who might be even thinking of building a new product to compete head on with one of theirs. The large companies have spent hundreds of millions of dollars to create an industry standard. They mean to reap the fattest reward they can from that precious investment.

The Intellectual Property Issue.   The issue is how the founder and members of the core team can leave their current employers and not get sued. We found that most engineers were vaguely aware that this question was important. However, several startup founders said that they later came to realize that doing something wise and practical about this issue was much more complicated than they realized. Several had found themselves in trouble with their former employers.

After this issue continued to surface regularly in our research, we spent time with leading venture capital attorneys to analyze it further.

Lois Abraham of Brown & Bain in Palo Alto, California, highlighted the fundamental issue this way:

> Individuals should be especially aware that there are two groups whose intellectual property rights are protected. One is composed of the employees, whose knowledge and skills belong to each person to do what needs to be done to earning a gainful living. The other group is the employers, who are to keep the fruits of labor of employees for the benefit of the shareholders. Both groups are strongly protected by the law. Finding the line that cannot be crossed is difficult. Good legal counsel is very important.

Here is a typical problem: After the seed round is closed, the CEO discovers that the startup's lead design engineer has three schematics of his last employer's related products in some old, forgotten file boxes that are buried in the junk in his garage. The engineer says the products never got to market, but the startup's counsel sees red flags everywhere. What should the founder tell the venture investors, who performed their due diligence last month and asked about this issue?

Potential Problems and Pitfalls. There is a long list of headaches to watch out for; here are some examples:

- Members of the startup's technical staff have taken boxes of work home from their former employer over the past three to nine months, particularly in the past four weeks. Included in the boxes are:
  - Copies of a few overhead transparencies that contain the bold capitalized header: "CONFIDENTIAL — COMPANY PROPRIETARY — XYMEX CORP."
  - Articles copied from electronics magazines that include these handwritten notes: "Good idea for new product," "Should be feature added to Xymex 6141," "Tell Mike and marketing staff."
- The founder cannot remember what he did with the last three backup tapes and box of diskettes. The former employer has just called with the information that these items cannot be found.
- The startup's marketing guru has just shown the founder a copy of a copy of a copy of the proposed pricing of Big Corp's Model 9999. An interviewee (still employed by Big Corp) left the pricing copy with the startup's marketing vice president.
- Your attorney turns green when told that the new company's core team has been designing product and writing their business plan at night and on weekends during the long-term planning session at Big Corp, where they are still employed. The startup's first product will be bus-and-socket-compatible with Big Corp's top-selling model 2219.

Given any of the above circumstances, an opposing attorney can skillfully present a damning case, twisting the facts to paint a picture of evil, scheming people who violated their employer's trust and stole company secrets.

Practices and Policies for Successful Prevention.   Table 4-1 lists some important rules to follow when leaving an employer. The secret to success here is *advance planning*. The founder's actions will leave a trail that will paint a picture of his character. An opposing counsel will seek to use—disadvantageously—every detail of the founder's actions and those of the startup's key employees.

The advice in Table 4-1 provides an overall plan that maximizes protection for the founders. Table 4-2 lists steps that should be taken that will increase the value of the startup's own intellectual property. The key factor to success here is *discipline*.

Successful CEOs insisted from day one on establishing and following selected policies and practices. The objective was clear: to make it clear to all employees and visitors that this company places the highest priority on retention of proprietary information. Sloppiness was not tolerated. New hires were carefully instructed on policy and procedures in their first week of employment. VPs were expected to set the example for the company.

TABLE 4-1.   Nine Commandments to Follow When Leaving an Employer

1. Take *nothing* with you.
2. Take no notebooks, meeting notes, schematics, drawings, business plans, or portions thereof.
3. Make no copies of anything, not even magazine articles with your handwritten notes in the margins.
4. Tell your supervisor of the whereabouts of any mag tapes, diskettes, or other electronic information storage devices that you had access to or used.
5. Do not write any portion of a business plan until well after you have left your employer, preferably months afterward.
6. Do not meet with cofounders until after all of you have left your employers.
7. Do everything you can to prevent the possibility of a lawyer twisting your actions into a story that makes you look like a sneaky thief.
8. After leaving your employers and upon your first meeting as founders, get your patent counsel and general counsel to write a letter to your former employers stating what business you plan to enter and asking what specific proprietary information the employers may feel you possess.
9. *Talk to no one* from or at your former employer until your legal counsel gives you the all-clear signal.

Sources: Skjerven, Morrill, MacPherson, San Jose, CA., and Saratoga Venture Finance

TABLE 4-2. How to Protect a Startup Company's Intellectual Property

1. Have all employees sign upon first day of employment an "Employee Proprietary and Confidential Information Agreement." It will help keep the company's secrets secret.

2. Install and enforce a written patent notebook procedure. It will strengthen your company's claims that its intellectual property is very valuable, as well as improve chances of obtaining desired patents.

3. Issue to all of the company's technical staff written patent notebook recordkeeping instructions. Be sure your people respect the importance of these instructions.

4. Be sure your VP of Engineering strictly manages the issuing and tracking of all notebooks given to the technical staff.

5. Keep on hand a good stock of the kind of notebooks required by your instructions. Do not use the kind of notebooks commonly found in stationery stores.

6. Issue to employees and all managers Confidential Disclosure Agreements that cover the following areas and instruct them to use the documents in dealing with non-employees:

   a. STARTUP, INC. and a third party exchanging confidential information.

   b. STARTUP, INC. receiving confidential information from a third party.

   c. STARTUP, INC. disclosing confidential information to a third party.

7. Require that your VP of Finance and Administration issue and control all Confidential Disclosure Agreements.

8. Prepare a document called "Submission of Inventions or Suggestions" for the use of third parties, typically nonemployees but also often nontechnical employees of STARTUP, INC.

9. Prepare an "Invention Disclosure" form that will clearly identify the holder of any proprietary information that STARTUP, INC. may be interested in using or developing.

Sources: Skjerven, Morrill, MacPherson and Saratoga Venture Finance

Case Study: Newtech Company

In October of 1985, Bill and Kim committed to creating their own startup. They quickly formed a core group of four and started drafting their business plan. They had worked closely together at Radco and they both had outstanding track records for creating the top three products that literally saved Radco from bankruptcy as a startup five years earlier. Radco was still trying to get to IPO. Their shares were fully vested, and neither liked the latest leadership of the company.

Bill had resigned from Radco earlier that month. He had contacted Kim, who had been consulting for nine months while working at home on prototype

product designs. They decided they needed a CEO as a leader in order to attract any venture capital and called Mike at Tech, Inc. They had gotten to know and respect Mike seven years earlier when all three of them had worked together at Tech, Inc. before Bill and Kim left for Radco.

After some consideration, Mike agreed to lead the startup. After two months of work on the business plan, he contacted his first venture firm, which immediately scheduled a presentation at Tech Ventures.

During the presentation, the venture partners became quite excited about the Newtech strategy. However, as the due diligence questions got around to technology, it became clear that nobody at Newtech had given much thought to the problems and pitfalls that might arise with intellectual property issues.

Moreover, an embarrassing moment of silence occurred when one partner asked how the shares were divided. Mike had not yet settled that with the other founders.

At the end of the all-day session, the senior partner told Mike in frank terms that he had handled the intellectual property issues very poorly. He gave Mike the name of a local law firm, and Mike was in its office the next afternoon.

Cathy represented the law firm and was the expert in technology problems. She began by asking Mike for a retainer, which Mike paid out of his personal funds. She started questioning the founders in her office the next morning.

Cathy soon uncovered the following:

1. *Mike had created no problems with his way of handling the departure from his last employer. However, there was some related general product marketing information that might be a problem. He had obtained it at Suma, from a friend. Newtech would compete with Suma. Cathy put that problem aside for the time being.*

2. *Kim had indeed left Radco nine months ago; that was true. However, she had not told Mike she was still on retainer to Radco. Nor had she told Mike that she had signed a nondisclosure agreement the day she left, and that the related information was vital to the technology strategy of Newtech. Kim's Southeast Asian cultural background always led her to withhold troublesome information until the last minute. Cathy had to pull the facts out of her using the best inquiry techniques she could muster.*

3. *Bill thought he had departed from Radco in a very professional manner, on good terms with the president and his boss, the VP of R&D. Cathy soon learned that Bill had cleaned out his office the day he departed. He had tossed four cartons of paper into a trash bin himself and had left six mag tapes in the cubicle of an MIS operator who was gone at the time. In addition, he had put two bookcases of materials of all sorts into cardboard boxes that he had obtained from the copy room; these were now stacked in his garage at home. He had little idea of exactly what was in those boxes. Cathy told him to bring the boxes to her office for an inventory of their contents.*

By Friday of that week, Cathy had a list of the contents of Bill's boxes. They contained copies of presentations to top management, clearly marked CONFIDENTIAL and COMPANY PROPRIETARY. There were several old engineering notebooks and many copies of technical articles and papers on products that were related to Radco's leading-edge products.

That same afternoon, Cathy received a phone call from Bill. His voice sounded quite shaken. His friend, the head of R&D at Radco, had written him a letter containing some legal-sounding wording, including this sentence: "It has come to our attention that you may have in your possession six mag tapes, two schematics of Radco Model 34340, and other proprietary documents that belong to Radco."

Cathy met with Bill on Monday morning. Bill wanted to call the president, talk to him, and straighten things out in person. Cathy advised him to wait until the following day and turned her attention to learning from Bill the basic technology and strategy behind Newtech's fundamental business plan.

She learned that Newtech intended to design its first product, the Newtech 1, to be pin-and-socket- and board-compatible with the Radco 34340, except that it would run on a 32-bit bus and be four times as fast. The speed advantage would come from Bill's and Kim's design skills. The next products would become an ultra–high-speed family of products designed around the Newtech 1.

When Bill left at 4:00 p.m., Cathy firmly told him not to talk to anyone at Radco until further notice.

On Monday evening, the regular weekly meeting night for the Newtech core team of eight people, Kim did not appear. Calls to her home got only the telephone answering device. Mike became concerned. Bill said he would try to lunch with Kim on Tuesday and find out what was happening.

At 6:30 p.m. the next day, Mike met Bill at a local restaurant. He was shocked to learn that Kim would not be joining Newtech after all. The president of Radco had made Kim a counteroffer and told Kim to accept it or face years in court with tons of legal bills, a ruined reputation, and all her friends angry at her. Besides, he had argued, Newtech would never get funded with a big lawsuit facing it. And the president had gone on to say he knew all about Newtech's plans and the technology belonged to Radco and its hard-nosed venture capitalists. Mike and Bill left at 7:05 p.m. in a very despondent mood.

The next morning, Mike got his third call from Tech Ventures' senior partner. How were things going? When would Mike have the intellectual properties issues resolved? Mike stalled him, said "Soon," hung up, and went to pick up the day's mail.

He sorted through the stack while he slowly walked back down the driveway to the house, but he stopped short as he immediately recognized the Radco logo on a business envelope. He tore it open on the spot and read a detailed description of the general technology direction that Newtech was planning to take; that Radco considered its patents and products to be proprietary; and that any hiring

*of Radco employees or of those who had recently left Radco would result in
immediate, severe legal action by Radco's law firm against Mike personally,
since Newtech was not yet incorporated.*

*Mike called Bill to talk things over. During the conversation, Bill slipped and
told Mike that he had gone over to Radco on the previous Friday to try to talk to
the president. (At the meeting on Monday, Bill had only talked about wanting to
talk to Radco's president, whereas in reality he had already done so!) The talk
had ended with an offer to consider some sort of joint venture, and Bill had then
told the president about the product plans and strategy for Newtech.*

*At 10:30 a.m. on Thursday, Mike made up his mind what he had to do. He
called the senior partner at Tech Ventures and told him that the founders of
Newtech had decided not to proceed at this time.*

Protecting Your Own Intellectual Property

To what degree is it important to protect a startup company's intellectual
property? One experienced venture capitalist answered that frequently
asked question for us in these terms: "We realize that the new business
enterprise could go bankrupt. And while we do not plan on that sad
event, we do seek to have something, something of worth, something
tangible to offer for sale if all else fails. That is why we shy away from
companies that get their worth mainly from intangibles such as services.
We much prefer to invest in companies that will generate a new technology, a real and valuable way of doing something better and something
very valuable to customers. The CEOs of the companies in which we
invest had better protect that asset with all of their diligence, or we will
find someone else who will."

Procedures and Practices.   We found that all startups kept their secrets
closely held to some degree. The consistency varied widely. Enlighten-
ment came for a few on the shocking day that they received the IBM
"SWAT" squad, who told them what secrecy really meant and how to
build secure rooms, etc., before IBM would deliver its latest computer for
alpha testing at the startup's new-products development lab. Microsoft
was among those companies.

However, we discovered that any security problems were not in the
companies' physical defenses; rather, they were in the legal area, where
most CEOs lack experience. In addition to the personal inexperience of
founders, there have been recent shifts in the U.S. Patent Court, and
court or trial results in areas like copyrighting microcode, that affect the
security of intellectual property.

Table 4-2 lists nine practical steps for protecting a company's intellectual
property. Allen MacPherson, a patent attorney in a San Jose, California

firm, was good enough to share these steps with us. He has developed customized programs, policies, and practices for his startup clients based on these recommendations. According to Allen, "The key is to develop a *documentable practice* that is followed by your employees as a matter of daily habit. You want to be able to demonstrate to a judge that your actions showed how vital and valuable to the company was its intellectual property."

Ken Allen, of Townsend & Townsend, Palo Alto, California, told us how important it was to "start right from the beginning with a foundation built on guidelines established up front by the legal counsel who will have to represent the company in related legal actions."

Case Study: Extro Electronics, Inc.

Just how practical legal advice is was demonstrated to an electronics startup CEO who recently recruited a top star from another startup that was floundering. Sam, the engineer, had impeccable credentials, an excellent track record, and a good cultural fit.

Jack, the CEO, was elated and greeted Sam personally when he saw him report to work at Extro on Tuesday. All went well until Sam failed to report to work on Friday.

After a few phone calls, Jack learned that Sam was at his desk, at work at Discus Systems. And Sam was not returning phone calls, either at his office or at home.

Jack called in his longtime assistant and had her pull Sam's personnel file. He found, to his great surprise, that the file was practically empty—no signed acceptance of the offer of employment from Extro, no signed nondisclosure agreement, nothing but a copy of Sam's resume.

"Now what do we do?" he lamented to his assistant. "We told Sam about our plans and technology, and Discus Systems could use that information to scoop us in the marketplace!"

At the time of this writing, the case remained open, with Sam still not answering phone calls and Jack still worried.

Patents, Trademarks, Copyrights, and Trade Secrets. Each of these—patents, trademarks, copyrights, and trade secrets—plays an important role in the startup's overall intellectual property strategy. Each calls for special expertise, to which good legal counsel can direct the CEO.

What we found missing most often was an overt, conscious plan to use these legal elements to construct a thorough effort to use intellectual property as part of the startup's overall plan to succeed.

And these elements fit nicely into a complete legal plan that reinforces the company's plan to build and reinforce a sustainable competitive advantage.

Incorporating the Company

It is always a pleasure to see the joy on the faces of the founders of a startup as they say enthusiastically, "We're a company, a real, live company." In legal terms, they are now a registered entity, a thing called a corporation. And they are subject to operating within all the state laws and regulations that govern such a business entity. Good legal counsel is a must.

The Role of an Attorney. Although it is technically possible to save a few dollars by doing one's own incorporation, we found that everyone advises against it.

The startup's counsel will help choose a company name, file all the papers with the secretary of the chosen state, and pay all required fees. There are also tax documents and filing papers to be created before the company can go into action as a corporation. In addition, the attorney must draft closely related legal documents for incentive stock options, and they must be scrutinized by the Secretary of State of the state in which the startup is incorporated.

It all goes together as a package that good law firms have set up as boilerplate on word processors. Their clerks are ready to move the paperwork through the bureaucracy and pay the fees on time. And the good firms do not charge much for this; for example, in California it's often less than $1000.

Picking a Company Name. We found a great deal of chaos in picking the startup's final name. We were given dozens of ways to select one and as many reasons for picking a certain kind of name. In the end, few people even cared.

What *is* important is picking a name and getting on with life—with raising the money.

For the less experienced, here is a summary of the consensus of opinion on picking a good name:

- Do not spend much time or money on it. The CEO should decide on a name if the founders cannot reach consensus in a day or two.

- Do not pay professional name finders to get you a name. Only if a product or company needs a *lot* of differentiation—as is usually the case with consumer-intensive companies—should the principals expend a great deal of effort on name choosing. A name earns its reputation over time, no matter which one is chosen.

- There is about a 75 percent chance that the first name will be changed within 18 months, according to startup company veterans.

Reserving a Name. Each state has a method of checking to make sure a proposed company name is not being used already and of letting a startup reserve that name for a few weeks. This procedure allows the founders to work out incorporation documents with their attorney. It is possible to call a telephone number in many states, pay a fee for an extended holding time, and thus get the name the founders have fallen in love with.

Cost to Incorporate. It should not be expensive to incorporate a company. A reputable law firm will charge around $1000 to get the job done. The startup should use the firm chosen for general legal matters.

Several top law firms familiar with venture capital startup companies told us they used paralegal talent to do routine incorporation work, which allowed them to charge a lower-than-normal fee for it

Typical Agreements. Each state has its own set of documents that are needed to incorporate. The firm of Morrison and Foerster in Palo Alto, California, gave us a list of the more important documents needed in that state. These are typical, and are listed in Table 4-3.

The stock shareholder documents are closely interlinked with the other legal papers.

Some CEOs thought it advantageous to postpone incorporation until the seed round was completed. They wanted to avoid pressures from VCs on founders to contribute a lot of personal cash to the founding capital of the new company. The founders *must* put in capital, and the attorney will explain how much is necessary.

TABLE 4-3. Typical Startup Incorporation Documents

1. Memorandum of Action of Sole Incorporator of STARTUP, INC.

2. Closing documents and personal checks for purchase of shares by founders

3. Unanimous Written Consent in Lieu of the first Meeting of the Board of Directors of STARTUP, INC.

4. Proprietary Information and Inventions Agreement

5. Letter to Internal Revenue Service for Election Under Section 83(b) of the Internal Revenue Code of 1954, As Amended

6. State form called: Commission of Corporations: Notice of Transaction Pursuant to Corporations Code Section XYZ3333(f)

7. Statement by Domestic Stock Corporation, to be filed with the Secretary of State

Sources: Morrison & Foerster and Saratoga Venture Finance

Problems and Pitfalls. The number-one problem cited to us over and over was picking the wrong legal counsel. Nothing beats experience in working for startups.

The next often cited problem was getting the general counsel to do specialized work for which they were not well qualified, such as intellectual property work.

Other pitfalls high on the most-often-mentioned list included:

- Using a giant law firm lacking in practical street smarts needed by startups.
- Picking a firm for its reputation and not for its know-how with the specialized technology in question.
- Finding that the startup company is a second-class citizen compared with the other clients serviced by that law firm.
- Switching attorneys in midstream. It is important to pick the best firm and stick with it.

Summary

Remember: your choice of lawyer will be with you for a long time, so pick carefully! True, the CEO can fire a law firm—but that is much more awkward to do than it sounds (we found no startup that had decided to fire its legal counsel, in spite of some black stories about poor advice and expensive, low-grade service). So do your best to pick the best the first time. One CEO told us he thinks his choice of lawyer saved him millions in negotiations with investors. Another CEO said he grew to appreciate the business advice he got from his lawyer.

The startups also said what a pain it was to have to work with an inexperienced lawyer: one such member of the bar forgot to check off the tax form box that would have prevented the CEO from having to pay taxes on his shares each time they vested! A veteran investment banker said that going public without the best lawyer experienced in securities law was like going through hell.

We are convinced that the choice of a good law firm is one of your most important decisions. The choice of the particular partner is even more important, whether it be for corporate law or intellectual property advice. In addition to helping to get your firm incorporated, the lawyer will be experienced with business plans and able and willing to read and comment on your first drafts. Our next chapter will help you get started writing a top-quality business plan that will not only impress your lawyer, but more importantly, impress the people with the money to invest in your startup.

5

Preparing the Business Plan

When you prepare a business plan worthy of being financed, it will stand out. Venture capitalists told us time after time that most of the plans they see are "just plain bad."

CEOs who succeeded in obtaining the funding they wanted told us why their plans were funded. Our research revealed that the heart of their secret for success was their ability to document the startup's distinctive competence, the company's competitive advantage, and the management's plans to *sustain that advantage.* The greatest danger was in creating a plan without advantage.

In this chapter we have incorporated the work of leading business thinkers. Peter Drucker classifies entrepreneurs' strategies; Donald Clifford and Richard Cavanagh of McKinsey identify what to look for in winning companies; Michael Porter of Harvard helps top management focus on doing useful strategic thinking; and Tom Peters talks about how to test your company's uniqueness.

This chapter provides an outline to show the startup CEO what a venture capitalist looks for in the body of a written business plan. It explains how to create financial projections using a personal computer and spreadsheet software, so that the budding entrepreneur can get off to a head start, save valuable time, and have more days available for strategic thinking.

This chapter analyzes a new participant—the CPA firm. Picking a good CPA firm is analyzed based on interviews of startup CFOs and CEOs.

This chapter is devoted to helping the founders of a new enterprise create the core of a business plan that will have a better chance of succeeding than the other 1000 business plans it is competing with.

Unlike most of the literature on startups, this chapter will not spend much time on the outline: that is not where the heart of success lies. Rather, we will focus on the findings of successful people—venture capitalists, CEOs, and some of the giants who have dedicated their careers and personal lives to analyzing and improving the practice of modern business management—people like Peter Drucker—who have recently published research findings regarding successful and failed new companies. Their findings may shock you.

The diligent reader will be able to apply this chapter's pragmatic suggestions and significantly improve his or her chances of raising needed capital.

Required Material

Like a résumé for a job interview, a business plan is required material. And just as a résumé alone does not get the applicant a job, neither will a business plan get a founder financing; the funding will depend on how well the founder manages the process of high tech capital formation. A business plan is expected to cover certain details, which we will spell out later in this chapter.

Opinions on when and how to use the business plan to raise capital varied considerably among those interviewed. CEOs who were successful said that deciding when to use the written plan was a key element in their tactics. The founder must know when to submit the business plan, to whom, and how to present it. (We found several clever methods used.) *Do not start by mailing business plans to a lot of venture capitalists.*

Confidentiality

Confidentiality was of concern to all CEOs. But venture capitalists told us it was impractical for VCs to sign nondisclosure agreements; they see so many deals that to do so would invite legal trouble. And we were told in confidence of business plans clearly marked "Confidential and Company Proprietary" that were handed out by venture capitalists to other startup companies.

Participants strongly advised careful control of the number of copies made and to whom they were given. Several CEOs required VCs to return the business plan, uncopied.

Timing

When should you submit your business plan to a venture firm? Many CEOs told of sending copies to 10 to 20 venture capital firms, but receiving virtually no response. The reason for this is simple: A three-man venture capital office receives about 1000 business plans a year, or about four per day. At that rate, the office could be doing nothing but reading plans, if it chose to do so. Instead, the VCs work out a method of screening the plans and read only certain ones. The rest are either scrapped, returned to the sender in one to four months, or in a few cases, filed.

An entrepreneur's goal is to avoid such a fate and instead get the startup's plan to the top of the hot deal in-box for careful scrutiny by the managing partner of the venture firm.

Attention Getters

How is this accomplished? Here are some tactics that worked for successfully funded startups:

- *Always start with a personal introduction.* This was the *major* recommendation by everyone, including the people with the money to invest.
- *Visit first. Do not send a plan until after at least one personal meeting.* This saves everyone time. The VC will not go further if he or she has decided to keep out of a particular kind of business. And the founder can ask how many competitors the VC firm has invested in or is about to invest in.
- *Be frank and find out.* Some CEOs had extensive sessions with a certain venture firm that resulted in a "No, thank you," then later read in the paper about that firm funding another directly competing startup. "Be sure you do not get pumped for the wrong reasons," said founders that learned the hard way.
- *Present the plan, tell your story.* Marketing CEOs especially recommended this be done as soon as possible, preferably in the second meeting. The CEO can control the flow of information better and can be specific in how it is presented in response to the questions of the venture partners present. More information can be kept confidential this way than if you mailed the business plan.
- *Negotiate, don't teach.* One CEO put it this way: "After weeks and weeks of work, several presentations, and reference checks galore, the

venture firm said 'No'! I got angry when I realized they were learning our business on our nickel!" He went on to say he'd never again spend time with a venture capitalist who had no hands-on experience in his or a related business.

- *Treat every contact as part of the overall negotiation for money.* Put each question into the context of pricing a deal. Then you will not be surprised later when the lead partner says, "We think we need *n* percent (which is 10 percent more than you had anticipated) of your startup, because you said a few weeks ago that you did not have much [management experience or whatever . . .] and that is critical to your company's success or failure, in our opinion." In other terms, focus on doing a deal from day one; never assume that the venture capitalist is just being a nice guy, talking to you about your neat ideas. After all, he is in business and is just as short of time as you are.

- *Realize that business plans are everything and nothing.* This paradox is easy to understand. History favors the reality that the successful startup usually abandons its original plan in some significant way as it gets into business. "People, we always start with the people," was so often said by VCs that one wonders why a plan is even necessary. Yet the plans are agonized over, read and reread. And the final funding decision depends a great deal on how it impresses the venture partners. We concluded that what is really going on under the surface, consciously or unconsciously, is a search for the missing sustainable competitive advantage. (More on that later in the chapter.)

- *Write a super executive summary.* Because that is all most readers take time to read. They then attend the first presentation meeting to take the rest in. One partner will take on the role of lead partner and will read the plan in detail. He will be the founder's primary contact, and the deal's life or death will depend upon his degree of responsiveness during the course of the investigation.

- *Write well.* Most plans are awful, say the luckless readers. Use a word processor with a spelling checker. The goal of the startup's founders is to stand out—but not for bad composition. The poor VC has an in-box piled high with unread business plans and will appreciate one that is concise, clear, and informative.

- *Be neat without overdoing things.* In this day of desktop publishing, documents can be stunning. However, a great strategy is worth much more than beauty.

- *Keep the packaging crisp, not drenched in gold leaf.* Like school term papers, content is what counts. We've seen VCs tear off and throw away expensive, bulky covers and binders, fancy pictures, and fat sections of copies of magazine articles.

Deal Flow

Deal flow is the behind-the-scenes power game that can suddenly turn a CEO who has worked hard into a star, or result in a soft, "Sorry, but we have decided to pass on investing in your deal—in this round." Deal flow is a kind of Monopoly game of venture capitalists: "Sam, we'll let you in on Super Corp. run by Dr. Wunderkid—if you let us in on your next super deal . . ."

Any deal becomes one of the playing cards. And if Power VC Firm drops a hot deal in the lap of the startup's lead VC, the CEO may suddenly find the phone ringing with the "Sorry . . ." response. Not surprisingly, the substitute deal could be with a direct competitor. It happens, and increasingly so, with more than 2000 venture firms competing with more than $30 billion of venture funds to invest annually.

How can such an outcome be avoided? We asked that question of our interviewees and they summarized their strategies as follows:

- *Get hot and stay hot.* In the end, deals are decided on emotion. A CEO must not let a deal cool down or lose momentum.

- *Always have alternative sources of funds.* The sharp CEOs were able to create competing groups, all vying for the deal. But there is the danger of becoming shopworn. Avoiding this requires sophistication and skill. The startup's legal counsel, CPA, and startup consultant can help immensely here.

- *Never count the cash until it's in the bank.* CEOs lamented about the closing party that took place before the funds were in the bank—and the funds never got there. Closings are delicate. A CEO needs all the help available to secure a solid closing.

- *Always remember that deal flow is at work.* The CEO should not be too disappointed when the "Sorry . . ." call comes in. It should be expected. Even great salespeople expect mostly "no's." It's not the end of the world.

Due Diligence

The founders must assume that *everything* written in their business plan will be checked, particularly details of marketing assumptions. The VC is looking for hidden traps, oversights, oversimplifications, and upside opportunities. When the weeks and months of due diligence work are finished, the VC will try to find the silver thread woven through the business plan: It will be in the form of a simple, one-sentence line that will become his or her reason for saying yes to your invitation to invest in this startup.

What Investors Look For

Now let's concentrate on the perspective of the venture capitalists, so that you can better see what they are looking for, and looking out for, based on their successful and unsuccessful experiences.

The experienced investor looks for many things. We found a long list cited by the people with whom we spoke. (We'll go into this in more detail in Chapter 9, "Venture Capitalists.")

Our findings have been categorized into five sets of things venture investors look for in a startup. They are, in order of importance:

1. People/management that can get the job done
2. A brilliant technology that can be commercialized
3. A large, rapidly expanding market
4. Strategy for an "unfair advantage"
5. An attractive price per share

When asked which is most important, venture capitalists answered in resounding unison: *People management is number one.*

Management Experience.   Investors want most a *complete* team, with a president, and with VPs for each function. (The possible exception is a VP Finance; the reasons for this are presented in Chapter 9 in the section "How a VC Firm Controls Its Investment.") Chapter 6 discusses the team requirements in more detail.

The general rule is: *The more complete the team, the more likely the startup will get funded.*

Investors consider it a valuable asset to their funding if a startup is run by a team that has been working together for 5 to 10 years. One example is Linear Technology, who walked out of National Semiconductor as a unit (sans VP Finance) and started in business with the key functions filled. That is the good news.

The bad news is that Linear was sued by National. At the time of this writing, the lawyers have yet to completely settle the matter. For guidance on how to avoid this kind of lawsuit, see Chapter 4, in the section called "Ethical Departure from an Employer."

Next in importance after completeness comes *competence*. The president must at least have a proven track record that has demonstrated the likelihood of success in the new venture. This does not require experience in a prior successful startup. Bob Swanson, president of Linear, had no prior startup experience; he had been with National as a manager for most of his career. Prior to the startup, he was general manager of National's linear business.

After competence comes *maturity*. It is very common to begin with an incomplete team, putting individuals lacking adequate experience as managers of people in the position of being corporate officers. The first management problem that venture investors look for is people in positions for which they are not qualified. A former salesperson in the role of president will not be well received if he has no prior track record as a general manager, no matter how well he has succeeded as manager of a national sales force; such people are viewed as looking for something other than financial business success. Consequently, the VCs carefully scan the management section of the business plan that contains all résumés.

A core group of high tech people frequently label themselves vice presidents, with one becoming president, creating a problem later when there are personnel to be managed and business goals to be met. In the raw seed stage of funding, VCs investing in that portion of the life of a company may reluctantly accept an existing set of self-assigned officers, but with the proviso that such people step aside when the seed venture capital firm recruits experienced leaders who are more satisfactory to investors.

Emerging Incompetence. Emerging incompetence is a common malady in startups; it is hard to avoid. What happens over time is that the founders and early hires are almost always outgrown by the exploding growth of management problems in the expanding company. This commonly happens before the initial public offering.

It is especially evident when times of trouble inevitably come. The board of directors, dominated by the venture capitalists, will try to talk such managers into stepping aside, but all too often intense personal emotions and egos enter into the fray, especially by founders, and a fight then becomes bitter:

Founder: "I started this company; I want to remain president!"
Venture Capitalist: "If you don't step down, this startup will never get another nickel of the capital it needs to survive!"

However, the fight is usually quite brief; eventually, the board members have a brief squabble behind closed doors, agree to act as a single united body, and emerge with their unalterable decision. And out go the (often not fully vested) resisting employees, regardless of their titles, personal sacrifices, or prior contributions to the startup.

We only hear about the startup management heroes, the giants on the cover of *Business Week* like Hewlett and Packard, Sporck and Noyce and Sanders, and billionaire Bill Gates. For each one of those, there are probably a thousand stories of founding managers who fought and lost as their startup outgrew them. There are also successful stories of early team members who stepped aside and stayed, at least for a few more years.

In general, the management team will be incomplete at first. Because of this, the investor looking at the startup will want to hear a plan for filling out the team with people having the skills necessary to help the startup succeed.

Brilliant Technology That Can Be Commercialized.   Simply put, can the idea become a commercial reality? Can the high tech team convert it from a laboratory success into a device that can be manufactured by the thousands at a low cost? How high is the risk in the technology?

Ben Rosen was asked what his firm looks for in a startup. He told the *Wall Street Week* television audience, "We look for blinding technology!" He would quickly add that there must be a reasonable chance to convert a brilliant flash of an idea into a wave of manufacturable product.

Large, Rapidly Expanding Market.   It is almost obvious that investors are looking for a rapidly expanding market. Yet, exceptions create the color—as well as a clarification—of this fact. For example, there are often the "as-yet-not-yet-started" markets: The Sony Walkman was an amazing success, but it was started even though market research showed very little consumer interest. Biotechnology engineering spawned Genentech even though investors and industry analysts were unable to predict the future potential. And consider successful Linear Technology, whose analog integrated circuit market was well established and grew more slowly than the digital IC market. VCs have committed millions to superconductor startups without any existing applications or markets.

In the case of Linear, the sustainable competitive advantage was founded upon a unique phenomenon of analog technology: the designers of linear integrated analog circuits are generally much more experienced and more scarce than digital designers. By attracting the top analog designers to a single, analog-only company, a case was made to create a startup company in a mature industry.

As for new, untested markets: that is what most startups are all about. In fact, it is probably the single greatest challenge to a startup marketing leader, which is why hiring a VP of marketing with prior startup experience is so valuable. The VCs are familiar with this reality and go about testing the realities of business plan claims by various means, including sessions with Dataquest and other market research firms.

However, we found the VCs most favored method was to telephone a couple of potential users and ask them about the likelihood of their buying the proposed product. A CEO should have a prepared list of such potential buyers for the venture capitalist to call. It may ensure that the VC says yes.

Strategy.   Cutting across all the above investors' concerns is a priority consideration of how the startup management plans to get ahead and stay ahead. We were told that the VCs spend the most time on this issue. Because of its importance, we have devoted two sections later in this chapter to strategy, "Sustainable Competitive Advantage," and "Creating Your Company's Strategy." The individual who understands those sections is well on the way to success.

Overview of a Business Plan

There is no magic about what should go into a good business plan. Table 5-1 provides a generic outline of the eight sections that should be included. Following is a brief outline of what should be covered in each section.

Executive Summary.   It should be brief, and it must be *great*. This is about all most readers will ever scan, let alone read. It must catch their attention, answer their key questions, and entice them to read further. It should be treated as a comprehensive miniplan. Your unfair advantage must stand out clearly.

Customer Need and Business Opportunity.   What is the startup going to build and how? Why would a customer want it? How well will it perform? Include your product technology here. Marketing strategy discussion starts in this section. Start building your unfair advantage in detail.

Business Strategy and Key Milestones.   This chapter summarizes the startup's strategy. It includes a one-page chart showing sequential, cumulative headcount and cash flow at each significant milestone.

Marketing Plan.   A great deal of time should be spent on this section. When the VC finishes reading it, he or she should be confident of how the startup will position its first products and why customers will value them relative to the competition.

Operations Plan.   This section should contain enough detail to show how the startup will design and manufacture its first products. The VCs will grill founders on the realism of the schedule to get to first customer shipment. Show total headcounts and facilities requirements.

Management and Key Personnel.   This should be kept as short and focused as possible. The emphasis should be on directly related experience, especially track records as managers. Irrelevant experience can be omitted.

TABLE 5-1. Outline of a Business Plan

Executive Summary
   Business opportunity, technology, product, market, management
   Proposed financing
      Amount
      Use of proceeds
   Summary of five-year income statement and capital requirements

Customer Need and Business Opportunity
   Product and technology description, uses

Business Strategy and Key Milestones
   Include one page showing cumulative cash need and head count at each
   milestone.

Marketing Plan
   Customer need
   Market segmentation
   Channels of distribution
   Sales strategy and plans
   Five-year sales forecast
   Competition and positioning

Operations Plan
   Engineering plan
   Manufacturing plan
   Facilities and administration plan

Management and Key Personnel
   Incentive compensation program
   Detailed résumés
   Organization
   Staffing plan and headcount projections

Financial Projections
   Assumptions
   Five-year pro forma forecasts
   Income statement
   Balance sheet
   Cash flow statement

Appendices

Source: Saratoga Venture Finance

Financial Projections.   Use a simple spreadsheet model to project the startup's financial success and need for capital. Include forecasts by month or quarter for years 1 and 2, with annual summaries for years 1 through 5. Build in conservative assumptions. Details of revenue by product line, average selling prices (ASP)s, and so on, should be kept in backup files in case they are called for.

Appendices.   These are not often used. They can contain photographs or copies of market research projections. Appendices should *not* be filled with bulky backup data.

Presentation.   A total of 30 to 50 pages is typical of what is written. Try to cut it to 12 pages. The shorter the better, although short ones are hardest to write. Make about 30 copies of your plan at the copy shop, and bind about half in some kind of neat, sturdy folder—nothing gaudy. You will soon be making a lot of changes, so there's no need to run up a big copy bill for soon-to-be obsoleted business plans. Each grilling by the VCs will uncover weaknesses that need fixing, which allows the founders to build a better plan as they go along.

Resources.   There are some very good free resources for preparing a business plan. Some venture capitalists have guides they will send upon request. Here are two that are available from a couple of the best Big Eight accounting firms:

- *Outline for a High Technology, New Venture Business Plan*. Arthur Young.
- *Business Planning*. Peat Marwick, Private Business Advisory Services.

The larger firms have local offices in large cities nationwide that will send copies to people requesting them by telephone.

The Importance of Unfair Advantage

"What do you do better than any other company?" will be a question the CEO must be well prepared to answer. A vague answer is as bad as no answer at all. Potential investors are looking for that special ingredient that will give them confidence that a startup company will have an advantage over its competitors, an advantage that will survive copying and reverse engineering and brute force attacks by giants with a lot more money. An advantage that can produce enough products to make the IPO dream thinkable. An unfair advantage. A distinctive competence.

Because of the high failure rate in startups, the investor is a born skeptic. Critical comments from the sea of doubting venture capitalists are thus common. As our research shows, about 60 per cent of the funded startups go bankrupt, so they are right to be skeptical. A very high proportion of startups rely solely on their technology as the backbone of their distinctive competence. Yet history shows that a lot more than technology is required to be a long-term success in a new business enterprise.

"What do you have that will enable you to switch gears, shift, and sidestep if the market is a lot different than you plan on?" That is the question in the investor's mind as he or she listens to a CEO explain the startup's strategy. The CEO's responses must be well thought through.

Shooting Stars

Every investor shudders to hear the words "shooting star." That is the phrase used to describe the company that got off to a flying start, but failed soon after reaching the headlines. According to our interviews, a large proportion of emerging companies fall into this category. The goal of a startup's CEO is to avoid the mistakes that lead to such a demise.

"But who cares?" some said to us. "All anyone wants is to get through the IPO and get out as a millionaire." We asked that question of many participants in the venture business, and they had a similar response: "Institutional investors make up our largest source of capital. They are also the investors in IPOs. We can't sell them all the turkeys and expect to be in business for long."

Thus the venture capitalist takes the longest-term view when reading a business plan, asking a number of related questions at the very beginning:

- "Is this a product or a business?" The VC often sees ideas from high tech personnel that are best suited to be sold or licensed to an established company. Single-product ideas are good candidates to become shooting stars, and VCs tend to shy away from them.

- "Can the market support a company that will grow to more than $100 million in revenue in five years?" The venture capitalist cannot afford to invest in anything less and must plan on becoming liquid in order to succeed in his investment business.

Lawsuits from investors who lost money are one consequence of going public too soon, on a song and a hope that everything will turn out all right. In 1991 the courts were still working on the rash of investor class action suits that broke out after the IPO frenzy of the 1982 to 1983 personal computer boom.

Forbes **Study of Shooting Stars.** Why does it happen? How can it be avoided? One watchdog of IPO shooting stars is the self-appointed guardian of the capitalist scene, *Forbes* magazine. It published a special review of this kind of company in its issue of January 28, 1985. The article makes good reading and opened up with this salvo:

> Were you one of those investors enticed into believing that small companies—"emerging growth stocks"—were the only game in town? If so,

you probably have a long disaster list of your own. There are plenty to choose from. American Software down 21% in the last year, to under $16 a share. Hawkeye Bancorp off 51%. Lee Data Corp. down 69%. LJN Toys off 59%. Oak Hill Sportswear down 36%. Reeves Communications down 57%. Sandwich Chef off 40%.

Face it, you can't blame this on just a fickle market. The profits, indeed the revenues, of many hot little companies suddenly turned cold.

Why does it happen? Why do so many small, promising companies peak so early? Why doesn't success breed success?

The simple answer is that the thin capitalization and narrow product lines that permit spectacular growth also permit overnight disasters.

That a young firm should have problems is not surprising. To succeed, it must do five things:

- Get an idea that can be funded.
- Market that product or service.
- Maximize efficiency.
- Extend that idea through add-ons and variations.
- Come up with another viable idea.

Obviously, entrepreneurs can stumble in any of the five areas, but the last step—coming up with another idea—seems to be the killer. *Forbes* has been chronicling the rise and fall of small companies since 1979, and we are always surprised at how few fast starters turn out to have staying power. Of the top 100 companies from the *Forbes* Up & Comer Class of 1979, 25 were acquired, leaving 75 still independent. Of those 75, only 25 qualified for the 1984 list of top-performing small companies. So, even if one charitably assumes that the best companies were acquired, it seems reasonable to say that the odds against staying on top are, at best, only 50/50. Little wonder so many investors get burned on the stocks of hot little companies.

Here are the headlines of *Forbes'* mini-case studies that followed the above introduction. They suggest what to look out for:

- "The Market Sours"
- "The Fluke Factor"
- "Outflanked"
- "Last Year's Model"
- "The Grass Looks Greener"
- "The Skimming Trap"
- "Dropping the Baton"
- "Me-Too'ed by the Mighty"

The writers closed with these words:

> Why do so many emerging growth companies peak so early? Because in addition to facing decisions as difficult as those at IBM or General Motors, their slender resources often force them to bet the company.
>
> There are two morals to be drawn from all this. One is for entrepreneurs: Don't get carried away by your own success; overconfidence is as dangerous as excessive timidity. The other is for investors: There is a depressingly high chance that just about the time the insiders are offering you a ride on their fast-rolling bandwagon, that bandwagon is poised to go right over the cliff. The maxim that follows for entrepreneurs: Always run scared. For investors: Be skeptical of super-high growth rates.

What you need is something to lean on, at all times, in all circumstances. That is what sustainable competitive advantage is all about.

Sustainable Competitive Advantage

The two hardest things about a sustainable advantage are that (1) few are very sustainable, and (2) few have many real advantages.

When a business plan contains a sustainable competitive advantage it is like the little girl: when it is good, it is very, very, good, and when it is bad, it is horrid. So let's examine how to develop an outstanding sustainable competitive advantage. A venture capitalist with one of America's top 20 VC firms had this to say about what he called "the company's compelling advantage":

> We start looking for the technology or idea that is the core to the advantage of the startup. This has become much more important to us because of the sharp increase in competition for funding startups which has arisen since 1983.
>
> Prior to 1983, we used to be able to count on calmly reviewing business plans, picking the best with a high degree of confidence that our $2 million total investment would be invested in a startup that had a 2- or 3-year lead on the competition. . . .
>
> However, today we are having to deal with much different circumstances, something our partners call "the Steeplechase Effect." The VC community has so much money chasing so few deals that we are actually seeing six or seven startups launched over the same six-month time period to do the same thing.
>
> As a result, venture capitalists are much more sensitive to the competitive threat to a startup. And that threat now comes from very large corporations, many of which have become much more responsive and alert to where technology and markets are going. They are much quicker on their feet than they were five or six years ago. We look for all the sources of competition: from startups funded by other venture capitalists, from large companies, from other businesses, from other technologies, from other markets. . . .
>
> All this increase in competition results in a shortage of good management. It gets back to the basic problem of how the startup plans to fill its needed team.

Closely linked to good management is proprietary advantage. We examine it closely in our due diligence. . . . The proprietary advantage is very important to a venture capitalist. We have to see clearly what the company's compelling advantage is. Venture capitalists are looking for the *revolutionary*—not the incremental—advantage. Incremental technologies build incremental companies—usually with a short life cycle—unless there is an *outstanding management* team that can continue to pursue incremental advances with few dollars of investment. The big wins are where you pursue a major new development that blasts you into a new market.

The proprietary advantage does not have to be technology, it can be in a new concept; for instance, in how to market a business in a large, established marketplace. . . . We ask lots of questions about marketing and its relations to the proprietary advantage: How are you going to get to market? Is it a large, established market or a brand-new, untapped one? Is it splintered, served by a collection of small mom and pop companies? Why will you have access to customers?

The business plan does not have to be long. We see all too many generic business plans that extrapolate financial forecasts to a $100 million company in four years. Instead, the plan should spend more time on addressing the issues surrounding competitive advantage, the pros and cons of the key issues facing the startup.

In our final decision, we are very selective. The entrepreneurs must learn that and not be so disappointed when we say "no," which is most of the time. We are sent close to 4000 business plans a year, including a few referred to us by people we know well. We fund only 10 to 15 of those, with more these days going to low tech than prior to 1983. And as for ultimate success—the IPO achieved by a good startup—we believe there are only 10 to 20 such deals in a given year in the entire U.S. among all the venture capital funds. We fund only the best plans we can find. And there are too few of those.

The best analysis of sustainable competitive advantage we could find is contained in a *Business Horizons* article entitled "Sustainable Competitive Advantage—What It Is, What It Isn't," by Kevin P. Coyne. Coyne (1986) dissects the advantages of a competitor, presents what to look for to test the sustainable edge, and adds a section on how to think through other competitors' possible reactions to a strategy. We strongly recommend that prospective entrepreneurs read it. Here are some of the key points of the analysis:

- Sustainable competitive advantage (SCA) is
  1. a consistent difference in product attributes . . .
  2. that are a direct consequence of a capability gap . . .
  3. that endures over time.

- SCA is based upon delivering superior *value* to the customer (not necessarily the lowest price).

- The product attribute differences must be the customers' key buying criteria.

The article is rich in lessons on what else to look for in an SCA. A CEO can use it to prepare a checklist and then test the startup's own business plan against that list. Coyne concludes with these sobering words:

> Although an SCA is a powerful tool in creating a successful business strategy, it is not the only key ingredient. In fact,
>
> - Possessing an SCA does not guarantee financial success.
> - Producers can succeed even when competitors possess an SCA.
> - Pursuing an SCA can sometimes conflict with sound business strategy.
>
> Although its attainment is the goal of *competitive* strategy, sustainable competitive advantage is not an end in itself but a means to an end. The corporation is not in business to beat its competitors, but to create wealth for its shareholders. Thus, actions that contribute to SCA but detract from creating shareholder wealth may be good strategy in the competitive sense but bad strategy for the corporation.

He goes on to cite examples of bad strategic thinking, including one very familiar to high tech people: "Aggressive learning-curve pricing strategies that sacrifice too much current profit."

Figure 5-1 is Saratoga Venture Finance's interpretation of sustainable competitive advantage.

Creating Your Company's Strategy

This is how Tom Peters (1986) summarized the characteristics of an effective strategy in his column "On Excellence":

> What is your organization's uniqueness? Can you state it in 15 to 25 words or less? Does everyone in the organization buy in? Is the strategy statement printed on wallet-sized cards that are given to everyone? Is it immortalized in granite?

VCs seldom find that in business plans. The point is that too often the only foundation on which a company is proposed to be built is technology. That translates to phrases often spoken by technologists, such as "faster X4" or "six times the price performance," all of which some other high tech group will be copying just as soon as they hear of a startup's funding. "What else does a startup have besides technology?" The answer is a good test of how deep a company's strategy is. Venture capital investors want as much depth as they can get before parting with their precious funds.

The next sections are designed to help founders sort out their strategy.

Classification of Startup Strategies.   Table 5-2 is a summary of the types of strategies followed by successful companies. It is based on the work of the great management consultant, Peter F. Drucker, and is

FIGURE 5-1. Key Determinants of Sustainable Competitive Advantage

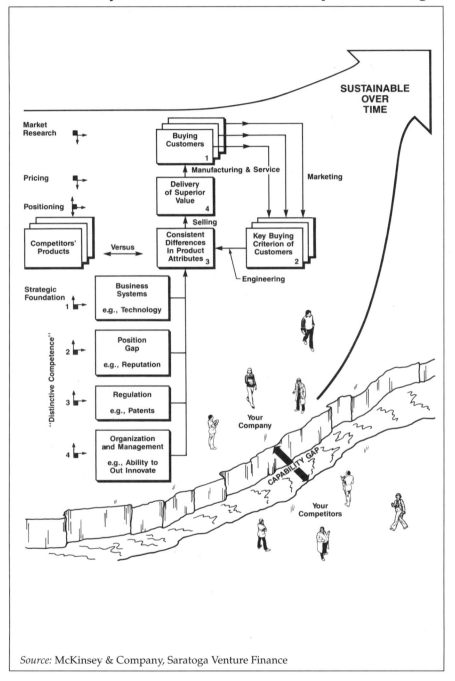

Source: McKinsey & Company, Saratoga Venture Finance

TABLE 5-2. Summary of Peter Drucker's Classification of Successful Business Strategies

1. **Be fustest with the mostest**
   Aimed at industry dominance.
   Examples: Apple (personal computers)
   　　　　　　Wang (office productivity via computers)
   - ⊹ If successful, highly rewarding.
   - ◦ Very risky, all success or all failure; seldom used by entrepreneurs.

2. **Hit them where they ain't**
   Aimed at market leadership.
   A. Creative Imitation
   Aimed at market dominance.
   Examples: IBM versus UNIVAC, 1953
   　　　　　　IBM versus Apple, 1980
   - ⊹ Less risky than "Fustest with the mostest."
   - ◦ Requires extreme alertness, flexibility, willingness to accept the verdict of the market, hard work, and massive efforts.
   B. Entrepreneurial
   Aimed at securing a beachhead, obtaining leadership position, and eventually dominance.
   Examples: Sony versus RCA and GE (transistor versus tube radios)
   　　　　　　MCI and Sprint versus AT&T (long distance)
   　　　　　　Japanese versus U.S. (stereo, TV, watches, calculators, copiers)
   - ⊹ Great for markets that are fast-changing or undefended by giants.
   - ⊹ Most likely to succeed for entrepreneurs.
   - ◦ Must accurately research market, remain market focused and market driven.
   - ◦ If done poorly, becomes head-on confrontation with giants in giants' area of dominance: "Fustest with the mostest."

(Continued)

digested from his book *Innovation and Entrepreneurship; Practice and Principles* (1985). A careful study of this table will help the reader sort out the kind of strategy the startup founders plan on using. Note how the risks vary with each type. CEOs may be surprised to find their strategies are not very strong. If this is the case, the weaknesses must be confronted and the business plan revised.

As Jerry Crowley of the startup Gazelle Microcircuits, Inc. explained to us, "Remember that a business plan is a living thing. It gets modified, shifts, and is altered along the way as the company progresses, hits barriers, fixes things, encounters competition, discovers opportunities, and gets a big break or two."

Readers of Table 5-2 should drop companies whose strategies they're acquainted with into the listed categories as they review them, and then

TABLE 5-2. Summary of Peter Drucker's Classification of Successful Business Strategies (continued)

---

3. Ecological Niches
Aimed at control.

A. Tollgate
Aimed at completely filling a niche small and discreet enough not to attract rivals.
Example: Alcon (cataract eye surgery enzyme)
+ Nearly impregnable.
- Very narrow position, nearly no room to maneuver.
- Once established, company can grow only as fast as customers grow.

B. Specialty Skill
Aimed at attaining controlling position in their specialty skill niche, and retaining it.
Example: Bosch (electrical systems for automobiles)
+ Most advantageous strategy in rapidly expanding new technology, industry, or market.
- Greatest danger: specialty ceases being specialty and becomes universal.
- Requires constant work to improve the skill.

C. Specialty Market
Aim is like Specialty Skill, except it is built around specialized knowledge of a market instead of around a product or service.
Example: Thomas Cook and American Express (travelers' checks)
+ - Same as Specialty Skill.

Source: Drucker (1985). Adapted by Saratoga Venture Finance

---

find the strengths and weaknesses of the companies. Try starting with the startup you most envy.

Positioning.   Practice can help the CEO use Table 5-2 to assess the strengths and weaknesses of the startup's major competitors. When these exercises are completed, the CEO must next position the company and its first products against its prime competitors. If the CEO avoids this step, the venture capitalists will expose the startup's softness in their rugged due diligence question-and-answer sessions. They will have no mercy on founders who have not adequately prepared their chosen strategy.

Positioning is very hard work and many books have been written about it, so we will not go into the detail here. Suffice it to say that a CEO who is uncomfortable with this work should call for help—from a startup consultant, a sharp marketing expert, or an experienced general manager.

No matter who is selected, the CEO should remember that the goal is to do top-notch strategic thinking as a whole company. *The CEO and founders should not expect to succeed in raising capital by leaving this vital work to a marketing person working solo.*

Strategic Thinking. Practical help in doing strategic thinking comes from Michael Porter, a professor at the Harvard Business School. Here is a summary of Porter's advice for CEOs:

> Every company, whether diversified or not, should have a strategic plan for each of its businesses. I favor a set of analytical techniques for developing strategy that have grown out of my research over the past 15 years. Whatever techniques one uses, however, a good plan should contain the following elements:
>
> - An analysis of the industry in which the firm competes.
> - Sources of competitive advantage.
> - An analysis of the existing and potential competitors who might affect the company.
> - An assessment of the company's competitive position.
> - Selection or ratification of strategy, built on competitive advantage and how it can be sustained.

Our research at Saratoga Venture Finance shows that startups that supply the above points in their business plan have a much higher chance of obtaining the funds they desire at fair prices.

The Role of the CPA Firm

The help of a good accounting firm is needed next. That means more than a good accountant. What is required is the services of a vast number of financial specialists, who can assist with the following tasks:

- Check the startup's financial forecasts.
- Verify the realism of startup's key assumptions.
- Prepare the startup's tax returns, which are required even though a company does not yet make a profit.
- Confidentially review the wisdom of key business plans and strategies, particularly the long-term implications of alternative actions the company could take today.
- Help set accounting policies for keeping books; this is particularly important in the area of setting policies that are consistent with those of other similar high tech enterprises.
- Arrange introductions to venture capitalists and investment bankers.

It may sound trite, but a CEO should remember that this choice involves engaging a whole firm; therefore the choice should be made thoughtfully.

We reviewed the amount of high tech practice of the most frequently mentioned accounting firms and ranked them in rough order of estimated annual billings for high tech startups as follows:

1. Arthur Anderson

2. Ernst & Young

3. Price Waterhouse

4. KPMG

5. Coopers and Lybrand

6. Deloitte Ross Tohmatsu

CPA firms can be much more than expensive bookkeepers—if a top firm is chosen. And a few strong regional CPA firms also have high tech practices. Above all, avoid being the first high tech startup for the chosen CPA firm in your local area.

Most startups will quickly be looking for customers overseas. A top CPA firm is already international. By comparison, venture capitalists are less helpful outside the United States.

Choosing a CPA Firm.   Our research showed strong consensus here: *one should go for a top name firm from the beginning*. No one recommended starting with a small firm and later shifting to a larger one; the pain of change and the animosity generated were not worth the possible fees saved with such a strategy.

However, our confidants recommended looking not just for a large international accounting firm, but also for one whose local office contains the most high tech experience in your area. Some firms have transferred top personnel into states that have lesser high tech experience in order to get such a practice started. *The founders should pick the firm with the most high tech veterans in the local office.*

The experienced high tech chief financial officers emphasized this: a firm should be selected based how well the accounting firm's manager and the startup's CEO and/or CFO communicate on business matters. They told us, "It's tough enough to get all the work done with limited resources without having to struggle to teach the CPA firm's manager what is practical and theoretical about an accounting reserve or expense accrual."

Accounting Fees.   New companies do not have to pay the going rate for accounting services. All the top companies will deeply discount their standard rates—if they get excited about a startup's long-term prospects. It is the CEO's job to sell them the startup's vision for the future.

The CEO must be sure to get the fee agreement executed up front. This agreement must include (1) all offices worldwide (several firms cannot guarantee discounted rates in their independent offices in Europe and elsewhere), and (2) all tax work. A CEO should be able to get a great deal of free time for the early days, particularly in the pre-seed stage.

A firm should not be chosen because of its low accounting fees. Other matters are too important. It is wise to get a commitment for the fees for an IPO. It is not too early and it is important to get the lower fee rates wherever possible. None of the fees related to raising capital are tax deductible (surprise!).

Making Financial Projections

The startup's consultant and CPA firm should review the financial forecasts. They must be told to do more than validate the accuracy of the arithmetic.

Their experience is valuable in verifying the founders' underlying business assumptions, such as the number of support engineers needed in marketing and engineering to care for customers spread out over the whole United States. It is not hard to project dollars per head; it is a lot harder to face the realities of the inefficiencies of tiny high tech startups that get spread too thin.

Modeling Financial Projections.   The CEO is about to do more numbers than anyone ever believed possible. A business plan is a document, a snapshot, of an ever-changing strategy. Change is a certainty.

To relieve the CEO of the bulk of the burden of building intricate formulas and basic structures of a financial model of a startup, you need a spreadsheet model of your business projections. The CEO can then start by plugging in his own revenue and headcount numbers, and end up with a five-year forecast.

The objective is to redirect the CEO's time from cranking out lots of time-consuming numbers to increasing the time spent on strategic thinking. That is where the big payoff is.

Calculating How Much Capital Is Needed.   Our experience showed that most business plan forecasts were off by a large order of magnitude in two areas:

- *Sales revenue.* Forecasts are particularly likely to be overly optimistic in predicting average selling prices and a larger-than-realistic share of the market. This is understandable in most cases—the CEO is forecasting into a new, untried market without much, if any, related track record to go on.

Venture capitalists know this and will still grill the CEO for the numbers. The real-world wide misses have turned most VCs we spoke to into doubting Thomases who were apt to make remarks like "Your numbers are off by a large order of magnitude," or "There is no way you will ever come close to those unit projections"—as if the VC is the expert in the CEO's industry. The CEO must be ready to face this.

- *Capital required.* We have been fortunate in being allowed to see original business plan forecasts years after the success of a startup. We found that most of them grossly underestimated the capital needed to launch the business. A few proudly told us they were right on plan. We often found unrealistically low expectations for (1) how long it took (much longer than planned) for the sales cycle to close on business, and (2) the cost of furniture, computers, telephone systems, and leasehold improvements.

Another great cause of trouble was the old nemesis, often called product slip. This condition occurs frequently when product development hits a snag and an additional six months to one year are required to finish the first prototype. This is almost a given for high tech companies. Yet rarely did any financial projections address this serious possibility. Our experiences have led us to recommend—as a matter of policy—that forecasts include enough cash cushion for a major rework of the first major product of the company, at least six months' worth of burn rate.

One consequence of this failure to allow for product slippage is that VCs have a habit of secretly "doing the double" in private: They quickly calculate the return on their investment in a startup company at the best price they think they can get, then assume they will have to double that in order to become liquid through either merger or IPO. They then adjust their first pricing to be sure of getting a good ROI, even if the extra capital is required. The founders' dilution is just part of the calculation. The CEO must decide on how much capital will be required; the figure must be as realistic as possible. It is surprising how many VCs tell founders to raise millions more capital than they originally asked for.

Other Capital Tips.   All the capital needed should be shown as one big number as a plug to the balance sheet and cash flow statement.

The financial structuring (preferred stock, etc.) should be left to sessions with the startup's consultant, accountant, and attorney.

Try to show all capital as equity. Bank borrowings and equipment lease-lines can be reconsidered after the company gets its first funding.

Do not forecast any bank debt until after one year of profitability. Thereafter, the startup can borrow about 60 percent of U.S. receivables. Inventory financing should be forgotten.

Wages should be loaded by 25 percent to cover benefits and related taxes.

No more than about 12 million total shares should be issued by the time the IPO is projected. These include stock options. A per-share price in the low teens will be desired at that time.

The CEO should consult the CPA for advice on how to deal with the uncertainties of the tax loss carryforward of net operating losses in a startup. After that the CEO can pick a tax rate.

Summary

This is a good place to begin your serious work. First, try writing the initial draft of your Executive Summary in less than one hour. That will tell you what you are missing in your thinking about your business plan. It's always the hardest chapter to write. The toughest portion is the first paragraph, in which you should summarize in three sentences or less what your unfair advantage is all about. Once you have surmounted that hurdle, the rest is downhill.

Keep in mind the following tips from the veterans:

- Spend time on creating a great business plan.
- Build the plan on unfair advantage—one that is sustainable against competition.
- Prepare for tough questions from VCs.
- Set up an adequate capital plan, with cash to spare for emergencies.
- Hire the best help you can to advise you in this work.

After you finish a draft you are satisfied with, ask friends to read it and comment. Your advisors will be glad to get in a few words before you lock in your final version. Also keep in mind that this is not a business plan as an operations manager thinks of it. Instead, it is a document intended to help both the company and the investor to better understand the business to be financed. So adjust your writing accordingly and, as you write, keep the audience in mind: the people with the cash to invest. They are always looking for hidden gems to invest in. Try to help them avoid having to wade through a badly written business plan to discover you. Instead, take the time to do a job you are proud of, and enjoy the reward from such a big effort as this, communicating the most important business idea of your life.

Now let's turn to the number-one topic for investors—the management team of your startup—and listen to what advice the veterans of startups give CEOs who are attempting to assemble their first core team of people.

6

The Team

Investors start reading a business plan by skimming the Executive Summary; then they jump to the section in the rear entitled "Management."

Our research showed that investors are increasingly reluctant to invest without "adequate management." The issue is what "adequate" means. This chapter will clarify this issue and will help the founders decide what additional talent they will need.

The Core Team

Each group of people who start a company has a core team around whom the company is built. Only a few of the original group are founders; most are additional talent that the leader feels will be needed soon after funding is closed. The core team should be picked very carefully, because its business and interpersonal style becomes the foundation for the company's culture and, like yeast, grows the value system that becomes the mark of that startup.

The founders should pick the most outstanding talent that can be found. These people will represent the company to the seed and Round 1 investors. They must make an excellent impression—not from a slick, smooth point of view, but rather from their track records and skills, and by their depth of experience in the areas most important to the sustainable competitive advantage of the company. Don't settle for a few average employees—this is the wrong place to compromise.

Experience. *Do I have a chance to attract venture capital if I do not have prior startup experience?* We found that venture capitalists generally gave the same answer to that question: They say that if it's a good idea, a new enterprise will always be welcome, along with the person who thought it up, but the chances of raising venture funds will certainly be increased if the founder has prior experience with a startup. However, most startups are not led by people with years of prior experience in new businesses. VCs will be frank and tell the leader if his or her experience needs to be supplemented by that of others with track records in startups.

The CEO's goal is to stack the deck in the startup's favor, and to get the needed capital at a fair price. If the founders believe that startup experience will improve the company's odds significantly, they must find it. For instance, ask venture capitalists for leads to people wanting to be CEO of a startup. Venture capitalists get hundreds of résumés from people who are looking for a startup. Founders can benefit from those contacts, even before asking the venture capitalist for money.

I am a technologist, not a businessperson. I think my idea can be a big success, but I don't know if I should proceed or not. What should I do? As consultants to startups, we are asked this question by people of many backgrounds. Our answer is always the same: Get started on the trail to getting your business financed. Complete your business plan as soon as possible; let that be the pacing process that you use to answer your important questions. Follow our guidelines for the early stages and this will raise the key issues you need to deal with. You can always get good people to listen to a good idea. And during the process you can attract the management talent you will need.

Now let us address a key issue for investors—completeness.

The Importance of a Complete Management Team

By the end of Round 1 of financing, the CEO will be expected to have filled all the key functional positions that report directly to him. Venture capitalists are particularly concerned if VP Marketing and VP Sales positions are not filled at that stage, particularly if the CEO is the lead technologist.

The investors see a race to finish the first product as soon as possible. Incomplete management teams slow that race down, and a window of opportunity may be missed. When a key person is missing, the CEO must take time to find, recruit, and train the new member of the executive team. That pause will probably delay introduction of the startup's first product, increasing the risk for investors, who will in turn price Round 1 accordingly, with more dilution to the founders.

What is the best sequence in which to add people? When should we hire a salesperson and a finance manager? The order in which startup founders added to their executive teams varied, but we discerned this pattern:

- Most start with the inventor and a solid VP Engineering. This secures the technology and creates an asset for the investors in case the company goes belly up.

- Most added an experienced CEO as soon as possible. This is preferred in all cases. Hopefully, that person can come on board in time to help close Round 1 financing.

- The VP Marketing is the next most important position to fill. Some investors insist that this person be a part of the creation of the first product. Increasingly, we find that investors are leery of placing any funds at risk in "a company in which technology is looking for a good market."

- The VP Sales was added about two months before first product was ready to ship. We were told that salespeople get cabin fever waiting for a chance to demonstrate their first product, live, to the first customer.

- The VP Manufacturing must be on board in enough time to get the first product ready to ship. Manufacturing management is responsible for meeting time, quantity, and quality commitments, all of which can be measured.

- The VP Finance and Administration position can be filled after the other positions are filled. This recommendation is controversial with some venture capitalists, and is discussed below.

Venture capitalists and the startup's chief financial officer are seemingly in the same camp, with the same goals of success. However, an experienced CFO is frequently an antagonist to some of the venture capitalists. They are most likely to argue over the need for capital, the price at which it is to be sold, and the degree of control over spending and hiring; which investment bankers, attorneys, and new investors the startup should do business with; what class of risk should be used to invest surplus funds; and how much leasing and borrowing the company should do.

In a nutshell, we found that venture capitalists are reluctant to turn over control of financial policy to a strong CFO. As investors, they want to keep close reins on their new child, particularly when it (inevitably) starts to steer off course from its original business plan.

Such control by VCs is not necessarily in the best interests of the entrepreneur and his core team. Some angry CEOs told us that investors had pressured them into dropping R&D projects so that the company's financial statements would look good enough to get the IPO done. Others told us that venture board members virtually took over running the company's financial affairs when a weak controller succumbed under the pressure of bad times. Other CEOs told of being threatened with expulsion and blackballing if they did not go along with the terms and conditions of the proposed next round of financing (which severely diluted the employees' equity but protected the prior venture capitalists because of the antidilution clauses in their contracts).

Needless to say, the founders and CEO had better be prepared to fight for the startup's and their own interests. It is easier with a strong CFO on board as early as is reasonable.

Lately we have been seeing proportionately more CEOs adding a full VP Finance instead of a controller. And the CFO is being brought on more quickly than in prior years. This may reflect the experiences of successful IPO companies, many of which attracted an experienced CFO early, near Round 1 time. This was noticeable for companies that raised more than $20 million of capital.

Completeness, Lawsuits, and Time.   Investors do not like lawsuits or even the likelihood of legal entanglements. The complete Linear Technology team left National Semiconductor together, got Round 1 monies almost immediately, and were promptly sued by their former employer. (Chapter 5 tells how to avoid this painful problem.)

Investors do like to see that two or three of the core team have worked together before. This reduces the risk to the investor by speeding the first product to market and reducing the time wasted in learning to get along with each other.

It takes time for people to learn to work together. We found all managements lamenting how long it took for the culture to form, gel, and begin to function creatively. Few business plans acknowledge the slip time associated with this "stranger phenomenon."

The Roles of Consultants and Contractors

Most startups use the buddy system to recruit team members through the first three rounds of funding. This is cheaper than using recruiters, tends to cement the culture, and creates a spirit of togetherness and participation by new employees. Newspaper advertisements seldom appeared until close to IPO time.

By definition, all startup companies are short of talent. Most startups solve this problem in part by the extensive use of contractors. These part-time personnel fill in for missing skill sets, and the company pays only for what it gets. Such personnel are widely available in the larger metropolitan areas and are regularly used in the life of emerging companies long after they go public. This phenomenon appears to have become a way of life for rapidly emerging high tech companies. It is now common for the stock option plans of startups to allow shares to be granted to key contractors.

Venture capitalists themselves make extensive use of part-time talent, often called "technology experts" or "due diligence associates." Venture firms can be helpful in recommending part-time consultants to fill any series of jobs that the startup needs done.

Contractors are common in engineering; they get paid by the hour, day, month, or project. Consultants are more often used in other functions. Some open and close the financial statements each month. Some run the personnel department for the early months. Still others work on market research or sales training. These contractors are usually highly experienced former operations professionals. Their compensation often includes equity in some form, ranging from grants to purchase stock to issue of stock warrants, as well as cash compensation.

These part-timers range from the recently unemployed to the financially independent person. The latter may have just finished a successful startup and cashed in at IPO time. Saratoga Venture Finance calls such people "49ers" (from the idea of financial independence gained by American pioneers in the California Gold Rush of 1849). The part-time working conditions gives both parties a chance to look each other over, possibly for permanent employment (without an expensive recruiter's fee). This part-time-to-permanent arrangement is frequently deliberately done, both by 49ers interested in becoming startup CEOs and the executives who hire them as contractors.

Recruiters are used as in larger companies—sparingly, but when the hiring is critical to success. A growing number of venture firms are keeping an active roster of VP and CEO résumés in a personal computer database, just to be able to supply needed talent to their startups.

However, investors have encouraged the use of recruiters in order to keep a startup on plan. Bodies are needed to get the work done. CEO recruiting seems to be on the rise, and VP work is steady for some recruiters, who told us they specialize in startups.

Impact on Valuation and Attraction of Funds

We believe that the pattern of high tech startup hiring practice we have described is commonly used. It is aimed at one goal: hiring as complete a team of competent professionals as the startup can attract, in order to execute its business plan on time and within budget.

The president of a very successful startup was asked for advice on what to do to be a successful startup, and he answered, "Hire the best people you can find!" Investors agree with him—the better the people, the less risk there is likely to be. The CEO should be able to translate management strength into negotiations that mean less dilution for the CEO and the founders, leaving more shares for more top people. As one veteran put it, "A players attract A players."

Interestingly, top-quality people often emerge from bankruptcies. Prior bankruptcy experience is valuable; failure has its rewards. Mature investors have seen six out of ten of their children go under. They know that it was not all the fault of every employee; the big breaks account for a lot of the outcome. Therefore, according to a number of wealthy, successful investors with whom we spoke, top managers from defunct companies are actively recruited to new startups.

In the end, the CEO will want to be able to present a solid core team to attract the first rounds of funds, while avoiding the sacrifice of too much quality or too many shares along the way. Compensation (equity and cash) for this team is discussed in Chapters 7 and 8.

7

Ownership, Dilution, Negotiation, and Valuation

The question most frequently asked by entrepreneurs is: How much of our company should we give up to get the money? This chapter is dedicated to guiding the startup CEO in answering that important question.

To assist the CEO in making this decision, we have done proprietary financial research on famous startups like Lotus and Apple, as well as on newer companies like Cypress and Convex and others. Actual data from SEC records were processed and summarized using proprietary software called the Saratoga Financial Synthesizer. Examples of the tables and charts are presented in this chapter and include these data:

- What percentages the founders retained, and how much the other employees received
- What percentage went to venture capitalists

- How much the investors really made
- Data from the results of the initial public offering

We will also discuss the process for dealing with venture capitalists and suggest tactics and negotiating tips gathered from startup CEOs—both the successful and unsuccessful ones.

This chapter presents key actions that lead to success in each stage of the capital formation process, from seed to IPO. It also presents a surefire formula for pricing a startup's financing, and explains how, why, and when preferred stock is used. And we discuss the delicate process of closing on a venture-financed deal, including why it is so important to keep your mind focused on success. Remember: success is achieved only when the money is in the startup's bank account.

Summary of the Campaign to Raise Capital

There are 13 financial stages in the process a CEO will go through to attract venture capitalists to a startup deal. Each stage has its own special nature, risks, and activities necessary for success. In the descriptions of the stages that follow, we have included the advice and insights that were cited most often in our interviews. There is plenty of room for creativity, yet a vast majority of funded deals follow this course of events, regardless of which round of financing is involved:

Stage 1: Set Funding Objectives.   Certainly the number-one objective is to get the money in the bank. But the founders must also answer these questions:

- How long are we willing to go on looking for money? When should we throw in the towel? Refer to Chapter 3 for a review of the overall process of marching to IPO.
- What is the rock-bottom point for dilution in this round? Be sure all founders agree before negotiations start!
- What amount of capital should be raised in this round? What is the minimum, the maximum, and the amount to ask for in the first session? This figure will be challenged during the presentations to venture capitalists. The founders must be ready to answer in unison.

Stage 2: Prepare the Plan to Attract Investors.   The founders must decide which firms to contact, how to get ahead of hundreds of other business plans that are ahead in the queue, and what to say to sell the firm of choice on taking the position of lead venture capitalist.

Founders need to plan this stage as carefully as any other critical business activity. It is a time for good minds to focus on how to succeed, given the resources on hand.

Stage 3: Pick the Best Capital-Raising Strategy.   To get started here, founders should review Chapter 5 and focus on their company's strengths and weaknesses. Investors will be looking for the hidden winner—the company with the strong unfair advantage. And they will closely scrutinize the founders and their core team personnel.

The CEO should talk strategy with experienced business executives outside the startup. Start with people who are avid supporters of the founders and leaders of the startup, and people who are excited about the business plan. Most of our clients are surprised at how helpful this can be.

The money-raising strategy must eventually have the full backing of the lead venture firm, the firm other investors will follow. They can attract other venture firms.

Warning: Many CEOs and CFOs have told us of a big mistake they made in raising capital. After the seed round, they assumed that their lead VC would raise the next rounds of capital while the CEO and CFO returned to running the company. This turned out to be a myth. The startup organizations that realized this soon enough survived; the others suffered or even died. The CEO of several startups has this advice (learned in the school of hard knocks):

> Tell all the founders that the only way to succeed is to raise the needed capital by themselves. Do not count on their well-intending lead venture partner to raise the cash. He cannot be counted on; he has too many alligators swimming around his fledgling companies, and he is frantically trying to help save his drowning turkey investments. Raising your own capital is too important an event to be trusted to anyone but yourself.

Case Study: Crown Semiconductor

Here is an actual profile of the objectives, plan, strategy, and tactics used by two founders to get Round 1 capital:

■ *Hire a household name veteran as CEO, someone highly competent whom we can respect and get along with.*

■ *Add three friends from our two seed venture capital firms who are heavies in our industry; put them on as advisors to the board of directors.*

■ *Present our company as the Blue Chip of the startups in this very new technology. Reinforce every word in the presentation with an image of top class.*

■ *Use our (well-known) law firm's top partner to introduce us to five to seven other top venture sources, at least two on the East or West Coast, whichever is opposite. Quickly follow those introductions with calls from our two seed sources.*

■ *Negotiate for at least $10 million, fully expecting to accept only $6 million. Cut off at that amount* [they built a reasonable spending cushion into their financial forecasts]. *Induce scarcity; competition among funding sources is our best friend. That will keep the price of this round higher, reducing dilution.*

■ *Make 30 percent for insiders (officers and employees) the minimum owner-ship dilution point at projected IPO time.*

■ *Give up only one more board seat to investors in this round.*

■ *Focus the sales pitch on (a) greatly reduced risk since seed capital came in: we got the first test part running, we got a top CEO (and other leadership from people out of the some of the best companies in Silicon Valley), and we are only five months from shipping first product; and (b) VCs, you'd better get in now, because there may not be a tomorrow: our business plan calls for this to be the last round before IPO.*

For the record, the above plan was implemented to the letter. The startup suc-ceeded on all points and got the cash in the bank at a favorable price per share.

Stage 4: Assign Tasks. The CEO's job here is to get the startup's little band all working to efficiently implement the capital-raising plan.

One person should be the keeper of VC contacts, appointments, and calendars. This gets quite complex if the CEO must get on planes and go around the country with a road show.

One person should be responsible for keeping the overhead foils and slides (35mm or electronic) up to date. These will be changed on the fly as difficult questions pop up from potential investors. These changes can drive the CEO wild unless there is a a sole source responsible for keeping order.

Practice your presentation, letting employees critique you. Practice makes perfect. Dry runs are necessary. Flops are created by people trying to wing it. VCs see the best every day; the CEO should make sure this presentation is in the top ten.

Stage 5: Launch the Campaign. Focus should be on how to efficiently get to the desired VC firms. It is a mistake to waste time teaching people about the startup's business. If they aren't in genetic engineering yet, chances are they won't say yes to a presentation from a genetic engineer-ing startup, certainly not as a lead venture firm.

A lot of people who have been through the process said, "It never goes fast enough, and you always get a lot of nos." Our interviews showed that there was seldom a group who found raising capital easy and swift. The founders must be prepared instead for a lot of presenta-tions and door knocking.

If the company is already running, the CEO must beware of losing business focus in this stage. If the CEO cannot afford to spend up to 20 percent of his or her time pitching sources of money, then tasks need to be delegated to someone else. Yes, CEOs spend that much time being deliberate about raising new money—some even hire and organize with that job specifically in mind. For instance, an experienced operations executive joined an electronics startup in San Jose, California, to run operations. As Mr. Inside, he freed time for the founder, born in Taiwan, to focus on his work as Mr. Outside, raising capital and managing the strategic alliances with Japanese and Korean companies.

Stage 6: Make Presentations. The CEO's goal in a presentation is to get his or her company distinguished from the dozen companies the venture partners saw last week. This doesn't mean that you should impress the VCs with your super high tech, but rather that you should make it clear that your company provides an opportunity for investors to earn a very high ROI in a short time. Yes, the presentation must cover the high tech bases, but the CEO must remember that cash flow and ROI are the measures of success for the venture capitalist, so these must be presented as part of the pitch. A CEO who is not familiar with how to calculate the right numbers and present them can ask the startup consultant, CPA manager, or attorney to provide these figures.

The CEO must wear a tough skin. The VCs are quite negative sounding in their questions. They have seen a lot of turkeys and have learned how to smoke them out. They are just doing their job, specifically the part called due diligence.

The first meeting is usually short, about one hour. Subsequent presentations are usually attended by more of the senior partners of the firm in a large room where the CEO will be center stage. By then, one partner has decided the company is worth looking at seriously. This is the key person in that VC firm for the CEO from now on. This individual will be the startup's "champion" and will pace the review process of that business plan within the VC firm.

The partners will expect to see a professional presentation, at least with overhead foils. Typeset desktop publishing output to laser printer hard copy is now the standard.

The CEO will get about two hours for the first formal presentation, including interruptions and many questions.

It is important to avoid presenting anything vitally proprietary, especially at the first meeting. VCs will not sign nondisclosure agreements. Their attorneys warn them that they see so many similar plans each day that the nondisclosure agreements may open the door to big trouble.

When the founders must open the door to reveal sensitive intellectual property, they can often do so instead under tight nondisclosure agreements from an expert hired for that purpose by the venture firm. That may happen anyway, particularly in the later stages when this VC gets serious about doing the deal.

A warning about hired experts. VCs do not always trust their own judgment on the technology or market, so they ask someone more qualified to be the technology judge. We have met several such experts, and a number of CEOs share our perceptions. Experts usually send in very negative reports, probably because they are hired to not be wrong. The use of experts is good in theory, but we have generally seen only negative results. This is probably why VCs with operating backgrounds from a single technology tend to stick together and invest mainly in that area. We advise clients to go to the VCs who are personally familiar with the startup company's technology and avoid the problem of negative experts.

The CEO must be prepared to answer questions about how the shares in this deal have been priced. Be ready to respond to a valuation question at any meeting, starting with the first meeting, even before things get serious. We found that startup CEOs and veteran VCs treat this step as the start of negotiations. The CEO must therefore be prepared to quote on the high side. When asked how negotiable the price is, the CEO's first response should be "Negotiable." If pressed to a number, be prepared to start the negotiations with a reasonable figure (see Chapters 7 and 8 for more specific help).

Stage 7: Feedback from the Presentation. The goal in this stage is to answer this question: How real is the interest of the VC firm to which we just made a presentation? This is a delicate state of affairs; the investors are not yet hooked. They are just nibbling. The big risk is that their interest in the business may cool.

Tough persistence and everlasting confidence are needed. We reviewed our logs of client work to see just how persistent one must be to communicate during this stage of raising capital. We found that the typical venture partner takes at least five calls before returning one. These are very busy people with a tall stack of unread business plans on their desks, five or six board meetings every other month, and another six investments that must be bailed out of real trouble. This is not the arena for the bashful or timid. A CEO seeking funds must be persistent, but polite.

However, many refusals should be expected for many good reasons, including the natural consequence of deal flow, which was discussed in Chapter 5.

Negatives can be turned into positives. When the CEO is told over the phone by the startup's venture firm champion at Top Gun Venture Firm that "You're going to do just fine. The plan is great. But we're going to pass on this round, the deal is just not right for us at this time," the CEO should be ready to counter immediately with "Tell me in more detail where to rethink our business plan." VCs like to give advice. Many of them are good at it, coming from years of operating experience in that industry.

Stage 8: Modify Your Plan but Retain Your Vision. Now the CEO must decide what and how much to change. The plan, the pricing of the deal, or even the entire business. Remember the success of the great Compaq: it took several *major* reworks of the first business plan to close on funding.

A founder must listen carefully to close advisors here, but most of all must follow his or her dream. That is important for the long haul, both to the company, and to the founders personal psychological well-being.

Stage 9: Due Diligence Time. Here the VCs find the nits and gnats that come out in their due diligence work. All references are checked, and then the VCs find references on the references. They call the market research firms, a half dozen of their friends who might buy the startup's first product, and attorneys who will be asked about every issue.

The startup's attorney and consultant are very useful here. A savvy startup attorney is worth a great deal during this stage. He or she knows the focus of the venture capitalists and can call VCs as a somewhat neutral party to detect any problem areas that may be bothering the VC. The startup consultant can also walk the CEO through any land mines in areas such as preparing the references for the kind of questions the VCs will be asking.

Your goal is to get through this stage as quickly as possible.

Stage 10: The Lead VC says: "Yes, we will!" The only thing left is for the VC firm to say one word: Yes. But that is easier said than heard. There is only one objective for the CEO during this phase: Get the VC with the money to say yes. But chances of influencing this stage are low.

One reason is that VCs are very busy comparing alternative companies, looking for ways to wisely invest their remaining funds. VCs meet religiously every Monday in their partners' meeting; that can be counted on. And there they make their decisions. Any given deal is competing against a dozen on the table for consideration that day.

Another reason is that VCs are always hard to reach. CEOs crack jokes about how soon it became obvious that VCs usually returned calls from an airport phone booth or on their crackling car phone at 7:15 p.m. as they rounded the entrance to their home's driveway. Try calling your VC champion at his office on Tuesday morning to learn how well your deal is looking to their firm.

Stage 11: Closing the VC Funding Contract.   The goal here is to convert the verbal yeses into written contracts, which are known as closing documents. And to agree on the last VCs to be let into the deal.

The biggest risk is that a bad surprise may scare off the lead venture investor. This sometimes happens because of questions asked by a follow-on investor.

The herd instinct is at work, along with deal flow, which is working for the startup at this stage. In a humorous way, CEOs said they felt their companies had become part of a venture version of a Monopoly game. Companies had become like the houses on Park Place, and were being offered in exchange for a futures contract on the next deal going up on St. James.

To succeed here, the CEO must cooperate fully with the lead VC, but never assume that the VC is managing the deal for the CEO. The CEO is the one who must lead the deal to completion.

Stage 12: Closing Week.   This is the week for the startup's attorney to really show his stuff. The documents must be prepared and agreed to by all parties. It is a mess to those unaccustomed to the paperwork and logistics nightmares.

A bad startup lawyer can kill a deal; we were told about several such cases. Also, weak lawyers take so much time to do things that they may easily double or triple their fees for the deal.

The CEO's goal is to stay out of the way, but to respond instantly to the attorney's calls. Needless to say, the attorney has to have briefed the CEO on the points to be negotiated well before this stage is reached.

Stage 13: Cash in the Bank.   At last! This week the founders count it twice, shout for joy, and go celebrate. Next week they meet their new bosses, the VCs sitting on the board of directors.

Roles and Goals of the Participants

Knowing what motivates each of the involved parties helps the founder reach a more satisfactory end result. Chapters 9 and 13 show how venture capitalists and Wall Street investment bankers make their money, how wealthy they can get, and therefore what they are eager to do with a startup. This chapter focuses upon the motivations of other participants as well, such as the attorney and accountant. The goal is to better equip the CEO and founders to negotiate the best deal they can get.

The Startup Consultant.   Some experienced veterans of startups earn a living assisting the founders along the way toward the IPO. This kind of business person makes money by providing the startup with certain services at each stage of the capital formation process, in exchange for compensation in the form of some combination of cash and stock (either as outright purchase or as a warrant, that is, the right to buy shares over the next ten years at a fixed price per share). This compensation makes the startup consultant desire the same success that the CEO and the founders do, thereby avoiding conflict of interest.

The startup consultant should be able to give advice based upon first-hand experience in startups. CEOs of the consultant's other client companies should be able to provide top-notch references.

Startup Attorney.   The company needs an experienced startup attorney as soon as it gets started. Chapter 4 discusses what startup attorneys can do. In particular, during these stages the attorney must competently walk the fine line between the practical and theoretical practice of law. One experienced venture capitalist told us that an attorney with a heavy practice working for venture capitalists is the wrong firm for a startup to use, mainly because the focus of the practice was very different from that of an attorney doing startups as his main practice.

The goal is to close on the financing. The terms and conditions can be real deal-busters, with the VC attempting to impose vetoes and other restraints on the CEO. The startup's attorney should be experienced at countering the more exorbitant claims of investors' attorneys, and must be able to counteroffer and do tradeoffs on the startup's behalf without losing sight of the goal: Get the deal done, now.

Attorneys charge by the hour. The CEO should expect a fee in the range of thousands of dollars—more if the opposing side's attorneys are not experienced with startup law practice. This situation tends to create a larger fee if the deal becomes protracted, which is not in the startup's best interest. Some law firms accept stock or warrants to keep their fees lower. We found IPO prospectuses that revealed stockholdings by the lead attorney in the law firm used by the startup, as well as by the general fund or trust in which the law firm puts selected forms of compensation.

We found that top attorneys really get into their work, eager for the client's success. We found only one situation where the fees were considered outrageous, and in that one it turned out that the chairman/founder and the attorney were close friends.

Another important point: an experienced startup attorney will know the latest pricing of the latest venture capital deal; which firms are toughest or softest; what degree of complexity and creativity is acceptable in structuring the deal; and what the CEO and founders should give up, give in to, trade off, and stand firm on.

The Accounting Firm.   The accounting firm helps the CEO keep a good sense of the balance between the price on a deal and its relative worth in financial terms. It provides advice on tax matters that affect the CEO, the startup team, and the company.

For instance, the accountant's estimate of the tax rate will affect the after-tax earnings of the startup, which in turn will affect the valuation of the company, which will affect the value of the percentage the CEO will own. But tax reforms have created large uncertainties about the operating loss carry-forward and how much a startup can expect to pay in taxes. The outcome of tax advice on that question is worth millions; an extra round of capital may be required if the tax treatment is wrong.

If the projections of the startup's financial statements are realistic, the CEO can better control the pricing of the deal. When there is solid backup by a top CPA firm, investors are less likely to argue that there is a lot of uncertainty in the business plan, thereby requiring the founders to lower their price for the deal. Founders must insist on good *business* advice from the CPA, not just good *accounting* advice.

The accountant will also be able to advise about whether the deal is priced too high, too low, or in the middle of the deals it is competing with. And he will advise you of several ways to calculate and measure value, based on financial statements. Experienced startup accountants have seen a lot of stock offerings of high tech companies and have gained experience they can pass on to you, quickly.

The CPA firm also charges by the hour. Its fees should not be high at this stage, not until the startup's books must be audited annually and examined closely each quarter. Advice sessions are usually not for fee; they are used to nurture the relationship and the account for the long term. Accordingly, the CPA is motivated to help the startup client succeed; he or she is on the client's side. It is anticipated that the IPO fees and annual work thereafter will make up for the low fees during the startup phase of life of the company.

Conflict of Interest.   It is important to always ask the consultant, attorney, and accountant whether they have any conflicts of interest. Some work very closely with venture capitalists—the very ones you are going to negotiate with. Others may be close to suppliers or customers that will be important to the startup's business. And there is always the chance that they have worked with a competitor with whom they are still close. Get the cards on the table quickly, and get on with the deal.

Venture Capitalists. The startup needs the venture capitalist. The VC firm has the money. The CEO's goal is to get the VC to give the startup some of the money the VC has been entrusted to invest.

The VC is paid according to a formula spelled out in Chapter 9. The VC's share of the startup's rewards comes after the VC firms' investors get back at least their invested principal. The VC gets his cash when the partnership that was formed to invest is terminated, that is, liquidated. That outcome will take several years; seven is normal, ten not uncommon, and top firms are extending terms to 12 years.

Accordingly, the venture capitalist wants the startup to become liquid ASAP, if not sooner. That puts pressure on the CEO to "dress up the financials" to look good at IPO time, which may not be in the company's best interests long term.

Furthermore, the venture capitalists have a chance to attract new money to invest only if the last partnership has done well. Thus the startup will be under pressure to raise several rounds of capital at regularly increasing prices per share. Short-term performance pressures become a reality soon, well before the startup goes public.

A pattern of higher and higher prices in a company is a delight to the venture capitalist, and to employees also. So where is the conflict? The answer is that the venture capital people want to start with as large a percentage of the company as they can, (a) in case of a huge success, in which case their values rise rapidly in absolute terms; or (b) in case of disaster, in which any forced dilution will be less painful to the investor trying to attract new capital under terrible company conditions.

The name of the game for the venture capitalist is ROI, return on investment, measured by percent per annum. The CEO's deal should also measure results this way. This should be pointed out in the business plan, and emphasized strongly in presentations to investors. The accountant or startup consultant can run the numbers for you correctly.

We asked several CEOs, "What are the realities of negotiating with venture capitalists?" We obtained many answers, which we have summarized in the next section. The CEO must be just as analytical in negotiating for startup money as for buying furniture or some other resource needed for the company. The CEO must test the quality, measure the availability, check out the post-sales service, and determine the fairness of the price offered; then decide and close the deal. After all, money is just like other necessities; it has a price. It should be treated that way.

Negotiating Phases: Problems and Pitfalls

CEOs have to negotiate smart at each stage of funding, but nobody is born knowing how this process works. For example, the first-time startup CEO wants to know the answers to questions like: When should I call the venture guy back? How much should I bother him; he hasn't called us back since last week? These are not trivial questions—someone who is too pushy can make the deal sound like a loser, but the CEO who is too laid back may lose the interest of the investor, who has a lot more fish to catch.

Here is a summary of tips for handling each stage of raising venture capital.

Seed. The earlier the stage of financing, the more risk there is for the investors, as well as for the founders and the startup team. Accordingly, the CEO will have to work hardest to get the money in this stage. He can expect to call on 20 or more venture firms and make at least as many presentations, time after time after time.

The first goal is to secure a lead venture capitalist.

Usually the seed capital is planned to cover payroll through completion of the first working prototype. If the financial cushion planned into the seed funds is inadequate to cover expenses up to the next funding (called Round 1), VCs can extract a heavy price per share (deep dilution) to provide an emergency round of funding (a "bridge loan") in order to keep the CEO from announcing to the employees that the company will miss its next payroll.

The main problem of negotiating at the seed stage is to get and keep the VCs' attention long enough to convince one of them that this startup is worth the investment risk. The special risks of a seed round have increasingly attracted specialists, firms that focus on investing in seed round deals only (see Chapter 9). These specialized seed investors will be more likely to put up with incomplete management and will be sympathetic to the need to get some money to build a prototype to prove the technology works.

A common pitfall is to rely on one source for the seed money. The best advice we found was, "Don't get all of your venture money from one basket." Competition does wonders for a deal.

First Round. Often referred to as the first "real" round of venture capital, these funds will be about $2 million to $5 million, 5 to 10 times more than the seed round. Stock will be labeled Preferred B, since the seed round took Preferred A. The price per share will represent a large increase over the prior round.

It all sounds simple, but problems are soon encountered. The first one is the problem of "business slip." This occurs when the startup finds that product development or market positioning are significantly deviating from the original business plan. The startup's first key milestone will be missed. Should the CEO expose the slip and admit it? Will this decision hinder or enhance closing of Round 1? What if the decision on disclosure should slow closing on Round 1?

The best response is to tell the truth. The bad news is better delivered by the CEO as early as possible. Otherwise, when it leaks out, the CEO's credibility will be badly damaged.

The cure for this dilemma is twofold: (1) Plan for at least one redesign of the prototype (or retry of the first key milestone) and raise enough seed round cash to do that, and (2) hire competent *managers*, especially a VP Engineering, then closely monitor, encourage, and coach the development work. These two approaches will help avoid slips, and help you achieve milestones on time.

The next problem is getting commitments from *new* investors. This will take a lot of time, especially if your lead investor is simultaneously fighting fires in three other investments. The startup's management must be prepared to raise the money without any help from the lead, and still keep marching ahead on schedule with the business plan. (Suggestion: This is the time to go back to your business plan schedule and rethink what impact product slip will have on raising capital. You may want to reschedule your milestones and plan on raising more capital per round.)

The CEO and potential investors will haggle a great deal on pricing the deal, and the CEO must be prepared to justify the pricing. For a favorable Round 1, the CEO should have competing VC factions vying for his deal.

Incomplete management teams scare off a lot of investors at this stage of a startup; a missing VP Marketing will probably bring the show to a complete halt.

The focus should be on demonstrating success early, with confidence that a lot more will be coming soon. And then it is time to close on the financing.

Multiple Rounds.   Later rounds of financing will all be "fillers," capital needed to grow the business and get the company into shape to go public.

These rounds vary considerably in price per share, depending on whether management has succeeded or badly botched the original business plan. During these stages, the CEO will have lived out the true meaning of what it is to operate with a "living business plan" that changes daily.

The statistics increasingly say that the CEO's time as a founder is drawing to a close. Rough moments will have come and gone at least a few times, with ups and downs much wilder than any roller coaster ride.

And the startup will still need more money. Venture capitalists told us over and over again that entrepreneurs are overly optimistic—they always underestimate the time needed to get the first product to market, overestimate the ease of getting the company operating, and need double the capital called for in the first business plan. The number one error is underestimating how long it will take from the first sales call to shipping the first product.

Drops in prices per share are likely. Lower prices are needed to attract capital under conditions of duress. In times of duress, a CEO quickly learns the meaning of all the boilerplate terms and conditions in the preferred stock agreements, particularly the antidilution clauses. Antidilution occurs when a predefined formula gives VCs more shares because the subsequent round of financing was sold at a price lower than the VC has paid in previous rounds. Founders must be prepared to lose a large percentage of ownership in these cases.

"We waited too long before going after our next round of capital!"— that was an all too common cry from the startup CEOs, several of whom never survived as CEOs beyond such fiascoes. It is never too early to start raising the next round of capital. The CEO should get set at least six to nine months in advance of missing a payroll, and add three months of burn rate to the company's cash cushion for added safety. In other words, the CEO should start raising the next round just after closing of the last round.

Mezzanine.   This is the last round before the IPO, about a year or so before the big event. It is another name for the unplanned funding that keeps payroll flowing while everyone waits for a rotten stock market to perk up again.

It is tricky to decide how much to sell at this stage. Some startups that did large mezzanine deals in 1983 survived, but paid a high price in terms of dilution. Waiting too long can be costly for management, but not for the investors (remember the antidilution clauses in the venture investors' contracts). But in the early 1990s, few investors appear willing to do mezzanine deals: mezzanine results have been poor.

Initial Public Offering.   By the time the multiple rounds begin, the first visits from the investment bankers will have begun. This interest initiates a game new to the CEO: the public stock market game. It ushers in promises of liquidity, fame, and fortune, and a host of new problems, which are discussed in detail in Chapter 13.

The CEO must become an expert in pricing IPOs even before the seed round is raised. You must work backward from the IPO pricing to the seed round pricing in order to make sense out of your VC pricing plans. The money markets that drive the venture capitalists are the same ones driving the IPO pricings. The startup consultant, attorney, and accountant can help the CEO develop the required expertise.

Structuring and Pricing a Venture Capital Deal

A venture deal is like any other financing, with a few special characteristics mixed in for good measure. The classic deals are based on experience acquired by a lot of people in America over more than 50 years of venturing. The not-so-classic deals reflect the creativity of the investors and entrepreneurs who make this kind of business so interesting.

We will now describe a classic venture capital deal and then some interesting creative alternatives that were very successful for all parties involved. Actual percentages and per-share amounts are analyzed later in the chapter.

It all boils down to answering this question: "How much of my company will I have to give up in order to get the capital I want?" The following process is what actually goes on in the classic deal.

Use of Preferred Stock. The CEO, founders, and employees will all own or get options to buy common stock. The investors will all own preferred stock. This is done to avoid a tax problem: as the per-share prices rise quickly, the Internal Revenue Service will try to attribute income to the prior round investors and tax their sudden profit. Separating the shares into rounds of preferred stock isolates the rounds from one another and protects the investors from this problem.

All preferred shares are converted to common shares at the time the company goes public. A conversion ratio of one share of common for each share of preferred is typical practice. Whatever the ratio of exchange, the important calculation is what percentage of voting common stock everyone gets after the IPO.

Each round is accompanied by a thick set of legal agreements that contain the clauses so important to investors. Table 7-1 lists the common items in the agreements. The startup's attorney will advise on which are to be deal-busters, negotiated, or given up. Strategy must be planned early.

TABLE 7-1. Typical Terms of Preferred Stock Issued to Venture Capitalists

1. Number of shares issued, price per share
2. Conversion price: number of common shares per preferred share
3. Antidilution formulas
4. Registration rights: mandatory; "piggyback"; number of shares
5. Veto rights:
    Next financings, acquisitions, mergers
    Sale and other disposition of assets
    Dividends
    Amount of stock issued
    Borrowing and leasing
    Compensation of executive employee staff
    Ownership, sale or access of technology
6. Rights of inspection
7. Right to elect board member, attend board meetings
8. Vesting rights of employees
9. Receipt of financial statements
10. Closing expenses

Source: Saratoga Venture Finance

Each round of investors typically adds one more member to the startup's board of directors. There is a desire to "represent this round of investors" at the end of each round. The trouble with this is that it makes the board venture-capital heavy. Most CEOs we met found that bias to be unwise. The startup veterans started out with a couple of strong venture capitalists on their boards and then insisted, as a condition of each successive deal, that no more investors would be added to the startup's board.

The founders will be expected to agree to some formula that takes shares out of their portion instead of the venture capitalists' percentage ownership if the startup's share price sinks for the next round or two. The CEO and the startup's attorney must negotiate hard on this provision.

Investors will want no obstacles to getting liquid. They will want to include clauses that get them cash or registered public shares if the founders ever sell the company to a giant. But such clauses can cripple the chance of even starting negotiations with a big company. Follow the advice of the startup's attorney.

Veto rights or their equivalent are common. They usually appear innocent until the CEO is forced into some undesired action. For instance, CEOs told us they were urged in desperation to get money from the Super Venture Fund, whose partners were archenemies of the CEO and whose style and chemistry clashed with the CEO and core team. We have also witnessed cases where complete irrationality took over under veto conditions while the CEO missed payroll after payroll and developed ulcers.

Vesting limitations are imposed by preferred stock investors. Vesting is a contractual agreement between the startup and the employee. It limits the employee by connecting the number of days employed to the number of shares the employee may acquire through exercise of stock options. These days, typical terms are vesting over four years, with a one-year waiting period before the first day of exercising shares may begin. For instance, a new employee will have earned 12/48ths of his stock option on the first day of the second year. Thereafter he vests (earns) an additional 1/48th on the first day of each successive month over the four years following date of employment. These four years represent the whole vesting time. The CEO must get the best deal possible for his employees. Valid Logic and other successful IPOs used three-year schedules to attract more people from scarce talent pools in highly competitive times. Some venture firms try to insist on five-year vesting.

Employees have the choice of exercising the granted stock option (buying the shares) or waiting until the IPO occurs, when virtually all employees exercise their options. If the IPO takes longer than four years, the early employees will have to exercise or lose their optioned shares.

How much cash will the respective founders put in? That varied a great deal among companies. Several issued stock to founders at less than $0.01 per share. Multiplied by 500,000 shares for a founder (that is, 10 percent of 5 million outstanding shares), that comes to $5,000. Founders should not expect a free ride—they must be prepared to sign a check as an investor. A minority of companies loaned the purchase price to key employees. This became the case most often when heavy management was added late in the life of the startup. Finance is creative and is where the startup consultant, attorney, and accountant will earn their keep. There are severe tax and liquidity implications to decisions to buy or borrow. The CEO and founders must get all the advice they can in these matters.

Pricing Each Round of VC Funding.　　There are several quantitative methods used to calculate the price per share of each round of funding a startup. The methods most often cited by venture capitalists and investment bankers who were interviewed are shown in Table 7-2. All of them should be used by the CEO.

TABLE 7-2. Valuation Quantification Techniques

Multiple ROI	How many multiples of our investment can we reasonably expect from the time we invest to the time we are liquid, that is, when the startup goes public? (Used most often by venture capitalists in seed and later rounds of private funding of startups.) One dollar in today's money will be worth how many dollars at IPO?
ROI per Year	How much will we earn per year by the time the startup goes public? (Particularly important for the investor in the earliest stages of a lengthy startup.) If we put one dollar into the bank, how much interest would it have to earn each year to be worth the IPO price?
Percent Control	How much of the voting stock will we control after this round of financing? (More important for actively participating investors than others.) What percent of the stock of the company will be owned by investors versus management and employees (counting all options as if exercised)?
Next Rounds	How much room is left for the next round of investors if the startup needs another round? Will that be enough to attract them, especially if the startup gets in trouble? Will we be able to avoid a writedown of our share price in the next rounds? (This is very important for funding a startup that needs a lot of capital.) If we price each successive round of funding by a ratio of 2:1, can we hit the desired IPO price?
Prior Rounds	Will the pricing of this round create too high a profit for the last round? New investors do not like windfall profits for prior investors; instead, the new money tries to keep the markup of shares below 3:1; in the early 1990s, 2:1 or less was typical in the pricing of deals.
Historical Multiples	Using the startup's historical financial statements, are the prices of this round reasonable when compared to equivalent companies? How many times revenue does this round represent?"
Future Multiples	Using forecasts of the startup's financial statements, are the prices of this round reasonable when compared to equivalent companies? How many times revenue, profit, book value and cash flow does this round represent?" (This is especially used for pricing initial public offerings.)

Source: Saratoga Venture Finance

Key Funding Issues. We will now go through three case studies, each touching upon key issues for the startup CEO who is learning to price VC rounds of funding. Each case has special characteristics and demonstrates how varied VC deals can be in real life.

Case Study: Network Equipment Technologies

Network Equipment Technologies, Inc. (NET) went public on January 23, 1987, after starting business in August 1983. Here is how the private rounds of venture capital and the initial public offering ended up distributing the wealth.

After the IPO, the company had 12,568,987 shares outstanding and had reserved shares for and/or had issued to employees the right to purchase another 1,287,588, for a grand total of 13,856,575 shares. The ownership of those shares was as follows:

Equity Ownership

	Percent	Shares
New investors at IPO time	*10.8%*	*1,500,000*
Private round venture investors	*57.7%*	*7,992,000*
CEO and VPs	*9.6%*	*1,327,555*
Subtotal	*78.1%*	*10,819,555*
All other employees' stock and options to buy stock	*21.9%*	*3,037,020*
TOTAL COMPANY	*100.0%*	*13,856,575*

The venture capitalists had invested a total of $24,956,000 for which they got 7,992,000 common shares. Those shares at IPO time were worth $16.00 each for a total of $127,872,000. Their ROI ranged from 67 to 85 percent per annum.

Over the space of 17 quarters, the cofounder and CEO, Bruce D. Smith, sold NET stock to investors in three rounds of funding:

Financing Rounds

Seed	*Preferred A*	*$4,332,000*
Round 1	*Preferred B*	*$7,499,000*
Round 2	*Preferred C*	*$13,125,000*
TOTAL		*$24,956,000*

The IPO raised $24 million of new capital for NET by selling 1,500,000 new shares of common stock at $16.00 each. An additional 1,000,000 shares were sold by several investors, NET officers, and other shareholders during the IPO. The company spent $3,480,000, or 8.7 percent of the offering, for the fees and expenses (none of which are tax-deductible) necessary to accomplish the IPO.

---

* The data are taken from the Saratoga Venture Tables shown in Appendix A.

The CEO owned 534,513 shares for 3.9 percent of NET; these were worth $8,552,000. The shares of several of the other nonfounder VPs were valued at an average of $2.4 million each.

On Thursday, July 21, 1987, NET shares closed in trading on the NASDAQ market at $23.25, up 45 percent in the six months following the IPO. And over the same six months, NET revenue per quarter grew and so did net income.

That is a classic startup success story.

Case Study: Chips and Technologies

A modified classic is the case of Chips and Technologies, known as Chips. Chips altered the classic pattern by taking only 21 months to get to IPO; it was an amazing business success.

Shunned by the venture community, the CEO and cofounder, Gordon A. Campbell, funded Chips first with personal bootstrap funds, next with a round funded mainly by Chips' landlord, William L. Marocco, and finally with corporate venture capital from Chips' key Japanese suppliers of chip foundry manufacturing services.

Financing Rounds

Seed	*Common*	*$97,000*
Round 1	*Preferred A*	*$1,705,000*
Round 2	*Preferred B*	*$1,528,000*
TOTAL		*$3,330,000*

That was all the capital needed to build a very big business. By June 1987, Chips was selling millions of semiconductors a month and accounted for sales growing quickly toward the $100 million per year mark. Net income was running 16 percent of revenue and return on ending equity for the quarter ended March 31, 1987, was an annualized 34 percent.

The speed of getting the first product to market and the burst of sales helped insiders retain a large proportion of the company.

Equity Ownership

	Percent	*Shares*
New investors at IPO time	*13.6%*	*1,750,000*
Private round venture investors	*32.3%*	*4,151,077*
CEO and VPs	*41.9%*	*5,388,077*
Subtotal	*87.8%*	*11,289,154*
All other employees' stock		
and options to buy stock	*12.2%*	*1,571,665*
TOTAL COMPANY	*100.0%*	*12,860,819*

The CEO ended up with 23.3 percent of the company, worth $15,010,000 at IPO date. The shares climbed, settling on July 21, 1987 at $24.75 per share. That made Gordon Campbell worth about $74 million at that time. His VP's (several were cofounders) shares at IPO time were worth about $2 million each.

The investors' ROI soared! Using the IPO pricing of $5.00 per share, their return ranged from 266 to 284 percent per annum! At $24.00, they deserved a place in the Guinness Book of Records.

Chips' success teaches lessons in how to modify, persist, and succeed. Campbell and his employees also deserve an award for sheer determination.

Case Study: Worlds of Wonder

Worlds of Wonder (WOW) made investors, founders, and employees a lot of money by IPO time. The company used a very creative financing structure. But after the IPO their basic business and personal fortunes soon crashed.

The prospectus filed with the Securities and Exchange Commission for the June 20, 1986, public offering tells the facts about how it was done.

First, Donald Kingsborough—a former executive with Atari—found the idea for a new enterprise in the form of a design for a talking bear with synchronous facial movements. Alchemy II Inc. of Chatsworth, California, had spent nearly a year looking for someone to build and market its design.

Next, Kingsborough negotiated a development and marketing agreement with Alchemy for exclusive rights to the design. This agreement was later bought out by WOW after that company was formed and funded by Kingsborough, who became its chairman. In exchange, Alchemy was granted separate royalties on sales of articles using the technology.

WOW commenced operations in April 1985, and product shipments began in August 1985.

During fiscal 1986, WOW issued 13,770,000 common shares to its three founders in exchange for $306,333 in cash, the assignment of the agreement with Alchemy, and assistance in obtaining bank financing. Such assistance was in the form of a $9 million standby letter of credit made available in August by a shareholder for the company's use.

Subordinated notes of $3,651,000 were issued in conjunction with the issuance of the above-mentioned stock. They bore interest at 10 percent and were due on June 1987 or at the initial public offering of WOW, whichever was earlier.

During 1986, the company also sold 2,433,000 common shares for $3 million to investors and 1,783,500 restricted shares for $178,000 to officers pursuant to employment agreements. (Unlike the vast majority of high tech startups, WOW top management had five-year employment contracts with large salaries guaranteed.)

The kingpin of this clever financing structure was capital in the form of wealth from the Abercrombie interests in Houston, Texas. Their representatives knew Kingsborough and had backed him in creating WOW.

Note also how important a friendly commercial banker was in this case:

- Explosive growth demanded fast, very expandable working capital financing be provided almost immediately. Sales jumped to $93 million in the first fiscal year!

- Manufacturing in Asia required large international letters of credit to support spikes in Christmas seasonal inventory buildups.

- WOW had no track record, no profits, no sales for the loan credit officer to rely upon. The above-mentioned letter of credit was vital.

- By March 1986, WOW was using $20 million of its large line of working capital credit at the bank (up to $110 million under certain conditions).

The auditors, Deloitte Haskins & Sells, scrambled to keep the bookkeeping clean during this explosive growth. The audited records were handy and necessary: the company filed its registration statement for the initial public offering 12 months after commencing operations. Sales were $93 million and profits $8 million.

At the IPO, 4 million new shares were sold by WOW at $18.00 each. Certain shareholders sold another 2 million as part of the registration statement. The $108 million IPO was large, compared with most high tech deals.

Smith Barney and Dean Witter co-managed the IPO. Smith Barney employs one of the top-ranked toy company research analysts. The underwriting cost WOW $7,535,000, or 6.98 percent of the capital raised in that offering. The underwriters and stock brokers got $6,780,000 for their efforts. The rest went to attorneys, the accounting firm, and the special printer of the prospectus.

At IPO time, Kingsborough owned 20.5 percent of WOW (assuming all option pools were granted and exercised) and was worth $88 million. His chief operating officer was worth $11 million and the average wealth of eight other executives was about $4 million.

Top brass owned 76 percent of the combined shares of officers, directors, and employees (owned shares plus option pools).

Investors owned 50 percent of the company just before the IPO.

The IPO shares accounted for 17 percent of the company after the IPO.

The investors' reward for backing this startup was high. Venture backers made from 577 to 1,392 percent per annum ROI. At $26.00 they did even better. WOW broke a lot of records at that time with its success and did very well for the people who decided to support it with their checkbooks.

In May 1987, WOW announced fiscal year sales of $327 million and net income of $18.6 million or $0.85 per share. Lazer Tag was a smash hit and Teddy Ruxpin sold well for the second season; alongside it were talking characters from famous fairy tales.

That same month, the company decided to raise more cash to finance future growth, as well as to allow founders to "cash in some chips" by selling shares. It registered a secondary offering of shares in the form of a debenture bearing interest and convertible into common shares, at a fixed price, over a certain period of time, under certain conditions.

By May 14, 1987, however, the common stock had sunk from a high of $26.00 to $ 15-5/8 per share.

On July 21, 1987, WOW shares closed on the NASDAQ at $10-7/8 after reaching a low of $10.50.

By January 29, 1988, the shares were at $0.75 each. The company was struggling to survive in Chapter 11 bankruptcy.

It was a very rapid climb to success, and an equally fast crash after IPO. WOW's financing plan was creative and got the job done even though it did not use classic venture capital.

Shooting Stars.   Another lesson to be learned from the Worlds of Wonder case study is how nervous investors can be about continued success. "Can WOW repeat its Teddy Ruxpin success?" was commonly heard after WOW's IPO. That is also the same question asked of any high tech wonder startup that must follow success after success in order to justify a high stock price set by investors who are interested only in tomorrow's possible successes (and failures), not yesterday's. What was WOW's sustainable competitive advantage?

Pricing.   As the above cases show, founders and investors did well in financial terms. The cases also show that the wide range of percentage owned by outside investors, and that the proportion owned by the CEO also varies widely.

Later in this report we present more details on how to translate all of this into the dilution the founders will have to accept in order to get money for their company.

In the meantime, a study of the Saratoga Venture Tables in Appendix A will provide information from the famous startups to help the CEO know what to expect when negotiating rounds of venture financing.

Ownership and Control

"I'll never sell more than 49 percent of my company to investors. My fellow founders are committed to controlling this startup. We do not want the vulture capitalists telling us when to jump and when to sit." As consultants, we have heard this often—from very well-meaning souls. And from some very naive founders.

This section is intended to help the CEO gain a more realistic expectation of what will happen to control of a company as the founders start to sell shares in it to outside investors.

Conventions, Practices, and Expectations.   The facts of life are that as soon as more than one person gets some claim on the equity ownership of the startup, the first founder rapidly begins to lose control as a sole proprietor.

First, state laws are quite strict about offering shares in new enterprises. The flim-flam and bogus company hucksters have, over the centuries, bilked so many investors out of so much money that Americans are subject in each state to laws that are on the side of the new investor, the one who is in the minority. These are the "blue sky laws."

The term *blue sky laws* is popularly applied to state statutes regulating the offering and sale of securities within the jurisdiction of the respective states. "The name that is given to the law," said Justice McKenna in Hall vs. Geiger-Jones, "indicates the evil at which it is aimed; that is, to use the language of a cited case, speculative schemes which have no more basis than so many feet of blue sky."*

It is dangerous, to say the least, to simply start selling shares in a company. The entrepreneur needs a good attorney who is experienced in these matters and in the home state's laws. Otherwise, a founder could easily end up with a lawsuit later on when the startup company badly needs classic venture capital. VCs shy away from companies with legal trouble.

Effective Control and Preferred Stock.   Classic venture capitalists do not control a startup in terms of shares voted. Even if they had the 51 percent of the votes, they would have to be very careful for the reasons noted above.

What really happens is demonstrated in this disguised case study.

Case Study: Yourco, Inc.

The founder succeeds in selling preferred stock in his startup, Yourco, Inc., to investors. He soon learns that the investment will be made via HiTech Venture Limited Partnership III. The general partner, Sam V. Enture, hands the startup's attorney his usual contract, which calls for one seat on the company's board of directors because he must represent the interests of Partnership III.

---

* Hall vs. Geiger-Jones Co., 242 U.S. 539, 550 (1917).

When the founder reads the fine print, he quickly sees that Sam will now be calling a lot of shots; future financings are going to involve virtual veto power authority by Sam. [Table 7-1 describes some of what can be expected.]

Next, the founder finds that Sam requires that Sam takes over as chairman. After all, the founder has never run an independent company before, and Sam is a veteran of many. Anyway, Sam's name at the top will attract a lot more investors of similar world-class stature. Everyone will benefit, he postulates.

At the first board meeting, the founder learns that the board of directors will hereafter be setting compensation policy, including, but not limited to, wage scales, starting with the founders, cash bonuses, and of course all stock option grantings to new employees.

If the startup doesn't already have one, Sam will advise (in a firm tone) using a top venture lawyer, and he'll have the attorney of his choice, Rick Jones, call tomorrow. Goodbye to the founder's friend, the less experienced guy who set up this whole deal in the first place.

And Jim, the founder's CPA buddy, will no longer suffice to do the books. Instead, Sam provides the phone number of Tom, downtown at the regional headquarters of one of the Big Six multinational accounting firms.

As the first board meeting comes to a close, Sam smiles and gives the founder his next assignment: at the board meeting next month, he is to present a summary of progress of Yourco, comparing it to the original business plan, complete with headcount and budget facts.

Welcome to the world of venture-capital-backed startups!

With a little better idea of what to expect, a founder can better prepare for what is to come. It is unrealistic expectations that causes many of the squabbles between the board and the CEO-founder. Like the Boy Scout motto says, "Be prepared."

Typical Agreements

Like all contracts, agreements with investors can be customized to fit any need and circumstance. The practice of securities law can be very creative.

However, venture capital terms and conditions have evolved since the 1930s when this form of investing became serious. The rules have made a lot of sense to a lot of people since then, and they have also enabled a lot of founders and VCs to become very wealthy. Companies were run within the bounds of the restrictions and many became successes. So we were not surprised to find CEOs telling us in interviews of the good results they had in spite of what sounded like onerous conditions.

The best advice the startup presidents had for the prospective startup leader was to get a good attorney. He will keep the founder from being subject to unfair restrictions and will help plan for the future.

Dick Riordon, who founded the Los Angeles law firm Riordan & McKinzie, told us, "The startup CEO needs to use a lawyer that will structure the deal today to take care of the events of tomorrow. That is why the lawyer needs to know venture capital well and also have a good sense of business."

The number of shares to be outstanding is aimed to be somewhere between 10 million and 15 million at IPO time. That will produce a per-share price in a range acceptable to quality investors, at least $10 and no more than $25 each. And the agreement specifies the exact number of shares in the voting control of the new investor. This starts to put bounds on what can be sold to other investors.

The conversion price is usually one for one. At IPO time, all preferred shares are converted to common, share for share. Underwriters will be expecting that condition.

Antidilution terms are tricky. The CEO should work out each combination of circumstances and do the calculations to see what the VC is expecting to happen to the CEO's percentage when the company gets into trouble and has to have extra, unplanned rounds of capital added to keep it alive. The startup's attorney will be familiar with what ranges are acceptable, common practice among the latest venture deals.

Registration rights also become key when a company goes public. Registration rights are the right to have your shares registered with the Securities and Exchange Commission so that the shares may be traded as public shares. Everyone wants their shares to become public as soon as possible so that they can be sold quickly, as desired. CEOs and founders do not want anyone in line ahead of them. Yet some investors try to get such a favored position. Common practice is to have everyone in the same boat, all getting registered together when such events arise.

The fights on registration rights are usually over how many of the founders' shares may be sold at IPO time. This is argued between the CEO and the underwriters as part of the underwriting agreement signed at the time of the IPO.

Veto rights are the implicit control items that were mentioned earlier. They are very real. A CEO must get to know them well. They fall into two categories: financings and stock related. In all cases the CEO must know what his authorities are under adverse conditions.

Rights of inspection are needed by investors so they can get into the accounting and legal books in case of trouble. Venture investors successfully sued Osborne and its auditor Arthur Young over accounting matters. Not many situations require such action. But since financial trouble can and does happen, a company's books must be open as soon as it takes money from the first investor.

Board member voting is where the power plays occur, particularly as venture partners vie for top gun position in hot startups. Being chairman of a raving success adds a lot of publicity and awe to the VC firm whose general partner is chairman. This VC hopes that exposure will get the firm a lot more first looks at great startups and will get it in on the few first-class deals over the next year or so.

As to the wisdom of having more or fewer VCs on the board of a startup, we found a lot of mixed opinion. The only consensus pattern of response was from CEOs whose company had gotten into trouble at some time in the past. A clear majority said that at such times most VCs are a big hindrance, more trouble than help. Some CEOs were bitter and advised keeping as few VCs on the board as possible, and to particularly avoid the arrogant ones who have not had much recent operating experience in meeting payrolls of struggling startups. The deans of venture capital speak often of the need for people that can become good board members. Those gray-haired VC veterans can be worth their weight in gold.

Vesting rights of employees is so commonly standard now that to compete with anything more stringent would put you at a disadvantage. The usual is to have four-year vesting monthly after a one-year waiting period. Be more creative if you think it will help in your recruiting, but check with your lawyer first.

The company must mail financial statements to investors. Investors will commonly call at times convenient to them to inquire about the numbers. They expect a prompt reply, usually immediately (drop every-thing and talk to me), because their time is so constrained and they want to get this call off their mind. Some write short notes, mail them, and watch to see how fast the CEO responds. (They'll remind the CEO at the next board meeting, in front of the other members.)

Closing expenses are an area for haggling, concerning both the dollar amount and who will pay for expenses, particularly for the VC's legal fees. Attorney's fees (which are paid for out of the capital raised) should be reasonable (check with your lawyer for local rates and practice), with excesses paid for by the VCs themselves. The company's attorney will advise on what "reasonable" is in a given region.

Those are the major points—those that will be worth thinking about before the company gets started.

Famous Startups: Their Private Deals with Venture Capitalists

We conclude the chapter with a description of the Saratoga Venture Tables in Appendix A. The information they contain is hard to get; it will help you plan and prepare for negotiations with investors.

The information in the Tables has been generated by proprietary software, the Saratoga Financial Synthesizer, which was developed exclusively by Saratoga Venture Finance. The Synthesizer digests and analyzes Securities and Exchange Commission documents, particularly the initial public offerings of famous companies. The result is a computerized database of private venture facts on new enterprises and their public offerings.

Selected results of selected companies are made available in the Saratoga Venture Tables. The data included are:

- Percentage owned by founders, employees, and venture capitalists
- Pricing of rounds of stock sold by famous private companies
- Cash compensation of executives
- Mix of stock between top management and employees
- Cost of deals charged by Wall Street investment banking firms
- Amounts of stock option pools
- Wealth of president and founders after going public

The Saratoga Venture Tables are divided into two groups:

- *Saratoga Venture Tables of Equity Ownership.* These quantify number of shares, percentage owned, value of holdings, options to employees, and IPO shares sold. They tell the story of venture capital funding from seed through multiround funding. They also tell how much top management compensation was, and how much founders gave up to key employees.
- *Saratoga Venture Tables of ROI.* These reveal how much the VCs made in each deal. Each round of preferred stock is analyzed. The multiples are calculated, and so are the all-important percentages earned, which are computed in terms of percentages compounded per annum. They also show how much capital each company raised, and how long each company went between rounds of funding.

Conventions and Assumptions Used.   The Saratoga Venture Tables are derived from SEC documents to which the reader can refer for exact details. While the Saratoga Venture Tables have been faithfully produced, they contain certain assumptions about some details of the private financings. Not all SEC documents were in complete enough detail to avoid making certain assumptions.

Note that the percentages of ownership are based on a special definition of the total number of shares outstanding; it assumes that all options in the option pools are granted and exercised. Using this convention helps CEOs plan better their allocation of shares to employees. The data required in the SEC prospectuses do not offer this important calculation.

Personal Rewards and Costs

In this chapter we will examine the rewards of doing a startup. And we will count the cost.

Our goal is simple: *to help entrepreneurs realistically examine what they are about to get into and to better prepare them for achieving their personal best.* The chapter contains some very frank statements by people we talked to. We have changed names and places to preserve the privacy of those who were willing to be frank about their experiences. We thank them for their concern for others' success and for their participation.

The first section concentrates on financial return; the other sections review professional and psychological rewards. After that we analyze the personal costs of doing a startup.

Potential Financial Return

Over the 50 years or so that modern venture capital has been in existence, there have been vast swings in all the factors that affect the formation of wealth: taxes, wage levels, inflation, depression, recessions, wars large and small, periods when business is viewed as the bad guy, and elation with business as the leader of all that is good for the country.

All this change adds risk. Yet the entrepreneurial-minded keep coming.

The basis for wealth formation in venture-backed companies is equity. It consists of all the leftovers after everyone, including the government, has been fully compensated.

To take on the level of risk of a startup for the reward of leftovers seems incongruous at best. To get a better handle on this strange phenomenon, we will start with the item that in the end is the only monetary thing that counts: cash—preferably, cash in the entrepreneur's personal account at the bank.

Then we will look at the cash value of being a founder or a later-stage employee, and how much CEOs and VPs are worth at initial public offering time.

Table 8-1 lists top guns of some famous startups and their equity. It shows what the founders were worth. Both the percent they owned and their absolute dollars of wealth from the startup are measured in terms of the price per share at IPO time. Later, some stock prices rose and others dropped by large percentages, for many different reasons. The number of founders is shown and the average owned per founder is calculated, as is the value of 1 percent of each company.

This table provides all the types of information any employee needs to measure the fairness of an equity offer:

1. What percentage of the company the employee will own at IPO time.

2. What each share of stock will be worth at IPO time.

3. How many shares of stock will be outstanding at IPO time.

The equation is simple:

Employee's percentage × Total no. shares outstanding × \$/share = \$Wealth

The CEO will be expected to predict these numbers for each employee hired, especially the key VPs and the veterans of former startups. They will insist on being given these numbers. This chapter will attempt to help by explaining the workings of the stock value calculations. In tables later in the chapter we will provide facts from other famous startups so that the CEO can set realistic targets for rationing precious equity for sale to investors and attractive employees.

To get even more detail—for example, to find out what the vice presidents by function got—carefully examine the Saratoga Venture Tables in Appendix A.

Now let us make some observations based on Table 8-1.

TABLE 8-1. Ownership by Founders and CEOs Just After IPO

Company	CEO		Founders* (Avg. per Founder)		Total Employees	
	Percent	$M	Percent	$M	Percent	$M (per 1%)
Cypress Semiconductor	2.1%	$6.8	0.9%	$2.7	16.7%	$53
No. people	1		5			($3.2)
Convex	4.3%	$5.6	4.3%	$5.6	19.1%	$25
No. people	1		1			($1.3)
Chips and Technologies	23.3%	$15.0	3.9%	$2.5	19.1%	$12
No. people	1		3			($0.6)
Network Equipment	3.9%	$8.6	2.5%	$5.6	25.1%	$56
No. people	1		1			($2.2)
Silicon Graphics	3.1%	$4.5	4.6%	$6.7	26.3%	$38
No. people	1		1			($1.5)
Worlds of Wonder	20.5%	$88.5	0%	$0	22.9%	$99
No. people	1		0			($4.3)

* Does not include the CEO.

Source: Saratoga Venture Finance

CEO's Share. There is a *wide* range of value in the worth of the CEO's wealth. Compare billionaire Bill Gates (Microsoft) to the CEOs in Table 8-1. And remember that we have included only the more famous startups in our table. A lot more leaders were worth a lot less.

Gates had a rare success. And by startup standards, the company was very old at IPO time. Famous startups in the early 1980s typically went public in less than 3.5 years, while Microsoft waited until it was 11 years old. By 1990, a wait of 5 to 8 years had become common.

In an exploration of over two dozen companies in the Saratoga Venture database, we noticed that there is a bunching of wealth in the $6 million range for the CEOs. This is so predominant that we wonder if this is a rule laid down by venture capitalists!

The median of our selected companies has the CEO worth $6.8 million. The high was Bill Gates, worth $236 million (this rose to several billion in later years!). The low was seen occasionally, in companies where the leaders appear to have traded very high cash compensation for very low equity positions. Bill Gates and others who started their companies in the pre-1983 era took low salaries and got much larger percentages of their companies.

Seldom in recent years has the CEO owned more than 3 percent of the startup after IPO time. Yet here too there is a range of results. In our pre-1990 sample, the median CEO percentage at IPO time was about 5 percent; the high was 40 percent and the low was 1.6 percent.

Founders' Shares.   *Founders other than the CEO rarely owned more than 4 percent.* The founders' median is in the range of 3 to 4 percent.

Note that exceptions do occur: when the board of Silicon Graphics brought in a new employee to take over from the founder as CEO (the leader remained on as chairman and chief technical officer), the new CEO ended up with less than the founding leader, but was nonetheless the number-two employee in terms of ownership ranking.

Implicit is the obvious: *Those who are founders get a lot more wealth than those who join later,* even though people may join only a few months after the founding of the company. It seems that here the old adage is true: "The early bird gets the worm," or at least the fattest one by far. A late-joiner cannot qualify as a founder nor get the same number of shares as the founders. Founders take extra risks, such as leaving employment before any money is raised. Their equity reward is compensation for those risks.

Competence of founders relative to later-joiners seems to have little to do with these wide swings of wealth, according to several of the lawyers we spoke to. The individual who joins a year later as VP of sales or finance, for instance, can expect to get a very small portion of the company.

One noteworthy exception occurs when the board of directors decides it is time to add operational leadership while retaining the high tech guru who has been leader number one but is struggling to cope as a manager. This appears to us to have been the case in Silicon Graphics (we are not picking on or criticizing its successful management, just using the organizational changes to make a point): McCracken—a veteran successful general manager from Hewlett-Packard—joined three years after the founding of the company and ended up with 3.1 percent versus 4.6 percent for the founder. The successful startup chairman, who stayed on, continued leading the company's advanced technology work.

Attorneys warned us that such a big bite of stock for a new leader—and the attendant dilution—usually comes out of shares controlled by insiders. And in some cases when the founder-CEO chooses to leave or is forced out by investors, because of buyback conditions in the company's policies on stock, the shares for the new leader come out of the holdings of the former CEO and the remaining management and employees. The VCs do not want to share in such dilution proportionately with the remaining management and employees.

Employees' Shares.   After founders, the other employees share in the remaining pool of stock via incentive stock options. The median size of the ownership pool for all non-founder employees in the companies analyzed was 19 percent of the company, with the high at 26 percent and the low at 17 percent. We found that the founders and investors worked out various schemes for creating enough shares to attract a lot of new employees. A deliberate scheme is needed to avoid running out of enough shares to draw in the top players that will be needed in the ranks of the middle management as well as in all the other positions in the company. Saratoga Venture Finance does this with a proprietary software model based on case histories. Whatever scheme is chosen, be sure there is enough stock available, in terms of both percentage and absolute dollars.

The non-executive employees' pool of equity ranged from a high of $145 million to a low of $12 million with $38 million as the median. The first was in a mature company, 11 years old; the other in a company only a little more than 21 months old. Those pools were created in the form of options to be shared among all employees in each company. Each had a widely varying number of employees and per-employee distribution of stock, according to our analysis. It seems that here each company makes a significant statement about its culture and character. Some spread the wealth more widely, others focus shares in fewer hands.

Case Study: Cypress Semiconductor

*One example of special use of equity is that of Cypress Semiconductor. It used stock options to make Cypress stand out as a motivator, with equity for all. First, the leader, T.J. Rogers, shared founders' shares among **six** people, including himself (two or three founders is much more the norm; see Table 8-1). The founders were almost all key functional employees at the VP level.*

During the private years the company granted bonuses in the form of stock to all employees, tied to milestones that are a part of the culture at Cypress called "turbo MBO." Literally every employee works daily with detailed goals for the week and month. Success resulted and the employees shared in more equity.

Additional stock options were granted to all levels of the company along the way, including top management. To veteran investors this is rare; seldom are top managers ever granted more stock than the original amount they signed up for when they were first employed by the company. The reason is not clear, based on our limited interviews. We have nonetheless formed the hypothesis that it happens because most startups go widely off their original business plan, go over budget, are late with first product, are profitable much later than first planned, and are managed poorly.

Cypress ended up going public 3-1/2 years after starting in business. At that time, the founders did well by most measures. The CEO owned shares worth $6.8 million; the average for the five other founders was $2.7 million, and the *pool for its 336 other employees (including both the granted and the remaining available pools of options) was worth $53 million.*

Cypress continued to perform well after the IPO. And the stock rose to close at $11-7/8 on July 21, 1987, up 32 percent from the $9.00 IPO price.

Rogers was paid a total cash package of $122,325 for the 12 months prior to the 1986 IPO. His VPs earned in the range of $91,000 to $93,000.

Just before the IPO, the founders and employees had claims to stock accounting for 26 percent of the company. Private sales of stock had brought venture capitalists' holdings to the remaining 74 percent, including 3 percent owned by an important early corporate partner, Monolithic Memories.

What Is One Percent Worth?

The final variable in the equity equation is the value of 1 percent of the company at IPO time. When using this measure, our data in Table 8-1 shows a wide range of value among the companies .

The low was Chips at $0.6 million for each percentage point. That later rose by a factor of five to $3.0 million as the IPO price of $5.00—issued in a very soft IPO market—rose to $35. Within four more months the stock had settled near $25.

The high was Microsoft, which should be no surprise after 11 years of adding successful value. A 1 percent share was worth $5.9 million.

The median value was $1.5 million per percentage point. This varied considerably between companies because of many variables, including maturity of the company and consensus by Wall Street analysts on projections of the companies' operating earnings, cash flow, and return on invested capital.

Other Findings.   Here are some further observations based on our research:

- Our proprietary databank suggests that *the greater the amount of capital to be raised, measured in absolute dollars, the lower the percentage retained by management and employees.* More analysis is required to confirm this hypothesis.

- *What is not visible is probably as significant as what is.* That is, how much did the founder CEO *plan on* giving up, versus how much did he *have to* give up because he grossly underestimated the capital actually needed, or missed development schedules, or found out that the market was much smaller or slower to grow than he had expected?

- In simple terms, *startup CEOs that get to IPO in less than five years can look forward to becoming millionaires*—typically, they acquire about $7 million; tens of millions is rare. Note that in the examples we chose, one does not see the wealth of those CEOs who left before the IPO, for whatever reason—because the board dismissed them, they got tired and quit, or they just wanted to get out of the stress and see more of their families and friends.

Participants' Cash and Equity.   The name of the game is equity formation. Cash compensation plays a small role relative to stock options. Bonuses do occur; typically, however, they occur only after the company has been profitable for several quarters. Some venture capital firms are fiercely against large cash bonuses of any kind.

One trend we detected was that *the level of cash and equity have reversed direction and relative importance since 1983*. That year seems to have marked a watershed:

- *Prior to 1983, it was common to find CEOs working for $50,000 per year and ending up with a company in which outside investors owned less than 50 percent of the stock.* Everyone hunkered down, lived on a lean and mean salary and waited to make up for lost wages when the stock went public in five years.

- *After 1983, salaries moved up to become much closer to those of employees of public, established corporations.* More money meant more startups needing to pull more managers out of successful, well-paying, established companies. CEOs have shown up at IPO time earning closer to $100,000, and VPs and those reporting directly to them have been earning salaries a lot closer to the going rate for people with their experience and skills.

- *Equity took the reverse trend. It has now become rare to see startups at IPO time with more than 35 percent owned by management and employees.* Investors typically took 65 percent to 75 percent of the company by the time the IPO was over. Prior to 1983, those statistics for equity were reversed, with the larger percentage going to founders and employees.

Our sample in Table 8-2 shows the holdings of common equivalent shares, including all pools of options, both granted and available, just *before* IPO time. The valuation is measured at the IPO price. The definition of employees is the total of all founders, VPs, and employees, whether optionees or actual shareholders.

The company holding the highest percentage for employees is Microsoft at 95 percent. It is also the oldest company in the list, founded in 1975.

The lowest company holding is Cypress, at 25 percent. However, its management was close to Microsoft's in cash compensation.

TABLE 8-2. Ownership by Employees and Investors Just Before IPO*

Company	Employees†	Value at IPO ($M)	Investors	Value at IPO ($M)	Equity Capital ($M)
Cypress Semiconductor	25%	$74	75%	$176	$40
Convex	29%	$36	71%	$72	$32
Chips and Technologies	63%	$35	37%	$21	$3
Network Equipment	34%	$70	66%	$128	$25
Silicon Graphics	33%	$49	67%	$78	$22
Worlds of Wonder	50%	$187	50%	$172	$13

* Includes all options granted; excludes remainder of available option pool. Value is measured at IPO price in millions of dollars.

† Everyone except investors.

Source: Saratoga Venture Finance

The median is 39 percent ownership for employees, 61 percent for investors.

Companies with low venture capital requirements like Chips ($3 million), Worlds of Wonder ($7 million) and Microsoft ($5 million) sold proportionately less to investors.

The largest capital-requiring companies—requiring $25 million to $40 million had to sell the largest percentages to investors.

Big Fish, Little Fish

At this juncture we must bring up a familiar issue that we hear about quite often: Is it better to be a little fish in a big pond or a big fish in a little pond?

In the parlance of startups that is rephrased: Is it better to do a startup that requires $3 million in capital and grows to $20 million in annual sales; or one that needs $30 million to get to $100 million? Will the dilution to me in the bigger pond outweigh my lower absolute wealth in the little pond?

The answer can, fortunately, at least be quantified with simple arithmetic. Then the entrepreneur must decide which strategy has the best chance for fulfilling the startup's business plan. This of course focuses only on the financial aspects of such a decision.

Control seems to be a swing factor in settling this issue. Both small capital requirements and speed to market auger well for selling less to outsiders and retaining more control. However, as cited in Chapter 7, investors quickly get into control, regardless of percentage owned.

Most of the classical venture capitalists argue for the larger pond, which is in their best interest. They have a great deal of capital to invest, and it takes about the same effort and time to invest $1 million as $10 million. The venture capitalist is not in the business of getting the founder the best deal in town; that is up to the founder.

Cash: Wages and Bonuses. Venture capitalists approve of paying cash wages, but just not too much. The CEO's job is to determine how low a wage he can personally exist on, and then expect no increase in cash compensation at least until the startup becomes profitable years later, two or three years at least.

Cash bonuses are more common today than in earlier days. Sales VPs all got commission compensation; marketing VPs less commonly so, even if they were responsible for sales. But the proportion of cash taken out by the top executives of a startup as bonuses was rarely in the same proportion as in large, established companies.

High salaries did exist in some cases, typically in wildly successful companies with sales at IPO time already in excess of $100 million per year.

To generalize, the universal attitude is classically a "lean and mean" attitude toward cash compensation. The CEO should be prepared to step down by at least 20 percent or so from the nice base plus bonus package at his former BigCo Inc.

Day 1 wages for startup CEOs in the seed stage were rarely over $90,000 during the 1980s, and were more commonly in the range of $70,000 to $80,000. Nonetheless, there are important exceptions, and the trend in the 1990s is toward larger cash compensation—with less of the company reserved for the CEO as a consequence.

Is It Worth It?

I wonder if I'd be better off staying at IBM, or HP, or DEC or XYZ Tech? Would the payoff be worth it? Table 8-3 provides a quick calculation. A prospective startup CEO needs 44 years of wages to break even.

Vice Presidents. The numbers for vice presidents are not as varied as for CEOs, but still require a lot of years of wages just to get even. A VP earning $90,000 a year at BigCo Inc., who gets 0.5 percent of a startup, pays $50,000 for optioned shares, pays taxes at the marginal rate of 39 percent, and whose company is worth $1,500,000 per 1 percent requires 16 years of wages to equal the worth of his or her equity.

Note that in neither case—CEO or vice president—is any credit given in the above calculations for the cash wages paid by the startup.

TABLE 8-3. Cash vs. Stock: A Breakeven Analysis Example

- A startup CEO expects to own 4% of his company at IPO time.
- At IPO time, 1% of his company is forecast to be worth $1,500,000.
- His current and expected cash compensation at BigCo Inc. is $135,000 annually.

Gross value of equity	4% × $1,500,000 = $6,000,000
Cost of founder's shares	$5,000
Gross profit on shares	$5,995,000

Marginal tax rate:

Federal	28%
State	11%
TOTAL	39%

Tax on shares sold	-$2,338,050
Net after taxes	$3,656,950

Breakeven Analysis

Cash after taxes totals	$3,656,950
Taxes paid at 39% rate	2,338,050
Total gross wages all years	$5,995,000
Total gross annual wages	$135,000
Years needed to break even	$5,995,000 / $135,000 = 44 years

Clearly the comparative financial reward is attractive to a manager who is interested in doing a startup. The tougher aspect to measure is the risk of doing so.

The Downside. The CEO must be prepared to live for three to five years on the salary that he accepts with the first funding of the startup. Most startups do not get to the successful heights shown in our examples of famous high tech startups. Our research suggests that only 9 percent of the companies that are funded get to those lofty levels of success.

As a consequence, the prudent individual must expect to pay bills and meet family obligations on wages earned, or else formulate another plan. Here are a few of the more common personal plans as well as a few of the more creative ones we have encountered. All are real names, although some details have been changed for privacy:

- Sam saved enough to live without *any* income for two years. This provided enough time to resign, write a business plan, incorporate a startup, and work at lower wages until three years later, when he got a raise at the point the startup became profitable.

- Bob treated his reduced salary as an investment. He considered the incremental wages lost to be schooling in the world of the entrepreneur, regardless of the outcome.

- Charlie, an engineer, opened up a Chinese restaurant on the side with two cousins. His goal was to accumulate seed capital to start his own company. While his share of the profits turned out to be insufficient to start a company, the capital did give him enough to make up for the lower wages he settled on when joining the founding team of a new enterprise.

- After 20 years as an engineer, Jim found himself at the age of 45 without sufficient funds for retirement. Although he had become a very successful engineering manager, his string of startup company employers had not done well. Jim quit his latest job as an engineer and went into the real estate business. He bought and refurbished a five-apartment complex. After three years, he found the cash flow income to be enough for his eventual retirement. So Jim found yet another promising startup and went to work again in his first love, engineering.

- Philip Huang, the founder of Televideo worked a second part-time job at 7-11 stores to help him save the startup capital that he used to create Televideo.

- Jake and Sue were top salespeople who married to form a family and raise children. Both wanted to do a startup. They agreed she would go first, and she joined her former boss in his new startup. The company did fine. After nearly four years it went public. Sue emerged as one of the top salespeople. Meanwhile, Jake kept the bills paid on his salary. They saved his commission checks for rainy day emergencies. After Sue's company did their IPO, Jake left BigCo Inc. and joined a tiny high tech startup as VP/Marketing and Sales, taking a big cut in salary. Meanwhile, Sue got another raise, set another record as top salesperson. Now they switched roles. Sue's salary paid the bills. And the couple sold half her shares to pay for the extra expenses of their first baby and the construction of an extra room on their home in Silicon Valley.

- Jack decided to go for broke. He took out a second mortgage, guaranteed loans to his startup, and cut the family's spending to a pittance. This went on for nearly three years. Then his company went bankrupt. Although his wife is still with him, his kids remember every day of those three years, including the Christmas with gifts from the Goodwill store.

Tables of Cash Compensation. Table 8-4 shows how well paid top management was in startups that were successful. Shown is the total cash compensation that existed in the twelve-month fiscal year prior to the IPO date, including all bonuses and any other cash compensation. Equity-related compensation is excluded. In some cases, the Saratoga Venture Tables will indicate that the board of directors approved significant increases just prior to the initial public offering. Such increases, however, were not a prevailing pattern.

Here are some of our findings:

- *Cash compensation varies widely, and appears related to several factors.* The top compensation ranged from a high of $332,000 for the CEO of Worlds of Wonder to a low of $75,000 for CEO of Businessland. Businessland was started in March 1982, WOW in April 1985. And while both are retail related, WOW is classically consumer-oriented, in an industry that is well known to pay significantly higher compensation than electronics companies of similar size. Businessland required three times as much capital as WOW. Both companies took about the same length of time to get to IPO. WOW went public in six quarters, Businessland in eight.

- *The head of sales often earned more cash than the CEO in "hot" companies.* This occurred in both Chips ($100 million annual sales run rate in by IPO time) and Alliant. And the VP/Sales was a close second to the CEO in Network Equipment Technologies. Several startup CEOs told us that they had paid their head of sales on a commission structure to encourage beating the business plan by a wide margin. They wanted the compensation to be the result of hot sales, and not to be artificially limited to being a salary lower than that of the CEO.

TABLE 8-4. Cash Compensation in Startups*

| | ($ in Thousands per year) | | Range of VPs | |
Company	Highest Paid		High	Low
Cypress Semiconductor	$122	CEO	$93	$91
Convex	$86	CEO, VP R&D	$82	$78
Chips	$137	VP Sales	$125	$93
Network Equipment	$113	CEO	$103	$74
Silicon Graphics	$156	CEO	$138	$105
Worlds of Wonder	$332	CEO	$203	$167

* For the twelve months prior to IPO as reported to the Securities and Exchange Commission in the offering prospectus.

Source: Saratoga Venture Finance

- *The salaries of VPs naturally followed those of the CEO.* However, several chairmen said they had on occasion paid proportionately more cash to VPs than to CEOs because the VPs were not holding a large fistful of founders shares. This was most pronounced when the company decided to bring in a chief operating officer to run the show, as Microsoft did. The new leader is often paid a lot more in cash than the CEO, who is a founder and wealthy stockholder.

- *Here again, what is unseen is as significant as what is visible.* Compensation rates for private companies is difficult to obtain. However, since 1981, Saratoga Venture Finance has monitored startup CEOs' salaries and compared them to wage guidelines published by several popular compensation surveys. We found the closest correlation for high tech companies was with the private findings of the American Electronics Association salary surveys for small companies. Venture capitalists told us they also use the AEA findings to compare startup wages. A friend in a member AEA company may be able to advise you in such a matter. Or ask your startup consultant for assistance.

Founders' Shares.   CEOs often have questions about founders' shares. There is an awe, an air of extra respect, for "founders' shares," some unfounded and misleading. We found that this is due to a number of misconceptions. And we found that founders get into a lot of restrictions.

- *First, founders' shares don't really exist.* Everyone gets the same common shares as everyone else.

- *Founders get more shares than any other employee.* They are there in the first days, it is their idea, they took a big risk when they left their employers to start the company, and they worked very hard to create the business plan and convince investors to risk their money in the company.

- *Founders lose a lot of privacy.* Corporate laws identify a founder as such in the IPO prospectus and include compensation and shares compared with everyone else in the company.

- *But the founder has basically the same restrictions on shares as any other common shareholder has: Rule 144.*

Rule 144.   Rule 144 is meant to prevent founders and investors from selling their shares soon after the IPO and running away as the company collapses in ruins shortly thereafter, leaving the latest investors holding worthless shares. The rules are, as usual with the law, complex. But here is an oversimplified explanation of it all. (Be sure to talk to a good securities lawyer if this pertains to you.)

A founder must wait two years before selling his shares to anyone. The clock starts ticking only on the date the owner has paid for the shares in full; getting a loan from the company to buy the shares does not start the two-year countdown.

What a founder does not want is to wait to start the clock ticking the day after the IPO. But in order to own the shares, he must have paid cash to purchase the shares. That is more risky than waiting. The tradeoffs between waiting to purchase and purchasing early will have tax consequences, too, so a talk with a good tax advisor is a must.

Rule 144 does allow some sales of private, nonregistered stock. However, the restrictions on who can sell and to whom are quite narrow. Advice from a good tax and securities advisor is mandatory. There are frequent proposals for changes in Rule 144.

Employees' Stock Options. For most employees, including everyone other than founders who buy their shares on day one, the means of getting stock ownership is through stock options. There are no special rules for options for a startup. The option plan a company selects must comply with federal and state laws for such things.

How much the company grants to whom depends mainly on company policy. More startups these days are granting options from day one to all employees, hourly employees included. It is necessary to calculate the size of the pool needed over five years. That takes some real finesse, and a computer model can help save a CEO's sanity.

The company's lawyer can explain about the two types of options: ISO and Nonqualified. The former has better tax consequences, generally, but is limited to an absolute dollar value that can be issued per person. Since that is a problem for a lot of VPs who will be hired, the Nonqualified will be used for fixing that problem. The shares are the same, common stock, only the amounts and tax effects are different.

Vesting is now almost always designed to occur evenly over four years, with an initial one-year waiting period. The company gets the right to buy back any unvested portion, even if the employee has paid for the shares in full. This is the hook the investors use to keep the CEO at the office, working hard even when things seem impossible. And it is their main control on CEO performance: if the CEO does not deliver, they will probably fire him, buy back the unvested shares, and grant them as an option as part of the new CEO's employment package. Other vesting schemes do appear, and they are usually in favor of the investors.

Employment Contracts and Personal Loans. Although they do occur upon occasion, employment contracts for startup CEOs are rare. They are almost nonexistent before, during, or after IPO time. VCs hate them; most won't touch a round of financing for a company with contracts in place.

Personal loans are also very rare. The exception is in the form of loans to buy stock. But that is less and less common, and is seldom done for anyone other than a critically important executive who must be financially assisted to attract him to work for the new company.

Relocation. Relocation loans are rare for startups, but do occur from time to time. It is hard for a tiny company with $250,000 in the bank to squeeze out the extra money. Relocation of key employees is to be avoided. It costs a lot of time, takes a lot of emotional energy from your employee, and adds to the already high stress of doing a startup. This is especially obvious for startups in the high-rent districts, such as Silicon Valley, Boston, and metropolitan New York City. Another problem is that banks do not like to grant mortgages guaranteed by new enterprises of any size, especially those that may fail next year.

Venture Capitalists' Shares. Investors buy preferred stock that has the option of being converted into common shares under certain conditions, or is required to be converted into common at the time of the IPO.

As noted in Chapter 7, the shares have certain restrictions and requirements. They are like a contract, and the CEO is the party that must perform.

Watch out for the conversion terms. A 1:1 ratio is almost always used, but antidilution clauses may trigger a much higher ratio in favor of investors.

Case Study: An Engineer's Offer of Compensation

A.W. had decided two years earlier to start looking for a startup to join, and over the past eight weeks he had been talking seriously about joining one of two startups where he had been interviewed, PiTech and Saga Systems. Since immigrating to the United States from Taiwan, he had put in 10 years at two well-known companies. He held bachelor's and master's degrees in electrical engineering and had earned his Ph.D. at MIT 13 years earlier. A.W. had developed a series of successful chips, had three patents, and regularly contributed IEEE papers in his field of expertise. He had just sent his last chip design to the wafer fabrication lab at BigCo Inc., and was now ready to leave. He wondered what the offer from PiTech would be.

A.W.'s wife, Nancy, was a layout person at Chips and Technologies. Her stock option would carry the reserves they needed to support his parents in Taiwan. They had both talked about their dream house and decided they could never get it except through a big success in stock at a startup. Nancy had done well enough for the down payment plus the family reserve, and now A.W. decided to get the rest by going to a good startup in its infancy. He wanted the maximum stock he could get. They lived frugally and had no high lifestyle to support.

PiTech had been after A.W. for some time. Jim, the PiTech CEO and former director of engineering in the Logic Division of BigCo, had noticed A.W. during the past four years. In addition to being a very hard worker, A.W. was talented. He had pulled several key design projects out of the fire. This was important to the massive turnaround effort that Jim had been handed four years earlier.

During that time, Jim had been thinking of the value of his 30,000 share option at BigCo, at a price of $3.25. The electronics industry slump of 1984 to 1986 had plunged the market price to $2.10. His work had yet to be recognized at the bottom line because the Systems Division had fallen into the tank at just the time the Logic Division was getting into black ink. The hours had been long, there was lots of travel to key customers, often with few results to cheer about. Key engineers had left for greener pastures over the past two years, and innovation was not as common as earlier. A.W. had been a sparkling exception.

After much personal consideration, Jim finally contacted Frank at Elm Ventures. Frank was a former executive at a successful startup, Tecnic Corporation. Frank had met Jim at a seminar put on by the American Electronic Association. Frank took care to listen to Jim's guarded words and was impressed by the man and his track record. Jim left with confidence that some of his ideas for a startup business plan would be attractive to Frank once they were down on paper. Nine months later, Elm became the lead investor in the seed round for PiTech.

A.W. liked Jim, who during interviews at PiTech had mentioned that a slot as director of advanced engineering was available. But A.W. would report to a new VP of engineering, Mike, who had joined as a founder and was a close friend of Jim's. In A.W.'s mind, this increased the risk of joining PiTech. Mike had only limited experience in managing engineers at Digital Equipment Corporation. According to the grapevine rumors in the Route 128 region of Boston where Mike had worked, he was reputed to be one of the greats as a solo inventor and much less successful as a leader of a group of design engineers .

Jim had prepared a written offer and had it waiting in a manila folder on his desk. He had decided long ago to make every offer of employment in PiTech, at least up to offer number 100. Jim had carefully calculated how much to give his first 20 top recruits. Six of the last 12 offers had been accepted with no hassle or haggling, and only one had not worked out and left. Jim was confident that his offer to A.W. was generous and fair, both to A.W. and to PiTech.

The secretary ushered A.W. into Jim's small office and the two began the meeting. A.W. waited for the CEO to make the offer. After agreeing on a rather open-ended charter to design the next two logic chips, Jim got around to the offer.

"After careful consideration, we have decided to offer you $66,500 per year base salary and 30,000 shares," said Jim. He paused to see A.W.'s reaction.

A.W. did not move a face muscle but tensed up inside. He had expected higher numbers in both base and stock.

"May I see the written offer?" asked A.W. Jim handed it to A.W., who read it carefully.

"How does it look to you?" queried Jim.

After a long pause that made Jim quite uncomfortable, A.W. replied, "Well, frankly I am a bit disappointed." Pause again.

Jim groaned inside. "Why didn't I check with Sam over at NewCo? He would have helped me on this one. I haven't any support in human relations, I thought this was an attractive offer. His base is nearly that of our VP of engineering! How can I go any higher? But did I go too far below his old base of $83,000?"

"Well, perhaps I can answer any questions you have about your offer, A.W. All the guys want you to join us, and we thought the offer was really quite fair for a startup." Jim knew he couldn't say that everyone had taken cuts in pay, because that just was not true; in fact, two people had to be offered raises to get them to join.

"How many shares do you have?" A.W. said.

Jim stiffened visibly. He hadn't expected this seemingly quiet person to be so aggressive. A.W. noticed it and sensed defensiveness. "I wonder if he gets that defensive about everything?" thought A.W., who began to doubt his eager attraction to Jim as a leader.

"Well, that's confidential, of course!" barked Jim. He was now angry inside.

What Jim did not know was that A.W. had done his homework. Friends had given him details about PiTech and its backers. His friends had spent a lot of time coaching him on how to measure the wealth in the stock offer, and a lawyer friend had obtained PiTech corporate records in the state capital. A.W. knew exactly how many shares Jim and the other founders each had.

"OK, how many shares are outstanding?" said A.W.

"About five million," replied Jim.

"Is that including the venture capitalists' preferred converted to common?" asked A.W.

At that moment, Jim sensed he was dealing with someone more experienced than he was.

"No, you need to add another 5 million shares or so for that," said Jim. He waited, nervously.

"About 11 million in total?" inquired A.W.

"Yes," answered Jim. But Jim did not tell A.W. about the one million shares granted as an option to the equipment leasing company and a technical consultant. After all, they were not yet shares outstanding, at least not until the IPO time.

"What do you think the shares will be worth at the public offering date?" asked A.W.

"Oh, brother, this guy is sharp! I hope he designs as well as he does his homework!" Jim thought. "Well, the calculations I have made tell me we can get about $15 per share if we do our business plan," responded Jim.

What Jim did not know was that during the team interviews, Mike and one of the venture capitalists on the board had let slip that they thought the company could do $10 at IPO time. Jim had decided to skip that number. After all, it was a wild projection, wasn't it?

The offer letter stated that the stock for A.W. would be priced at $0.10 per share. A.W. had learned that the seed round had gone for $0.50 each after the Preferred A was converted to common 1:1. Jim pointed out that "At those prices, and as employee number 14, you would be practically a founder!" A.W. liked that idea.

"How many shares will be outstanding at IPO time?" responded A.W.

Now Jim really got nervous. "If I tell him, he'll learn that we need three more rounds of venture capital to get the $35 million that our business plan calls for. And the total 23 million shares will make his wealth, before the cost of $0.10 per share, worth less than $300,000. I hope he buys my $15 per share instead!"

Jim eagerly said, "Remember, 30,000 shares makes you one of the top 10 shareholders in the company!"

A.W. immediately revolted inside. "Who does he think he is kidding? I know what dilution is. I'll end up owning less than 0.1 percent of the whole company; that's next to nothing!"

Jim kept thinking he had already revealed too much. He disliked opening up with anyone, especially like this. Would A.W. get scared of the dangers of having to meet milestones in order to get the other venture capital that PiTech needed? "If I don't get this guy," Jim thought, "our first product ship will be set back six to twelve months!"

"OK, I'll give you $70,000 base and an extra 5,000 shares," blurted Jim.

A.W. decided he had enough, and said, "Could you put that in writing?" Jim immediately inked the changes and initialled them, handing the modified original to A.W. without making a copy.

"Thank you, I'll get back to you soon," said A.W., and he walked out the door.

As he started his car and eased out into the traffic, he thought the meeting over. By the time he arrived home he had made up his mind.

He would accept the Saga Systems offer of director of engineering at $85,000 and 0.2 percent of the company at IPO time from the 20-man startup. He wondered why he had been so excited about Jim in the first place.

Employee Benefits and Perquisites.   All startups have to be competitive with health benefits. That's a given. Several insurance companies are focusing on smaller enterprises and serving them well, with good rates.

Beyond medical and dental plans, the seed startup seldom offers a lot more in benefits. Glasses and other extras are usually reserved for post-IPO companies.

Vacations are two weeks, but one should not count on having time for more than a week at a time.

Cars are rarely offered. Field salespeople get car allowances instead. Car allowances for executives are getting scarce, partially because of their abuse in the boom times of 1981 to 1983. Startup companies troubles in this area can begin when the new VP Sales who will reside in the head office insists that he must have a new Mercedes (he cannot afford one himself and his current one must be turned in to his current employer when he leaves next month).

Fancy offices are rare. Furnishings are usually spartan or used. Even for the CEO.

Private secretaries are nonexistent at most new companies. Instead, one person does every administrative job imaginable.

Several startups told us they offer free use of computers in engineers' homes to encourage extra hours of design time. And several others offer either loans of personal computers (luggables and laptops), or inexpensive purchases through the company. The idea is to encourage more work and productivity in staff personnel.

The Professional Reward

Our research revealed that there are several nonfinancial reasons that people joined startups. Many people said that these were more important than the monetary reward.

Being a Winner. Becoming an early employee of a famous startup like Apple or Compaq, one that everyone talks about, is probably the most often mentioned motivator of those who think of startups. The next DEC, Sun, Genentech. "Wow! That would feel great," said people we interviewed. That overpowered the other responses of those we spoke to and observed over the past eleven years. Venture firms avidly encourage this desire. "Everyone loves a winner," is how the saying goes. "So try for one," says the venture capitalist.

However reality is sobering. Few are winners. Only 1 in 10 make it to the fame of attaining the ranks of those companies that got to IPO. And only a handful of those that get funded become household names like Apple. Yet all the people who start out seem to have faith that their company will make it. That is the stuff startups are made of. Everyone has to believe in the dream, the vision of glory and success.

Some startup veterans told us such dreams were unrealistic. A few said you just have to believe. Yet others were of the opinion that "It's better to have tried [a startup] than never to have tried at all."

Hot Startup Atmosphere.   We have learned firsthand how exciting it is to be a part of a company that is on a roll. When a startup is hot it is *HOT!* Just a walk into the lobby of Chips and Technologies as it was ramping up to $20 million of sales per quarter in early 1987 was breathtaking to us. The lobby was jammed with customers whose conversations were marked with accents from Texas, New York, Korea, Japan; five suppliers representatives were hassling the polite but very firm telephone receptionist, who said they all needed prior appointments; two walk-ins who were having trouble with English were getting help filling out job applications; engineering interviewees were coming and going like patrons of Baskins and Robbins on a 100-degree July day; advertising and PR agents were zooming through the lobby, racing for cars to avoid being too late for the next interview with reporters; several phone call pink slips from the BMW, Porsche, Mercedes, and Ferrari dealers' salesmen were waiting for attention; repairmen with their shiny aluminum toolkits were getting immediate access to the inner sanctum. The switchboard wouldn't stop ringing. And the air of hard work and look of confidence on the faces of the employees that swaggered through the lobby was obvious.

Once ushered into the inner sanctum, we walked past cubicles housing people bent over PC screens and workstations, and office areas filled with partially opened boxes of papers and books. The chart of daily stock price changes was posted outside a secretary's cubicle; it looked like a rocket flight path. Talk in the aisles was over new orders, ship rates, the next chip set just off the CAE system that looked solid after simulation; how the layout team had worked until 11:00 p.m. last night to get the final changes done on schedule; that the president had appeared in the *San Jose Mercury News* Business Monday section today. T-shirts and sweatshirts with big CHIPS logos were everywhere.

The air was filled with the feeling of success. Chips had accomplished in less than three years what most startups, even the famous ones, typically took five years to do.

The last memory of our visit was the article someone had ripped out of a newspaper and pinned to his cubicle fabric with a bent paperclip. The headline said something about the rumored timing of the next IBM personal computers. As we headed to our car in the hot afternoon sun, we recalled the familiar words from a recent article in *Forbes* on the "shooting stars" that so often are hot companies that quickly burn out; the writer had written that "entrepreneurs should always run scared."

Patents.   Regardless of which company we visited, engineers were quick to tell us that they had confidence that their ideas would lead to several landmark patents. They talked about that a great deal, especially since the U.S. patent court and the copyright laws had been changed in the past ten years. The desire to get a patent was clear, even if the company had all the legal rights assigned to it. Prior patents were visibly displayed in cubicles of many of the technical staff members that we visited.

Clearly, many engineers felt they had a much better chance to get patents in a startup than in a much larger company. When asked why, they cited fewer constraints on creativity, or that the entire business plan of the startup was founded upon the inventions (to be) claimed by the engineering staff. Their excitement seemed to stimulate ideas that led them to new heights of exploration, stretching the former limits of their technical capabilities.

Papers, the Media, and Conferences.   Presenting papers at technical conferences ranked high on the list of reasons to do a startup, at least for the technical staff. Marketing personnel talked about getting invitations to make presentations about their startup at industry seminars and conferences. Such highly visible forums were attractive to many people we interviewed.

Yet we found such visions in conflict with reality. Managers of startups lamented that their technical staff did not even have enough time to write the minimal technical collateral materials needed by the company's sales and marketing staffs. Papers on the company's latest new products, aimed by marketing departments for covers of magazines like *Electronic Design,* usually lacked writers. And there was such intensity for finishing new designs that some engineers lamented they had to turn down trips to annual technical conferences they used to attend religiously.

However, marketing staffs flocked to seminars and conferences. They cited their need to be abreast of current trends, and they wanted to influence the newsletter writers and media people that were invited to attend. Public relations included such activity, and employees seemed to search each issue of their favorite magazine or newspaper for tidbits written about their startup. If a competitor was mentioned but not a word on their own company, employees were quick to point this out to the VP Marketing.

Regis McKenna received top marks for setting an early example for how to use public relations as an offensive marketing weapon in the battles for setting industry standards. Since the winning companies so often included those that set and defended the standard, this partially explains why so many people on the marketing staff seek out the paper and seminar circuit with great intensity after joining a startup.

Local Business Accolades.   Coverage in the local news media was clearly pleasing to the founders of startups. They said the interviews and resulting publicity were "part of the game." The press promoted the good and the bad, making bums out of the heroes as fast as the rumor mills sent out faint signals that "Jobs is behind schedule" or "Osborne may not get its next model out on time" or "A former employee who refused to be identified said ..." Bad press could deliver news that caused customers to hesitate or even forgo orders that the startup counted on and needed badly. That simply reinforced the power of the PR push needed behind the startups. And the drive for headlines was renewed with more vigor and desperation.

The winners got the personal fame that goes along with such success. The companies and management of the losers, the majority, were quickly old news and never mentioned again.

Personal Growth.   Many people said they joined a startup to achieve much greater personal growth, to get out of a rut in BigCo. Our interviews revealed two very different groups of people in the realm of personal growth: one camp responded well to the demands of the startups they joined, learning on the job and adding experience after experience to their always-up-to-date résumés. The other camp was ground up, burned out, and left in worse shape by the startup experience.

Escape from stagnation in a large company was the attraction for many. They were looking for less politics, less waste, less bureaucracy. Most startup people believed they escaped from all that in a new enterprise. And this helped them grow personally.

Some people seemed to thrive on the stress and difficulties that a small company inevitably encounters. Some claimed to possess more drive or determination. Others attached credit to a religious belief. Others said they were just happy to have made it through in one piece. Whatever the outcome, a startup profoundly affects a person who becomes involved in it.

Some people picked up special skills on the job in their function, whether it was finance or manufacturing or whatever. But, as compared with the formal classroom learning sessions conducted by large established companies, startups spent little time on such things. Predominant was the classroom of the school of hard knocks and lessons learned on the fly. A vast majority of the people with whom we spoke had mastered sophisticated tools and techniques well before joining a small startup. New companies tend to use rather than create skills, especially those skills requiring heavy blocks of time to learn.

Management Climbing and Turnover.   Consensus was that promotion was a lot easier in a startup than in a larger company. However, it also seems a lot easier to end up without a job.

Part of the source of the problem of turnover lies in the hiring practices of startups. Veterans of startups kept telling us that management under stress tends to recruit the nearest warm body, rather than incur an expensive headhunter fee to carefully search out the best person for a key regional sales position or product marketing job or whatever. Sink or swim was a common phrase bantered about, and a lot of people sank.

Our hypothesis is that this hiring practice contributes significantly to the troubles so many startups run into and never recover from. Firing people in a startup has vivid morale repercussions. Recruiting and retraining is dreadfully expensive for a company with such limited resources as the new enterprise. Low turnover probably has a lot more to do with success than it is given credit for.

The Floundering Founder Phenomena

One observation became so predominant that we think it is a rule of a startup: at some level of sales or complexity or duress, the founding leader will find that he is failing miserably. This is often referred to as the Peter Principle—he has risen to his level of incompetency. It is painfully evident in startups.

As noted in earlier chapters, the board is dominated by VCs who very frequently fire the president founder who won't give up, even though the company is in a real mess. Few people enjoy this, or think it good. (However, we did find several old venture capital salts with the reputation of believing that it was both natural and healthy to ax the founders, because the companies that succeed always got to a point where that was necessary.)

The resulting bitter feelings are seldom forgotten. Spouses of such discarded employees told us of legal battles behind the scenes that were intensely fierce, angry, and devastating. Former friends had to choose sides and close relationships were severed, never to be renewed.

On a more optimistic note, the experience gained and the value of any vested shares are both worth a lot, particularly in the next startup job, even if the first one does not work out. One budding manager left an outstanding career at a large computer company to take over the presidency of a startup when that company was growing 300 percent a year just after going public. He inherited a lot more of a mess than anyone had expected and left after a short period of time. However, soon thereafter he was recruited to be president of a small private startup. Its sales soared and it shortly went public.

It would be an interesting and very useful study to learn how long founders last and why. Some leave because they have become independently wealthy. But few leave voluntarily; their lives seem to be so bound up in their startup, their baby that they have given birth to and nourished from the first day they got the idea for the startup.

The Personal Cost

This section is dedicated to learning the truth from both the losers and the winners. Our goal is to enable a person considering doing a startup to weigh—realistically—both the tantalizing rewards and the expensive costs of launching or joining a startup. We recommend that you undertake such an analysis; the world of the startup can be a jungle of terror for the wrong person. Table 8-4 compares the demands of a job in a startup with a similar job in a large division of a very large company. We will discuss each of the 11 areas mentioned in the table in more detail.

The findings, observations, and case studies that follow are collections of personal experiences of people we interviewed. Accordingly, names have usually been altered to protect the privacy of the persons involved. Our contributors wanted to give some firsthand examples of how it really is in order to help others make up their own minds more realistically and avoid some of the pitfalls and pain they themselves encountered while doing a startup. We thank all of our contributors for their courage and truthfulness.

Our conclusions can be summarized as follows: *The toll of a startup depends on how firm a foundation the employee has for his self-worth.* A startup is most dangerous for the personality whose personal worth is wrapped up in the degree of his success or failure on the job. The more independent one's self-worth is from the success of the company or personal job performance, the less expensive a startup is likely to be in personal terms.

The trick lies in predetermining the reality of what one's self-worth is actually founded on. This is not easy to do, even for the highly educated employees of high tech startups. Professional counselors and psychiatrists lamented that this is particularly difficult for people who work and live in a technical world and are uncomfortable with people problems. But that is where you must begin. Then you will be able to realistically consider doing a startup, with your eyes open.

Make a realistic assessment of yourself, of the possible personal cost to you of doing a startup, and of the chances of a startup adding or detracting from your finding fulfillment in life. Our goal is to assist you in attaining your personal best for you and your family.

TABLE 8-4. Personal Costs Associated with a Startup

As compared to the job demands of managing a division of a large public company with revenues exceeding one billion dollars, a core team member must face:

An increase in the general level of stress
> There is more likelihood of burnout, and of the breakup of any already strained family relations.

A much larger time commitment
> Startups require longer hours and shorter vacations.

An increase in the requirement to do it yourself
> There is no large backup staff to delegate work to.

Additional reporting requirements
> The founders must now report to investors and the board of directors.

Less time for exercise, fitness, diet, and health
> At a time of increased stress, the healthy stress-reducers are less available.

Increased psychological pressure
> The weak points in personal character start to stand out, and to affect employees and family.

Increased pressure to make right decisions, and to make them faster
> The founder's decisions now affect a small group of very close people.

A heightened awareness of the risk of failure
> There is more personal exposure, and a greater chance of failure and of seeing the company go bankrupt.

Increased pressure from peers to "succeed"
> Media and industry exposure grows noticeably, and with it the audience for success or failure.

A sharply heightened test of love and intimacy
> The founder's family reacts to the conditions noted above, seeing growing evidence of the related problems in your shared lives, including less time, less cash, and more interpersonal irritability.

A sharp boost in personal introspection
> Who am I? Why am I doing this? Where can I find personal peace, contentment, and fulfillment?

Source: Saratoga Venture Finance

Time Commitment. *How much harder do people have to work in a startup?* This is a question we are frequently asked. To put our advice in perspective, consider these findings of a 1987 study of executive work patterns. The research was sponsored by Accountemps, the personnel company, and included 100 high-ranking executives picked from Fortune's top 1000 companies. The average executive rose at 5:49 a.m., getting about seven hours of sleep a night. On the average, the executives left the office at 5:52 p.m.

As for startups, we found that people generally work harder in a new enterprise than in a billion-dollar giant. We found that certainly there was no "9 to 5" behavior that lasted for long, if ever. We did observe that many of the startup employees were the kind of people who were always going to work hard, regardless of the size of the company for which they worked. In fact, they did not work much harder in a startup. This seemed to be especially true of the seasoned CEOs who set the pace for the rest of the employees.

Case Study: Bill's Style of Work

One startup CEO—we'll call him Bill—never changed his style from the time he left his billion-dollar semiconductor employer as a division VP to the time he took his startup public. Bill regularly showed up for work at about 8:45 or 9:00 in the morning, well after other company personnel were hard at work. He did help the whole crew move into new quarters on a Saturday and worked with the troops over the first July 4th holiday to get the first product completed. But he was rarely in the office after 6:30 p.m. and seldom dropped in on Saturdays. Bill took his bag of work home and did administrative tasks in his study on Saturday morning or Sunday evening. He used a couple of breakfasts a week to interview candidates, and dinners were mainly for customers who came to visit several days per month.

Bill traveled on Sundays for Monday meetings with customers and used Friday to fly home from Asia or Europe, as well as from most domestic trips. He did not object to other employees doing the same. He traveled cheapest coach fare, except that he flew business class on cross-ocean journeys, and chose leg stretch-out lounge seats (at coach fares) for the red-eye from San Francisco airport to Kennedy.

Bill began this pattern starting the first day on the job, and continued in that style regularly after the first year went by. Some employees told us they had kidded Bill about it one day (after they had been putting in long weekends of work without Bill). He immediately snapped back that that was his pace and that was how he always would work, no matter what company he worked for. He said he got his work done in that amount of time and maybe others were not able to.

As it turned out, Bill's startup went on to grab a nice share of the market in the business segment it served. And when his company went public, Bill was worth in excess of $6 million. His VPs also did handsomely with their shares at that time.

Times of Trouble.   In times of trouble, however, we found enormous increases in the demands for the time of startup employees. Engineering teams frequently worked past midnight, occasionally napping on cots at work, to meet vital customer deadlines. Marketing and sales personnel slept five hours a night for weeks on end in order to get booths and products ready for demonstration at important industry shows. Even more pressing was the time demanded when the company came close to running out of cash; then the number of hours put in by all employees rose enormously. In circumstances as desperate as these, it becomes very clear that startup employees work much harder than Fortune 1000 personnel.

Fortune 500 and Other Executives.   We compared our findings with more formal surveys and concluded that startup executives work about as hard as CEOs in low tech companies and in America's largest corporations. A 60-hour work week is the standard for high tech executives, according to a 1986 survey by Heidrick & Struggles, the Chicago-based international executive search firm. That finding came from their survey of about 350 executives at independent, private, and public technology companies, all with annual sales of less than $450 million and at least 15 employees.

And a 1987 survey of chief executives of America's largest corporations found nearly two-thirds claiming to work between 10 and 11 hours a day, Monday through Friday. Most of them also reported working on weekends; nearly 60 percent claimed between one and five hours of weekend work. Half travel seven or more days per month.

Stress.   How different is the stress in a startup from stress in a large company? We asked that of employees and managers. We found an interesting and important paradox. On the one hand, we did find nearly everyone claiming that startups put *more* stress on an individual than do large corporations. On the other hand, we found several veterans of more than one startup claiming they had *no more* stress in a startup. How can it be that startups that people claim induce more stress produce people claiming to experience no more stress? The paradox is explained as follows: startup stress is different—and to many better—than large-company stress. For instance, in a startup, there is:

- Less back-stabbing and big-company politics, but more exposure to failure (or success).
- More creativity, but more chance of pet projects being canned. For instance, in the case of a computer-aided design startup, the company dumped a hard-working engineer's completed software project because of a last-minute board ultimatum to reduce the high cash burn rate. As a consequence, the CEO had to suddenly junk a promising, nearly finished new product, in spite of angry outcries

from the demoralized engineering and marketing staffs. The tiny company could not afford to introduce the product that the engineer's software ran on. The startup simply had too many products that cost too much to sell and support.

- More chance to finally show what you can do (and get promoted) but also more danger of being canned for really messing things up.

Terror.   For the CEO who has never been there, starting a company will be terrifying, with no one to share those fears. Most CEOs we spoke with believed wives to be unable to cope with the reality of the chances of company bankruptcy. This meant that there was often no one at home with whom to share the inevitable troubles and problems. And no CEOs we met said they had an employee with which they shared intimate feelings triggered by stress. Close friends also seemed to be missing. So the CEO was left alone with his troubled emotions.

This situation was vividly portrayed in a stunning story in the February 1987 issue of *Inc.* magazine, which was entitled:

> **Entrepreneurial**
> **TERROR**
> **Starting a company? Get ready for the**
> **most terrifying experience of your life.**

The article produced a flood of letters to the editor, most of them poignantly identifying with the author, Wilson Harrell, who had the guts to tell his story as he experienced it. He struck a lot of nerves. He and the *Inc.* editor should be congratulated for their courage and their contribution to the managerial literature on startups. The article has to be read in its entirety to be appreciated, but here are a few of the more stinging observations. Wilson opens with these lines:

> I would like to address a few words to a particular group of readers, to those of you, young and not so young, who are starting your first company. By that act, you have joined a very special organization. Admission is automatic; permission is neither needed nor sought; tenure is indefinite. Welcome to the Club of Terror.
>
> I myself have been a member of this club, and have known this terror, for close to 35 years. I can assure you that it is unlike anything you have ever experienced before. No longer do you have to be bothered with such ordinary feelings as concern, or frustration, or even fear; those gentle things are the least of your troubles now. You can put them away as a child puts away toys. From now on, you will be in the grip of a human emotion that the good Lord, or more likely his nemesis, created just for entrepreneurs.
>
> Now, I realize that you didn't bargain on this when you started your company. Terror is something that entrepreneurs don't expect, can't escape, and have no way of preparing for.

Harrell goes on to explain the terror of which he speaks, both the positive and the negative terror. He goes on to give personal examples of how this terror occurred in his life, and tells how he conquered it. At the end he shares a high point in his moments of positive terror (some call it the sweet smell of success, but not Harrell). He concludes with this:

> You will have your own highs to share once you have conquered your terror. In the meantime, you should at least be aware that you are not alone—far from it. There is a whole gang of us out here living with the same monster. And you can take some comfort in knowing that terror is an integral and necessary part of every new business started by anyone, anywhere, at any time. Which means that, for every company in existence, there is, or was, some poor soul who bore the cross of terror for all of the people who have benefited. Whether the name was Mr. Kraft, Mr. Pillsbury, Mr. Ford, or Joe Blow, they all shook hands with the devil and joined the club.
>
> My own belief is that the ability to handle terror, to live with it, is the single most important—and, yes, necessary—ingredient of entrepreneurial success. I also believe that it is the lonely entrepreneur living with his or her personal terror who breathed life and excitement into an otherwise dull and mundane world. From that perspective, the Club of Terror is a very exclusive one. Welcome.

The letters to the editor from readers of the article were just as soul-jerking. Here is one example, signed by a "Founder and Chief Executive Officer":

> My terror is not unlike that which I knew as a Vietnam soldier. I also know that while I have control of my entrepreneurial terror, my beautiful wife does not and knows more terror than I ever will. Will our precious sons have a home, a father, college if we get through it this time? It's no wonder that as I embark on another "terrorific"-filled joy ride, she wants out. Who can blame her?

We talked with "winners" and they told us of the same terror. Bill said it hit him hardest when he delivered his first semiconductors to distributors and then waited, and waited, and waited to see if they would move off the distributors' shelves, into the computers of customers. His road to glory at IPO time was filled with terror. Yet the public relations stories left all that out as they put his picture on the front page of the business section of the newspaper and talked about "focused strategy," and "leading-edge technology."

The Workaholic.   The workaholic is the character type most likely to be damaged by failure in a startup, or failure in his family because of his devotion to the new enterprise. The problem here is just like that of an alcoholic or sexaholic: how do you get the person you are concerned with to recognize that they are this type of personality?

For years we have successfully used a simple test to assist our friends and clients in detecting the workaholic symptoms in themselves or friends or employees. It is taken from an excellent practical handbook entitled *The Work Trap* (Engstrom and Juroe, 1979). We recommend that the test be taken by any individual considering doing a startup.

Burnout. Burnout is very common and dangerous to CEOs of startups and their key employees. The author has personally experienced near burnout in his first years while managing a software startup and has assisted friends who were going through burnout in high tech companies.

Since its "discovery" in the sixties by a New York psychoanalyst, Dr. Herbert J. Freudenberger, burnout has been accepted as a serious disorder among people who work hard. Dr. Freudenberger experienced it himself. Our friends in psychotherapy in Silicon Valley reported that burnout is a common and serious problem, often leading to executive dropout, divorce, drug use, and mental derangement that ruined lives.

The *San Jose Mercury News* featured several Silicon Valley therapists in an article in *West* magazine entitled "Can Engineers Become Human?" It dealt with the special personal problems of people in the Valley. In the July 27, 1986 issue, *West* interviewed six counselors and therapists who talked about what they encountered and how they tried to help. It was clear that problems, including burnout, abound, whether the troubled individual's company has or has not been successful.

To assist you in the most practical terms, we recommend Dr. Freudenberger's paperback, *Burnout: How to Beat the High Cost of Success* (1980). The recommended therapy works well and even better with the help of a good counselor. The book includes a simple test that has helped individuals detect burnout before it is too late. Here is Freudenberger's definition of burnout:

> BURNOUT: TO DEPLETE ONESELF. TO EXHAUST ONE'S PHYSICAL AND MENTAL RESOURCES. TO WEAR ONESELF OUT BY EXCESSIVELY STRIVING TO REACH SOME UNREALISTIC EXPECTATION IMPOSED BY ONE'S SELF OR BY THE VALUES OF SOCIETY.
>
> Many men and women who come to me in pain report that life seems to have lost its meaning. Their enthusiasm is gone. They feel uninvolved, even in the midst of family and friends. Their jobs, which used to mean so much, have become drudgery with no associated feeling of reward.
>
> All their lives, they have undertaken tough jobs and prided themselves on their ability to master situations . . . a difficult child, an exhausting job situation or economic reverses. They had enough determination and will power to lick anything. Now, however, no matter how great their efforts, the only result seems to be frustration. Some vital spark inside these men and women is burning out, leaving a terrible void.

Our advice is that no one should even attempt to do a startup if he is on his way to burnout in the current job. And those already burned out because of a recent startup, take heart: Dr. Freudenberger and many other therapists have successfully treated the burnout problems of many people. The author of this book is a good example of how professional help can lead to a complete cure of burnout.

Fitness, Diet, and Health

How destructive is a startup to a person's health? is a concern we often heard expressed by people considering a startup. How you handle your well-being can have a profound impact on your ability to handle the pressures that inevitably confront entrepreneurs.

Exercise.   Demands on time are intense in a startup, and that adds pressure to keep going without the "frills" such as exercise. Yet the facts about the behavior of small-company personnel show that such concerns are not warranted. In May, 1987, *Venture* magazine published the results of a survey of 2,463 subscribers: "Not only do a panting three-quarters of respondents exercise regularly, two-thirds do so frequently—three times a week or more." The report went on to say, "According to the 1986 results of a Harris Poll commissioned by *Prevention* magazine, 77 percent of American adults get regular exercise."

Venture reported that "Steve Smith, president of Executive Fitness Center, New York, a health club that specializes in fitness training programs for executives, works with company founders and observes, 'They have high-pressure jobs, and exercise can be a time to be alone, in contrast to the teamwork required at the office.'"

Some managers have become innovative and disciplined about this problem. One VP at Chips and Technologies rode his bike 20 miles each day instead of taking a long lunch hour. Silicon Valley is full of lunchtime runners, racquetball players, and swimmers. A CFO told about his daily discipline of prebreakfast runs no matter where he travels: in London parks, Paris shopping marts, beside Belgian canals, and along Munich's winding streets.

Like *Venture* magazine, we have found a vocal group of CEOs of new enterprises avidly claiming that their regular exercise program was a vital contributor to their excelling in business. Sharper minds, feeling better about oneself, and longer endurance while managing troubled startups were often cited as reasons for a startup executive *needing* regular exercise more than other business people.

Sleep.   We found sleep patterns and duration to be similar in startups and larger companies. Again, the difference appeared to be nil if any between the executives of new companies and established corporations. The *Venture* survey reinforced our findings: "But it's hard to guess when some company founders find time for working out at all. Although a quarter spend a restful eight to nine hours sleeping, the majority (70 percent) catch only five to seven hours of sleep. Yet they typically put in a long day and work many weekends. Forty-six percent work 8 to 10 hours daily, while 38 percent work more than 10 hours. And on weekends, founders are often at the office: 54 percent give up more than two weekends a month for their companies, compared with only 31 percent for non-founders."

Diet and Alcohol.   We found that alcohol was shunned at almost all the lunches we attended, starting with the CEO, who set a strict example regardless of the occasion. However, wine was popular for business dinners when customers and other VIPs were entertained. Yet even over dinner, we found executives forgoing dessert and telling guests that they were watching their weight. *Venture* found that "diet was as important as exercise to the survey respondents. Sixty-nine percent supplement their meals with vitamins."

Smoking.   As to smoking, a standard exists: "Don't!" There is a clear trend: startups are starting from day one as 100 percent no-smoking companies. It is a strong factor in recruiting decisions. *Venture* confirmed that "smoking is not a problem for most: Only a tenth of the respondents smoke cigarettes."

Doctors.   With all the commitment to fitness, we were surprised to find that only a minority of startup executives have annual physical examinations. Perhaps this is a consequence of the limited health benefits offered by new enterprises—few insurance plans paid the costs of annual physical examinations. However, several individuals said they personally paid for annual exams. This finding was reinforced by the *Venture* survey report, which stated: "As for keeping an eye on their bodies, a wise 43 percent have had a physical checkup within a year and another third were examined in the last couple of years."

Importance of Fitness.   Fitness businessman Steve Smith closed the *Venture* report with these words, "Only the fit survive [in business], and that not only means the smartest but also the most physically fit." We remind readers that Steve is selling fitness and may not be the experienced executive that can comment on years of experience with business survival. However, we did find that medical doctors and psychotherapists strongly recommend more exercise, no smoking, and care in diet for everyone, including the startup executive. "Some of my patients need exercise as much as food," said one counselor. The trick is to juggle time commitments.

Sudden Changes and Accompanying Problems

One poignant situation cited over and over again was the personal danger from violent changes in lifestyles during the post-IPO period. After the IPO, people suddenly found their bank accounts and personal egos swollen by the success and publicity of their company. In reaction, many changed their lives dramatically, many for the worse. Sad personal stories ranged from the lonely bachelor who buys a huge estate in the mountains and quits work to live on cocaine, to the executive who suddenly decides the spouse is no longer right and gets a divorce.

Drug Abuse.   Drug abuse during the 1980s was believed to be common among some high tech employees. But we could not find a quantified study that compared high tech companies to other industries. Nor could we find a definitive study that showed to what degree this problem existed in startups and emerging growth high tech companies. Therapists talked about what their patients told them in the July 27, 1987, *West* magazine article in the *San Jose Mercury News*. Bill Hazle is a psychiatrist and the medical director of the Alcohol and Drug Treatment Program at Stanford University Hospital in Palo Alto, California. Here is how he described the drug situation that he must deal with daily:

> "I have two populations of engineers," he comments. "The older group is over 40. These men are alcoholics. They've been working for the same company for over 25 years; they're dedicated, hard workers. Things haven't worked out quite like they'd expected. Over the years they've chemically isolated themselves from their families and the world. My challenge is to bring them back to reality, to help them feel.
>
> The other group is mid-30s or younger. This guy moved to Silicon Valley five years ago; he's worked for four different companies and doubled his salary with each move. He's at the peak of his professional life, but there are 25-year-olds who know more than he does. His professional life expectancy isn't looking good. Coke is the perfect drug for him: It gives him high energy, euphoria. And he lives and works in a culture that makes coke available and acceptable. This is the guy who tells me he thought he'd *arrived* the first time he had coke delivered to his office. Six months later he's in *my* office.
>
> About two-thirds of Hazle's clients are sent to therapy by their wives or employers. "Denial is the big word," he says. "Both age groups come in here wanting to be normal drinkers or drug takers. They want me to fix their stress so they can stop tooting up their BMW payments or learn to drink socially. But I hit them with the reality that *everything* has to change: what they do, who they do it with.

We found no one openly advocating use of drugs. However, we did find private testimonials that the special form of stress in startups led a number of startup executives and key employees to do drugs. Counselors told us of their experiences; for example, two psychiatrists were called into an emergency situation by the board of directors of a new software startup. The company was holding up the worldwide introduction of one of America's top computer corporation's hottest new products. Upon arriving, they found the three-person project team doing cocaine in an attempt to meet the severe product delivery deadlines imposed by a management threatened with loss of their jobs and possible lawsuit, and by investors facing the company's bankruptcy.

And pot seemed to be an open joke among several of the leaders of well-known startups and recent IPO companies whom we got to know. Fortunately, the anti-drug advocates seem to be winning at this time.

Wives, Children, Family, and Divorce.   How likely is divorce for a startup executive? Would you believe less than 26 percent?

Some insight is provided by a 1986 Heidrick & Struggles survey of high tech CEOs of 350 independent, private, and public technology companies, all with annual sales of less than $450 million and at least 15 employees. The survey's findings suggested that high tech executives are more likely to be divorced than CEOs of America's bigger, lower technology companies. "While 71 percent of high tech CEOs said they're married to their first spouse, more than a quarter—26 percent—have been divorced or separated. More than 81 percent of Fortune 1000 chiefs say their first marriage is intact." As one startup CEO veteran sadly put it, "You have to earn twice as much in a startup because your ex-wife will get half after the IPO." Yet we also found happily married couples who had gone through startups and remained together.

As for the impact of a startup on raising children, we found no studies in this area, so we will comment from firsthand observation. CEOs seemed to us to be successful in raising their children and being loving parents, whether they are in larger, established corporations or in startups. The choice is there: a startup does not automatically rule out the time or ability to be a responsible parent. We personally know of executives at famous high tech startups who raised healthy families.

Wives told us that they had the same attitude toward a startup or a big corporation, as long as the business took secondary priority to the wife and the family. This seems to be where the problems begin. Many CEOs and VPs of new companies have never before been responsible as executives. For a wife who has never before experienced the hours her husband must put into new job as CEO, the startup looks like the culprit.

The issue seems to us to be more of a measure of the normal demands on a top executive than of the special demands of a startup.

However, people told us that they grew to find work all-consuming and one day just decided they did not want to be married any more. Again, to us the issue seemed to be one of choices, of personal values: What was personally more important, what got top priority when the going got rough—the company or the home?

One of the biggest single negative impacts on the wife of a startup CEO can occur when he decides to mortgage the house to get the cash to survive. This is not uncommon. The author was in that situation once and his wife was terrified for two years.

Security is not the stuff of which startups are made. But in this day of layoffs from even the largest high tech companies around the world, there is no real security anywhere, only blind hope. That can be frightening to children as well as spouses. We have known kids who became bitter toward their father because they felt they lost out on material and psychological security when the startup went sour, whereas other children got things the startup CEO's kids wanted: more time from parents, assurances of no divorce for dad and mom, and deeper intimacy between the family members. These were the things that the counselors advise parents to provide when one of them is founding a high tech company.

Fear of divorce tops the list of concerns of kids in the United States today, according to recent surveys. Stress from a startup can trigger such an event or contribute to the cracks in a marriage.

And success can be as hard on a marriage as failure. One famous example of this is the divorce history of Apple cofounder Steve Wozniak, who is now divorced from his second wife. Steve's wealth was estimated in 1987 to be in excess of $50 million.

Right and Wrong, Morals and Ethics

Startups and emerging growth high tech companies get into special circumstances that challenge the integrity of employees. Here are some issues that we have encountered and that were often noted by startup managers as especially difficult to cope with:

- **Intellectual property theft**. Chapter 4 dealt with problems of this type. Managers find themselves under a spotlight these days, yet naïve but well-meaning engineers can and do take the wrong materials and ideas with them. Does a CEO of the company receiving the stolen property stop the startup in its tracks upon learning of such a problem?

- **Promises to venture investors.** Hard selling to investors can distort the truth. We have experienced the selling of a business plan several times. How tempted would a CEO be to bias the facts in the company's favor during the due diligence sessions on competition?

- **Missed milestones.** As the inevitable occurs and early products fall behind their introduction schedules, there is a temptation to cover up all the bad news to the hostile VCs on the board of directors.

- **Capital shortfall.** Startups are always short of cash. The multiple rounds of fund-raising will occur during times of varying success in a startup. What should the CEO tell a prospective investor who has just asked how the latest sales backlog is developing, when the CEO knows that the top three customers just called to say sorry but they will not be buying after all, and when that investor is the last of 23 VC firms contacted to still be interested in making the necessary investment the company needs to avoid bankruptcy?

- **Missing payroll.** New companies are very likely to run out of funds and miss a payroll or two. This happens with both good and bad managements when they encounter a period of bad times. What does the CEO tell employees when investors scheduled for visits call to cancel and decline to reschedule? How does an executive remain honest and yet keep the ship from sinking, still keep people working instead of dropping everything to start looking for new jobs?

- **Bad news for the board meeting.** The bad news comes as sure as winter follows summer: missed shipments of new products, over-spending, bad publicity in the top newspaper, anger by a key employee who surreptitiously went to an investor, an archrival company that just eclipsed the company's core product line, and so on. How tempting is it to proclaim the good news and minimize the bad news (that kept the CEO from sleeping the past three nights)?

- **Recruiting stories.** Key personnel can be the difference between success and failure. The pressure is very intense to tell a lot of the dream without the negative side of the story. What should the CEO tell the only test engineer the company can attract (and who is vital to getting your first product to market before the window closes) when he inquires about how important it is to get this first product out on schedule? (The company is already five months behind and the board is furious with the CEO-founder for the company's poor results.)

- **Tales for the customers.** Marketing pressures mount as potential customers are lined up and first shipments begin. Engineers said they listened with dismay to promises of product performance that the company had no possibility of ever building with its technology.

Should the vital customers be told that the promises by the VP Marketing are not likely to be kept?

■ **Tales for the investors.** When it comes time to mark up the stock for the next round or to go public, there are enormous pressures to "make the books look good." Should the CEO deliberately postpone the next new product development project in order to get more short-term profit to the bottom line? Or create bookkeeping reserves to pad (boost) earnings for the next quarter?

These are categories of issues special to new enterprises that confront the CEO and his or her closest advisors. Board members also have to face such issues. There may be escape from big company politics, but there is no escape from the testing of character and integrity. Anyone scared by those issues should perhaps reconsider doing a startup.

Soul, Spirit, and Religion

Our findings in this section were gathered from personal observations over the past ten years in Silicon Valley in an attempt to cover an important area in our lives that is rarely reported or researched. We have disguised names and circumstances when we were so requested to do so.

We don't read or hear much about the private lives of startup CEOs or their top management teams. Most seem to prefer that the spotlight be confined to the business side of their lives. The public rarely gets a glimpse of the intimate side of their natures, their souls and emotions. It wasn't until Silicon Valley was booming that the *San Jose Mercury News* began a special section in its Saturday edition devoted to religion and ethics. But in spite of what appears to be a non-issue or one that many would prefer to avoid, religion, with its related issues about philosophy, morals, and value systems, does operate in centers of high tech activity, including startups.

We met a number of men and women along the way who told us that they believed that their ability to survive the terror of a startup was due entirely to their religious beliefs. They said that they had found peace in a storm by trusting the God of the Bible and Jesus Christ instead of just themselves. We also found people in high tech companies that looked to Mohammed and Buddha, or to Hindu and Shinto beliefs for guidance through the minefields of startups. They felt strongly that there must be more to life than the fame and fortune of startups.

Individuals told us that the intensity of startups can produce problems of such a huge size and degree that even the most stalwart leaders are overwhelmed. Counselors confirmed that this was their experience with many of their patients who were embroiled in startups. Failing as a manager or losing all the money of investors is often too much for the self-worth held by many a man or woman. They quickly see themselves as abject failures and fall into clinical depression and worse. Escape via drugs or sex or thrills can set in. Burnouts abound. Marriages fall apart. Hearts are broken. It is in conditions like these that we found people turning to religious teachings as the answer to finding personal peace, meaning, and purpose after experiencing failure in a startup. And remember, getting rich and famous can spell failure for some people as well.

And then there is the ultimate price to pay for doing a startup: your life. Heart attacks seem to be no more common in new companies than in larger, established ones. However, we found no studies to document this hypothesis. Veterans of Silicon Valley recall such tragedies as the terrible after-lunch ride in a hot red Ferrari that flipped and killed its two occupants, one the founder-CEO of the then hot Eagle personal computer company. His successive replacements were never able to sustain the company through its later trials and tribulations, and today it is long gone and mostly forgotten.

Support Systems

We found numerous veterans of startups who implore individuals to especially consider the condition of their support systems before doing a startup. Expectations that turn out to be different than what really transpires in a person's life are major contributors to burnout and personal anxiety, according to professional counselors and psychologists. For instance, if you expect to be part of a company that gets to IPO and becomes famous, but the company becomes much less than that, such defeated expectations can lead to personal problems and intense emotional troubles. Here are some constructive words of advice from people we interviewed:

> *Get sanctions from your spouse and children.* It is unwise to attempt a startup at a time when your marriage is in need of a lot of attention or when your children are in trouble in their lives. Get them to be honest about how they feel about your doing a startup. Take their wishes seriously.

> *Caring friends are worth a lot.* This is a vast understatement. Buddies to talk to are very important when the troubled times come and the fear sets in. You need caring listeners who will stick close to you through the tough times.

> *Mentors are needed.* Solo leaders are very rare. CEOs said they sought advice regularly. You need a set of qualified mentors, people who can give personal time and professional advice.

Don't drop all your avocations, hobbies, and friends just to have time to do a startup. Strong advice came to do the opposite: adhere to and nurture those relations that are your current support system: your wife, children, and friends who will love you whether you are a failure or a success. Take time to garden, ski, read—whatever you are used to doing to make yourself feel better. Or if it is to try to save the whales or do nonprofit work, then continue. Don't stop. It is dangerous to cut out such activities under the guise of having no time to do them because you are doing a startup. Figure out your sources of strengths and adhere to them. They will help you maintain stability. Balance your life. Work on that.

Take vacations, make them short, take them often. This was a pattern we detected in CEOs and their VPs. Seasoned startup personnel said that is how they did it. It refreshes the mind and spirit, yet is short enough to not lose touch with the delicate situations under way at the startup.

Use consultants and counselors. They can give you objective advice based on periodic observations of you and your behavior. Their suggestions can head off burnout.

Pick a trustworthy employer. The dangers of losing your job are great enough without choosing employers randomly. Some bosses or boards of directors are going to be much less trustworthy than others. Personal stability is enhanced when you can seek to do your best while confident of the support of your employer.

Keep an ace up your sleeve, stay in touch with the job market, and prepare a personal backup plan. Be ready for the surprise that can result if you no longer have income from the startup. Talk to a headhunter or two when they call. If nothing else, it helps you set wage guidelines for your employees. Plan any alternative lifestyle carefully with your spouse. Don't expect your partner to automatically go along with your plan to sell the house and live in an economical mobile home if the startup goes bankrupt. Whatever you decide, create a well-thought-through plan for you and your family.

If the kitchen is too hot, get out. Life is indeed lonely at the top. Leaders are looked up to. Employees do not operate well when the boss expresses his anxiety to employees down the hierarchy. If you find yourself dumping on the company or talking often to people about your stress, consider moving to a less pressured means of earning a living.

Get in touch with yourself. That was repeated by many of the people we spoke with. Decide what motivates you: joy of work, love of wealth, the satisfaction of getting further than anyone expected, and so on. And decide what a failure means to you, as a person, as a company leader.

Decide on your purpose in life. Get this in place—before gloom and doom set in and lead to immobilization of you as a key decision maker and leader.

Decision: To Do a Startup—That Is the Question

In this section we address the question: What can I do to test whether I am ready to do a startup? We have gathered the opinions of CEOs, VCs, psychologists, and counselors. The findings are presented in two sections. The first is how to use professionals to get a perspective on the likelihood of sustaining the rigors of a startup. The second section is a pragmatic how-to guide for screening each stage of a startup and relating that to the choice to join at each stage.

Professional Advice.   Seeking professional advice is an important option to consider when looking at one's own suitability to handle the stresses of the startup environment. There is a modest cost that will be incurred, but it is not expensive and, compared with the high cost of a bad decision to join a startup, the cost of professional advice is minimal. The field of psychology has developed an array of tests that can accurately and objectively assess your strengths and weaknesses. Such issues as personality style, interpersonal effectiveness, vulnerability to stress, and intellectual ability are all important in such a venture. An objective opinion about these variables should prove to be well worth your effort.

In choosing the particular psychologist to provide this service, look for the following. The psychologist should be specialized in psychological testing and assessment. Either consulting or clinical psychologists can provide this service. Check with your local psychological association or family physician to find a psychologist. A thorough evaluation will include the following:

- Objective personality testing; options include the Minnesota Multiphasic Personality Inventory (MMPI), Million Clinical Multiaxial Inventory (MCMI), and the 16-PF.

- Projective personality testing, often using the Rorschach Inkblot Test or the Thematic Apperception Test.

- Tests of intellectual functioning; the standard test here is the Wechsler Adult Intelligence Scale-Revised (WAIS-R).

- Vocational interest and ability tests are also possibilities.

Guide to Doing a Startup. Table 8-5 is a guide to helping you consider the pros and cons of joining a startup. It follows the format of the 14 key stages noted in Chapter 3. The table summarizes advice from veterans of startups who were asked to comment on what to consider in the decision of whether or not to join a startup.

Under the right conditions, a startup can be just the right next step in some people's career paths. Under the wrong conditions, a new enterprise can be very destructive to other people.

TABLE 8-5. When to Join a Startup

Stage	Join If:	Do Not Join If:
1. Idea	+You have done a startup before. +You are highly motivated and very self-confident.	- Bankruptcy and missing payrolls sound awful to you.
2. Kitchen Table	+You have a close friend who will lead the startup. +Your know-how is vital to the success of the technology or marketing of the idea. +See #1 above.	- The leader is a stranger. - See #1 above.
3. Founders' Commitment	+Your savings will carry you for nine months. +Your family agrees. +The founders represent a powerful core around which to build a business. +Your lawyer says you are ethically clean and free to join a startup.	- You need a job to pay the bills. - Your wife and kids think your doing a startup is nuts. - You need lots more experienced management talent in the company.
4. Pullout from Employer	+Your nerves are strong. +Your lawyer has prepared a good plan to guide you in how to leave your employer without getting sued. +You are prepared to live on your savings only.	- You have not prepared a pullout plan with a good lawyer. - Your home budget does not exist. - You and your family are not prepared to make home spending sacrifices.

(Continued)

TABLE 8-5.   When to Join a Startup (continued)

Stage	Join If:	Do Not Join If:
5. **Business Plan Creation**	+You missed #4 above, and are a great business plan writer and strategist.	- You never wrote a business plan before.
6. **Filling the Management Team**	+You have read and analyzed the business plan. +You want a chance at a job in a strong leadership position.	- You just want more stock. - The key VPs are not in place yet.
7. **Capital Raising**	+You have missed the above stages.	- You could not stomach folding the tent because funds could not be raised.
8. **Capital Closing**	+Cash in the company's bank is important to you.	- You could not handle having to scramble for a job in 9 to 18 months because of disaster to the company, such as a layoff that bumps you off the payroll.
9. **Finding a Home**	+The key VPs are in place. +See #8 above.	- You would be bothered by a "flameout" affecting your career.
10. **Startup**	+You are sure the cash is in the bank. +You are very excited about the company and its prospects.	- You want more assurance of being part of an initial public offering (IPO) soon.
11. **Secondary Rounds of Financing**	+You like the progress that the company is making with its first product. +You need assurance of the staying power of the leadership and the investors. +You like the progress already made and plans for reaching the IPO goal.	- The IPO is too far away for you.

(Continued)

Table 8-5. When to Join a Startup (continued)

Stage	Join If:	Do Not Join If:
12. **Launch First Product**	+You like riding a wave and are confident of the future of the successor products.	- You want to see how well customers receive the first product. - You want to have several products succeed before joining.
13. **Working Capital**	+You want to wade in and help build momentum. +The customers are good names and are reordering the products.	- The company is struggling to fund its growth. - First products will not enable the company to get cash flow positive.
14. **Initial Public Offering**	+You want to get in just before the IPO. +You want some of the experience of a startup, but not much of the risk.	- You desire much more financial reward in your stock option and are willing to take more risk in earlier stages.

Venture
Capitalists

In this chapter we will guide entrepreneurs seeking to build beneficial relationships with that strange, enigmatic breed of businessperson known as the venture capitalist. Both experienced entrepreneurs and venture capitalists tell us that many myths have been created about venture capitalists—myths that mislead CEOs and contribute to startup failures.

Venture capitalists, the men and women with the money, have learned to create large amounts of wealth—for their investors and themselves as individuals—by following certain predictable and successful patterns of investment. By investing time in learning how venture capitalists make money, the entrepreneur will be better prepared to negotiate with them, and to operate a new company with realistic expectations.

We will start with the origin of venture capital money and show how VCs derive their wealth and control the startup companies they invest in. We then move on to suggestions from experienced startup people on how to make good presentations and end with tips on closing deals.

The Cost of a Venture Capitalist's Capital

The name of the game for the VC is return on investment (ROI). His money goes in as preferred stock and comes out as common stock at the time of the initial public offering (IPO) or sale of the company to a larger corporation. If the company is unsuccessful, its assets go on the auction block, including the technology; the preferred stock shareholders get all of the meager pickings, while common stock shareholders get nothing.

The amount of ROI that a VC must earn on invested monies depends on the relative returns of alternative investments that the VC's limited partners could have put their money into.

Figure 9-1 shows how private venture funds are linked to the huge stock markets. There is a serial connection:

- The IPO price for a company is set by a select group: powerful, famous portfolio managers assisted by their research analysts. This is an elite group, highly respected because of their investing successes, who have mountains of money to invest. Because their actions are eagerly mimicked by the vast number of other money managers, this select group is often referred to as the "lead steers," that is, the few leaders who are followed by the large number of less able investors who constitute the herd. Lead steers also set share prices of the Fortune 500 companies. They start with the ROI expected from investing in a "safe" security such as U.S. Government treasury bills, add their expected rate of inflation, and then add percentage points that represent premiums for taking on the risk of investing in a company. Each company must be expected to earn the resulting "hurdle" ROI or else the analysts will reduce the price for the stock of the company. If the company outperforms the hurdle ROI, they will increase the price of the company's stock.

- Venture capitalists start their valuation work by simulating the most likely IPO price for the startup in which they are considering investing. VCs use simplified rules of thumb to approximate the IPO price.

- Having calculated the probable IPO value of a startup, the VC then calculates the percentage of the company ownership needed at IPO time to get the high ROI target that has been set for the VC firm. The VC's target ROI or "hurdle rate" depends on several factors, including how well or badly the VC's other startup companies are doing. Our research shows that the range of ROI is wide at a given point in time, with many factors causing it to be greater or smaller. The key factors are discussed in Chapter 7 and elsewhere in this book.

- Each subsequent private round is priced this way, from seed to the last round just before IPO.

FIGURE 9-1. Stock Markets Drive Venture Capital Markets

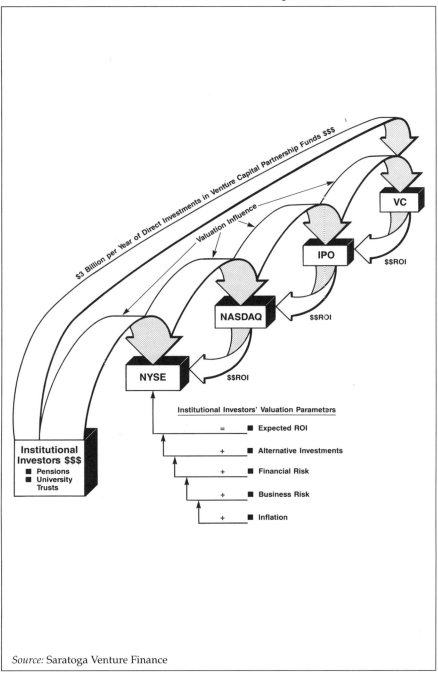

Source: Saratoga Venture Finance

Where the VCs Get Their Money

Giant pools of money called institutional funds dominate the world's money markets, especially in the United States. Research shows that individuals have been net dis-investors in stocks in America since 1945. Their decline in importance has been more than taken over by the pension plan and university trust pools of wealth. In 1962, individual investors owned about 82 percent of all the stock in American companies, according to the Securities Industry Association in New York. Today, individuals own less than 60 percent, according to estimates by Salomon Brothers in New York. And they account for less than 20 percent of the trading in the stocks. As Peter Drucker has put it, the pension plan money managers—and all of their "little people"—now own America's corporations.

With trillions of dollars needing to be invested each day, the trustees of those institutional pools of wealth have delegated the work to specialists. The trustees have put their funds in the hands of people called money managers. These money managers make a living by competing for the chance to be given some of those funds to invest. The goal is to earn the highest ROI possible in as short a time possible, for as many years as possible. They earn a fee for their efforts and in some cases share in any of the profits that may result. Venture capitalists are one variety of this type of professional money manager.

The goal of money managers like venture capitalists is to outperform the stock market. If they do, institutional pools of money will give them a chance to manage more money. VCs who do not perform will lose the second chance. It is a case of survival of the fittest.

Venture Capitalist of Venture Capitalists

There has been a huge surge of money into venture capital since 1983. The annual rate tripled to $3 billion per year during the 1980s, but declined as the 1990s began. The pool of VC money now stands above $40 billion, capable of creating over 5000 new enterprises every seven years and affecting the lives of more than five million people. Venture capital has arrived, becoming a significant economic factor in America.

As successes mounted in the late 1970s, pension fund trustees were increasingly approached by very successful venture capitalists whose early track records produced very high ROIs, in excess of 50 percent per year. The trustees of a few pension funds began to dabble in venture capital by investing through the VCs, and others soon followed. This phenomenon still left many conservative money managers wondering (and having doubts about) how to consistently make prudent investments in what appeared to them to be the wild and wooly game of high-risk venture capital.

Several pension and trust funds turned to specialized venture investor experts for advice. An early pioneer is Hal Bigler and his people who manage a fund of funds of venture capital. Located in Hartford, Connecticut, this firm specializes in monitoring, measuring, and comparing the portfolio results of the many limited partnerships that venture capitalists, acting as their own salespeople, try to sell to the institutional investors. Others have followed.

How good are the VCs? Bigler's research says that during the 1980s the average ROI was about 22 percent per year, compared with a 14 percent return for the Standard and Poors index of public companies. However, by 1990 that rate had fallen off and was struggling to stay in the teens. Venture Economics continues to report on the soggy ROIs of many venture capital portfolios, many of whom are lately returning single-digit ROIs to institutional investors.

But don't be fooled. That 22 percent per annum ROI is not what the VC will price his capital at for the investment in a startup company. Instead, the VC must add in the cost of the losers, the investments in companies that will go bankrupt or do poorly. That is why the VC's calculations will show that the entrepreneur will end up with a small percentage of ownership at IPO time.

The Life of a Venture Capitalist

For the startup CEO, the first contact at a venture capital firm is with one of several people who will collectively play key roles in the deal the entrepreneur wants to close. While there are still individuals who invest monies without help from other partners, the typical firm today consists of a couple of seasoned general partners who get along well and probably worked together in a prior company, perhaps even in a successful startup. These are the people who get the richest from profits on the investments made by the VC firm.

One or more other people help the senior partners. These range from green business school graduates to more experienced associates working hard to become partners and share in more of the wealth. The larger firms have grades of partners and some employ executive recruiters and public relations experts.

The week for a VC begins with a Monday staff meeting where investments are reviewed and decisions made to proceed with or stop further investigation on various business plans. The rest of the week is a hectic scramble of early-morning breakfast meetings, shuffling through an impossibly deep stack of pink telephone slips, and flying or driving madly between companies in cities throughout the entire country, but especially in the metropolitan region in which the VC's offices are located. Lunches and dinners are consumed while investigating managers-to-be and trading ideas with their vast network of contacts at universities, giant corporations, and the firms that service their beloved startups. Board meetings consume both emotional energy and several days per month.

Time in the VC office is used to interview potential startup teams, view their presentations, and read their business plans. Meetings with partners of other VC firms are frequent and on-the-fly, usually on the phone, as the deal flow between the venture capital firms goes on by the hour. The most emotional times involve closings on precarious deals led by a partner of the firm. It is not uncommon when visiting a VC office to overhear earnest long-distance phone calls to round up the last of the critically needed money from British pension managers, Italian industrial giants, and Japanese money managers.

The weekends and personal time of VCs often reflect the character of the companies that VCs invest in: fast-paced and risky. Only the rare few VCs who have become powerful kings of the VC community feel comfortable taking blocks of leisure time off from this hectic pace to enjoy life.

Fast communication is important to VCs. They always seem to be faxing something, and the Federal Express truck driver can find the way to the VC office with his eyes closed. And some observers think that VCs invented the cellular telephone—or at least the pressing need for one. Several of the partners in a VC firm carry their passports in their briefcases each day and keep a travel bag permanently packed for those unforeseeable emergency trips abroad.

How a VC Firm Makes Money

Venture capitalists can become very rich if they are successful. They are paid a percentage of the money they manage (the "carry") to pay themselves salaries and cover office and operating expenses, and they get a percentage of the profit of the money they invest. Details are shown in Table 9-1.

The first source of income (the "carry") for the venture capitalist typically equals 1 percent times the gross amount of capital invested by limited partners in a pool called a *limited partnership*. The venture capitalists are the *general partners*. The top venture firms manage several of these pools at the same time. The pools vary in size; $50 million is common, so the management fee for that fund will be $500,000 a year. That is typically used to operate a three-partner office.

TABLE 9-1. Economics of a Single Partnership Managed by a Private Venture Capital Firm

1.	Amount of capital raised for investment ("Capital")	$ 50,000,000
	Times	
2.	Profit on investments (25% per year for 5 years = × 3⁺)	$\times 3^+$
	Equals	
3.	Gross profit =	$152,587,880
	Less	
4.	Investment capital	- $50,000,000
	Equals	
5.	Net profit =	$102,587,880
	Times	
6.	Percentage for general partners ("Venture Capitalists")	$\times 20\%$
	Equals	
7.	Amount of investment income to general partners =	$20,517,576
	Plus	
8.	Cash compensation for general partners	+ $ (Included in the $500,000 of operating expenses)
	Plus	
9.	Operating expenses and benefits (cars, office) for general partners (= 1% × $50M Capital)	+ $500,000
10.	Net income to general partners before any profit sharing with others in venture firm =	$21,517,576

Source: Saratoga Venture Finance

The second source of income—profit on successful investments—is where the real wealth can come from. Usually, 20 percent of the profit goes to the venture capitalist general partners. If they successfully invest and earn a 25 percent per annum return for five years (i.e., return to limited investors three times their money in five years), then there would be $152,587,880 of gross profit. After returning the $50,000,000 of invested principal *capital* to limited partners, the remaining $102,587,880 is parceled out among the limited and general partners. At a 20 percent share, the three general partners of this fund would have $20,517,576 to divide among themselves, an average of $7,172,525 each, before any profit sharing with other employees of the VC firm. The example in Table 9-1 is for a single partnership; larger VC firms manage several funds at once, multiplying the financial return on the time they invest.

The Risk/Reward Tradeoffs: VC vs. Entrepreneur

According to the Saratoga Venture Tables research summarized in Table 8-1, a CEO of a successful startup can expect to earn about $6,500,000 within five years. So the venture capitalist sharing one-third of $21,000,000 can earn about as much as the successful CEO.

But the risk is higher for the CEO and employees of the company because the startup personnel cannot spread their risk, whereas the venture capitalist can diversify his or her bets and come out a net winner. Saratoga Venture Finance estimates that the risk of a startup CEO getting $6,500,000 is more than six times greater than that of the venture capitalist earning 25 percent per annum on $50,000,000.

If the risk is six times greater, why isn't the reward six times greater? Our analysis strongly suggests that the reason is that the venture capital markets are not yet "efficient." *Efficient* is a technical term used by money market economists to describe a market in which competition keeps small numbers of individuals or institutions from gaining windfall or excessive profits.

In this case, the evidence suggests that only since 1983 has competition clearly set in. One consequence was a move toward closing the disproportionate risk and reward gap between the venture capitalist and the CEOs of the companies they finance and lead. Here is what Jack Melchor, a very successful venture capital veteran, said in the July 1987 issue of *Venture* magazine: "The biggest problem right now is finding [well-priced] deals. Every time a good one comes along there is so much competition for it among funds that it raises the ante."

The article went on to say, "Anyway, Melchor reasons, he's now 61 and maybe it's time to retire." He also said that he figured he has lost money in about 30 of his 125 to 150 investments and has averaged a 30 percent annual return. That performance would be among the top long-term performers of all venture capitalists in history.

But by 1990, excesses, incompetence, and bad breaks had reversed the trend of early successes by new venture capitalists.

What that means for the startup company's founders is that competition for their deal is the best negotiating tool they can find. It means that with competition there will be less dilution and more potential wealth to share with fellow pioneers and risk takers. It also means that such competition must be created and nurtured, because it won't occur naturally.

What Motivates a Venture Capital Firm

Venture capitalists are expected by their investors to produce an ROI of about 20 percent to 25 percent per annum, according to serious studies that have been made on portfolios invested over long periods of time. Table 9-2 shows the findings of six studies that have reached the public. Little else has been made public about this very private world.

That ROI is excellent, compared with the performance of alternatives available to institutional investors. Figure 9-2 compares the VC's ROI with the ROI recorded over the same time period for leading indices of money market alternatives. If such 20 percent-plus ROIs can be maintained, fresh money will continue to flow to the VC pools. Institutional investors will be eager to invest.

Venture investors get their overall ROI from a mix of investments in startups. Table 9-3 shows the details of a typical portfolio of a venture capital partnership in a good year such as 1987. It represents an agglomeration of actual data gathered by Saratoga Venture Finance from this very private VC world. Although seven years old, this typical portfolio is still active. Although some IPOs have resulted in liquidations, all the proceeds have yet to be liquidated and turned over to the limited partners. The portfolio has earned a 19.7 percent p.a. (per annum) ROI to date. Unless one or more of the last of the surviving companies—those that have neither gone public nor gone bankrupt—somehow turns out better than shown, that 19.7 percent ROI will be recorded as the final result. It is very difficult to get actual data on venture portfolios. Most claims made by venture capitalists of their ROIs are hard to substantiate, particularly because the partnerships go on for 12 years or longer.

TABLE 9-2. Venture Capital Rates of Return

Source of Study	Year of Study	Period of Study	Compound Annual Rate of Return
Venture Economics	1984	20 years	26%
Stanford	1984	20 years	24%
Harvard	1984	15 years	25%
CIGNA	1985	14 years	over 20%
Horsley Keogh	1983	10 years	35%
First Chicago	1985	9 years	24.5%

Sources: Crossroads Capital, *Pension & Investment Age*, *Venture*, Venture Economics

FIGURE 9-2. VC Annual Rates of Return Compared with Other Leading Indices, 1976-1985

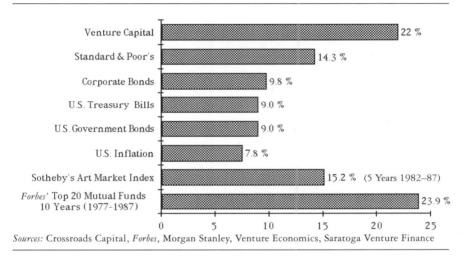

Sources: Crossroads Capital, *Forbes*, Morgan Stanley, Venture Economics, Saratoga Venture Finance

Looking closely at Table 9-3, we can learn some important lessons:

- About 60 percent of the companies that get funded eventually go bankrupt. Yet several VC partnerships investing today claim to have one third to one half fewer bankruptcies per portfolio company.

- Another 30 percent are sold off for pennies per dollar invested. "Zombies" get profitable, but remain too small to go public. Others are sold for their technology. And some reach the auction block.

- "Wild ones" like Apples and Compaqs are rare and seldom seen in VC portfolios. More common are "winners," famous IPOs—companies that are still hot and in the news after their public offering.

- A large proportion of the investment companies never get to the IPO stage. Private buyouts are common in the medical, biological, and genetic engineering industries. Investors still consider this an excellent channel to liquidity. The ROI for such deals can equal that from a company that gets to an IPO.

- Most employees of startups are working for companies that will not get into the limelight, will be denied the fame and the fortune that occupies most of the media's articles, or will go bankrupt.

- The winners subsidize the losers. This is very important for the CEO of the startup to grasp. It explains part of the reason for the high dilutions that VCs consider a necessary requirement before they will invest the money that they manage.

TABLE 9-3. Typical Venture Capital Partnership Portfolio in a Good Year

$50 million portfolio

Average investment per startup $1 million

	$ Invested ($M)	$ Mix	Gross Results 5 Yr. ROI (% p.a.)	Gross Results 5 Yr. ROI Multiple	Net Return ($ M)
Bankruptcies	$30	60.0%	-100.0%	0.00	($30.0)
Breakeven	$6	12.0%	0.0%	1.00	$0.0
Fire Sales	$5	10.0%	5.4%	1.30	$1.5
Zombies	$4	8.0%	9.9%	1.60	$2.4
Solids (IPO)	$3	6.0%	51.6%	8.00	$21.0
Winners (IPO)	$2	4.0%	109.1%	40.00	$78.0
Wild Ones (IPO)	$0	0.0%	300.0%	1024.00	$0.0
Total Portfolio	$50	100.0%	19.7%	68.70	$72.9

Source: Saratoga Venture Finance

How to Convert ROI to Percentage Sold in a Given Round of Financing

The CEO must learn to translate the VCs' ROI hurdle rate into terms of dilution. Use Table 9-4 as a guide; it is close to the median of deals done by successful companies we have studied. Begin with the end point: calculate the IPO value of your company; start with 3 times sales. Use the Saratoga Venture Tables to split the wealth between investors and the rest of the company. Set aside stock option pool shares needed each year. Next, plan each round of financing: cash raised, price per share, and date. Then calculate the ROI for each investor: divide your predicted IPO price per share by your desired price per share in each round; VCs call this the investor's "multiple." Then calculate the interest the investor would have earned if he had put $1 in the bank for the number of years to IPO to earn the multiple that you just calculated. That interest rate— i.e., the ROI percentage—is the VCs' goal. The ROIs should smoothly cascade downward for each round of financing because the risk drops each year. And remember, there is no fixed formula—every negotiation is a free market! It is up to you to make the best deal.

TABLE 9-4. Typical Return-on-Investment Hurdles Set by VC Funds

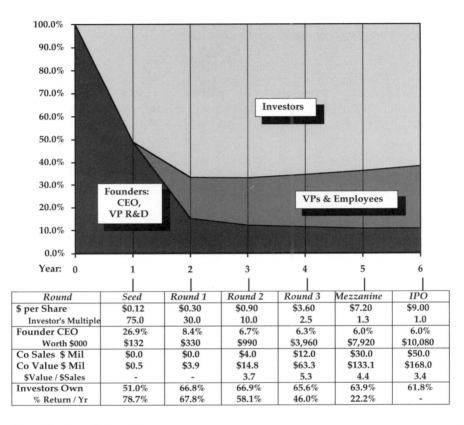

Round	Seed	Round 1	Round 2	Round 3	Mezzanine	IPO
$ per Share	$0.12	$0.30	$0.90	$3.60	$7.20	$9.00
Investor's Multiple	75.0	30.0	10.0	2.5	1.3	1.0
Founder CEO	26.9%	8.4%	6.7%	6.3%	6.0%	6.0%
Worth $000	$132	$330	$990	$3,960	$7,920	$10,080
Co Sales $ Mil	$0.0	$0.0	$4.0	$12.0	$30.0	$50.0
Co Value $ Mil	$0.5	$3.9	$14.8	$63.3	$133.1	$168.0
$Value / $Sales	-	-	3.7	5.3	4.4	3.4
Investors Own	51.0%	66.8%	66.9%	65.6%	63.9%	61.8%
% Return / Yr	78.7%	67.8%	58.1%	46.0%	22.2%	-

Source: Saratoga Venture Finance

Trends and Winds of Change

There are several shifts under way in venture capital portfolios. The marginal performing venture capital portfolios that were funded in 1982-1984 are dropping out of the race. Money is more cautious. Fewer startup frenzies—such as disk drive startups—are likely.

The trend most often noted is a shift from trying to hit a home run on each investment to a strategy of hitting more singles, doubles, and triples. The overall results can be in the same range as the 22 percent per annum ROI noted above, but the mix is different; there are proportionally fewer bankruptcies (more like 30 percent than 60 percent, say our sources), but there are fewer big-ticket winners.

We find these trends encouraging. Theoretically, if there are fewer bankruptcies, the rewards are increased and the personal cost for the entrepreneur and family and supportive friends is decreased.

The trends also suggest that more competition or less excesses can improve the risk/reward potential for the founders and employees. Most of all, it strongly suggests that everyone is making wiser, more prudent investment decisions. Entrepreneurs may be pitching less junk and more quality (although most VCs still lament the poor quality of the business plans they see).

And leading venture capitalists claim to be putting money into better deals more often.

Now if we all could learn to convert such wise initial decisions into higher ROI results, we would have a lot more wealth to share at a fraction of the current cost in terms of personal livelihoods.

Other Motivating Factors. Venture capitalists are people too. They have emotions like the rest of the human race, and are subject to the same internal pulls and battles. The up-and-comers struggle like the CEOs of startups. The established VCs labor to retain their positions of supremacy against both other established firms and the newer firms. It is important for the CEO to understand the emotions that startup work provokes.

Pride is a top motivator, especially in the powerful people who have gotten to the top. They are multimillionaires—Fred Adler was believed to be personally worth over $100 million in 1988. They are not only financially successful, they are noted as guiding lights to the successful companies that they backed, as the men and women who were the leaders that made a significant difference to the success of the famous IPO companies. Anything that tarnishes that reputation of success will be harshly dealt with by such wielders of power.

Feelings of belonging are another key motivator—the sense of belonging to that exclusive fraternity of winners, of venture capitalists who are revered by onlookers. Each wants to belong to the inside group, the one that attracts the top deals, gets the accolades, does the best ROI, structures the most famous IPOs.

Feelings of worthiness are also important. If they do well, they feel good about themselves. If an investment does not perform, that reflects on them. They are very personally connected to the success or failure of the startup's CEO and the company.

Feelings of competence are very intense for these people. They deal daily in a world of very high risk, like tightrope walkers over the

Grand Canyon. To the newcomer it looks frightening, but to them it is just another day at the office. VC leaders like to associate with winners and shun those people and companies that sound like average Joes or losers.

Emotions run high in VCs. The risks are high. Yet fear is not something the VCs talked about much in our interviews. They spoke more often about being angry at the incompetence of a CEO, or at the trouble an engineering group was having getting the first product working properly, or about trying to cope with a company on the ropes and nearly bankrupt. In spite of track records of fired founders and bankruptcies, we found no one saying he felt guilty about his own behavior or his own treatment of startup personnel. Love was never mentioned, except to describe a successful company. Greed was also never mentioned, but the degree of intensity of the negotiations for successive rounds of funding tells how vital maximum financial reward is to those who play this game in life.

The CEO-to-be should know that the venture capitalist is living a life of high risk and high reward. That high-stakes game is deadly serious—this individual is not investing money that he or she intends to lose.

The VC is also living life with a dilemma. Most VCs we have met stated over and over that they really intended to do more than just bring money to the party. They wanted to help the fledglings avoid the mistakes of the past by handing down their experience, which was learned in the school of hard knocks.

However, when bad times come, VCs will instantly switch from backing the incumbent management team to doing whatever must be done to save their investment in the struggling company. If the CEO is in the way—viewed as a hindrance to survival and the success of the next round of venture capital—that can cost the CEO his or her job and unvested shares. The CEO will also live through the emotional struggle of seeing friendly supportive VCs and board members turn into nasty antagonists. The CEO should be prepared to face this reality.

Finally, remember that each VC firm has a style and character unique to itself. The generalizations discussed here are no substitute for meeting the partners of the firm that wants to lead your startup's investment syndicate. The venture capitalist community is filled with fine, ethical people with good intentions, many with special experience that can make the difference between a startup being a successful or a poor investment. The CEO should take the time to pick wisely and carefully.

How a VC Firm Controls Its Investment

Founders often talk about their plans to retain control and to avoid selling out to venture capitalists. Such intentions are strong, and founders often deliberately avoid VCs just to fulfill such a goal.

This attitude stems from the horror stories they have heard and perhaps from painful personal experience when venture capitalists exercised control to change a startup and its management during times of duress or special significance, such as getting ready to go public. The more bitter people label the venture capitalists as "vulture capitalists" and "sharks." Their experiences or beliefs have led them to be eager to structure their next deal without any venture capital at all.

In the world of reality, few successful high tech deals ("We went public!") are done without classic venture capital. There appear to be relatively more non-VC successes in the nontech world, particularly in consumer goods.

The venture capitalists' degree of influence on a startup can be circumvented by attracting corporate venture capital and offshore money from Europe or Asia. Others have begun to seriously consider the controversial Toronto and Taiwan stock exchanges.

However, the most likely path will be to the doors of the venture firms, so entrepreneurs should prepare for the high likelihood of having at least some venture capitalists on their board of directors. The seat on the board of directors is the first level of control the VC uses. There the VC influences salaries, options of shares granted to employees, structures of deals with suppliers and customers, and the timing and pricing of the next addition of capital. The ultimate power is the hiring and firing of the CEO.

The next level of control is that of approval of the spending and cash burn rates. Approval of budgets and annual operating plans sets goals for the CEO. Missed goals are cause for termination of the CEO. Missed product development schedules and lower-than-forecast sales can also cost the leader his or her job, particularly if that trouble causes the company to run out of cash.

The next level of control is the exercise of the special covenants in the terms of the contract for the preferred stock that was sold to the VC. Those terms and conditions can include veto power over the next round of financing and can cause a major shift in the power in the startup. Fights are common during conditions of duress. The goal is to stay cool and rational. But according to managers of some of the troubled startups that we spoke to in private, spite can cause powerful VCs and stubborn CEOs to act irrationally.

When the startup needs more capital, the CEO will find the VCs on the board trying to stick together as much as possible. Because they do not want to be kept out of the next hot deals led by other VC firms, the VCs on the board will exercise a powerful influence on the choices of the next sources of money. This is common behavior mentioned to us in strictest privacy by several CEOs whose startups found their VC board members exercising their power to interfere with the CEO in the process of raising multiple rounds of capital.

A Positive Side of Control.   Other CEOs told us they appreciated the controls put on them by their VCs. We found a strong correlation between the degree of success and the degree of praise for a VC's positive contribution. The more successful the company was, the more was the praise of the VCs (and vice versa).

For instance, John Warnock, president of the highly successful Adobe Systems of Palo Alto, California, had this to say about one of the VCs that invested in his company:

> We were fortunate to have experienced venture capitalists from successful startups on our board from the inception. They have an immense range of experience, with excellent insight into when a company is running well or not. They acted as our parachute and safety net.

Other CEOs noted their deliberate choices of VCs having personal track records in operations and industries that could be directly applied to increase the startup company's chances of success. Jerry Crowley of Gazelle Microcircuits of Santa Clara, California, hand-picked leaders of Gazelle, including the board and the advisors to the board, who were world-class veterans from the semiconductor industry, executives from National Semiconductor, Signetics, and Texas Instruments.

"Success breeds success" is a common phrase in venture circles. This seems to have some degree of truth to it. In application, we suggest that the founders pick their VCs as carefully as they pick their key employees. It will greatly influence the degree of success the company can have.

Door Opening and Other Assistance.   Finally, VCs will gladly go out on a limb for the startup CEO when necessary. They will give a lot of their time to interview key personnel, get world-class companies' presidents to consider becoming early customers, and much more. VCs are fighters; they are also going to try to help their investment do well through the tough times. Many have a lot of operational experience and almost instinctively know what to do when the alligators are neck high and the cash flow is getting very negative.

When it comes time to do the IPO, the VC firm will help plan and carry out the tactics that attract a top Wall Street banker to do the underwriting. Muscle and power plays are often going on behind the scenes, invisible to the CEO. It is one explanation of why the VCs hang on so long to the treasury function and to setting financial policy.

The Process of Raising Venture Capital

Chapter 7 dealt in detail with the techniques and methods of raising venture capital and suggested a model of the process the startup will go through. We will concentrate here on the aspects closely linked to the individual venture firm.

Finding Venture Capitalists.   Venture capitalists now exist within easy reach of virtually any corner of the U.S. Some operate in Europe and Asia. It has been estimated that in the United States there are more than 2000 actively venturing individuals and over 500 VC investment firms.

Appendix B, Resources for the Entrepreneur, lists good sources of venture capitalists. An entrepreneur should start with those firms in his geographical region, and look carefully at the types of investments each firm says it is interested in. For instance, it is a waste of time to contact a firm that does later-round deals when the startup is looking for seed money. The tactics suggested in Chapter 7 will help avoid mistakes and wasted time.

Choosing a Venture Capital Firm.   CEOs should pick a VC firm as carefully as they pick the startup's most important employee. Here are some reasons for making a careful choice of your VC:

- The VC will be with the company a long time, and the founders want the best they can find for the long haul.
- Each VC firm as its own character; compatibility with the CEO is important.
- A VC's references must be checked. The VC firm should provide three or more names of CEOs of companies in their portfolios. And the entrepreneur must insist on talking to at least one that got into serious trouble or went bankrupt. Character comes out best under duress.
- The entrepreneur must review the VC's portfolios—all of the companies, including the turkeys. It is important to discuss the losers as well as the winners with the VC who will be the lead.
- What do competing VCs think of the firm? Other VCs should be asked what their experiences have been with the firm. Check with out-of-town VC firms as well.
- The investigation should conclude with an evaluation of the VC firm that is as thorough as the VC firm itself will do on the startup's potential as an investment, or as the CEO would do on a vital key employee. It is important to check for integrity, ethics, and honesty.

Other Sources of Information.   The pages of *Inc.* magazine feature articles on venture firms and their partners. Venture Economics publishes a helpful monthly journal, *Venture Capital Journal*. It is now in many libraries and most venture firms have it handy. Each issue tells of deals done recently and analyzes trends.

Many firms provide a carefully prepared written description of the character of their firm and the kinds of investments they are looking for. We have reprinted some of them in the appendix, Resources for Entrepreneurs.

How Venture Capitalists Differ from One Another.   Until the fledgling CEO has dealt with several venture firms, it is hard to grasp just how different each one is from the other. Some opinions on how they differ are shown in Table 9-5. The observations presented were collected from interviews of managers of startup companies, CPAs, and lawyers.

The firms in Table 9-5 were selected to show contrasts, not to recommend those firms over others. They will give the startup CEO a taste of how unique each venture firm is, according to the opinions of managers who have dealt often with the venture capital community. Actual experiences with each firm differed among the people we interviewed. Only personal meetings and careful research should be used to reach conclusions on this important aspect of raising capital for a startup.

Presenting to Venture Capitalists.   Like a job hunter, the CEO's primary goal is to get the invitation for the first interview. This is a golden opportunity that must be carefully prepared for. It should be treated like the presentation of the annual plan to the board of directors at one's former employer. The CEO should be just as thoroughly prepared to field tough questions and should practice beforehand. Homework is vital.

The VCs' attitude at presentations will be deceptively simple, casual, and informal. This is partially because the partners want to see the person behind the presentation and at the same time make the CEO comfortable with them. They also realize that good managers are very hard to find and that competing VC firms will be eager to contact the qualified CEO.

The presentation must be done well. Desktop publishing is being used to make presentations look very slick and convincing. Handouts should be kept to a minimum, talk to the maximum. And the CEO must *never* leave any proprietary material on the first visit, if ever.

The degree of teamwork used to make the presentation will also tell the VC that the startup is likely to be an organization that will work together effectively and smoothly.

TABLE 9-5. Comparison of Some Venture Capital Firms

Venture Firm	Comments
Brentwood Associates Los Angeles and Menlo Park, California	Manages large amount of funds. Takes strong lead position. Invests in companies in California and other states in U.S. Also does leveraged buyouts. Very experienced partners, well connected in venture community.
Crosspoint Venture Palo Alto, California	An experienced seed round firm. Willing to invest without complete management team in place. Amounts are usually under $500,000 per investment. Experienced in electronics.
Kleiner Perkins Caufield & Byers Palo Alto, California	One of the older, most experienced firms. Distinguished by its operational involvement in startups, often acting as CEO until launch is successfully achieved. Likes being lead investor. Strong in life sciences and electronics.
Arthur Rock San Francisco, California	Considered by many to be the "father" of modern venture capital. Operates quietly from a small office in San Francisco. Often invests in referred business deals.
Sierra Ventures Management Palo Alto, California	Broadbased investors, classical in approach but willing to listen to unusual ideas. Acts in concert with other top-name investors, but likes taking active lead and board seat. Focuses on people and sustainable strategic advantage.
TA Associates Boston, Massachusetts	Operating one of the largest pools of capital, TA usually takes the lead role. It makes multi-million-dollar investments in a wide variety of technologies. Less interested in operational involvement. Avoids mid-round deals. Strong in software.

Source: Saratoga Venture Finance

What VCs Look For. Table 9-6 shows selected issues that VCs told us they especially look for. It should be used as a checklist well before the presentation at the VC's office.

Some day the startup will go public—at least this is the plan of both founders and venture capitalists. Here is what one influential group looks for in a company ready for IPO. These criteria can be compared to

TABLE 9-6. Issues Venture Capitalists Are Sensitive To

1. The CEO's credentials as a successful businessperson.
2. Caliber of the founders.
3. Completeness of the management team.
4. Degree of drive of the core team.
5. How revolutionary the technology is, its breakthrough qualities.
6. Why is the competitive advantage going to be sustainable?
7. What is the distinctive competence of the company?
8. Does the company just have a nifty product, or is this a business?
9. Size of the market, intensity of competition, and revenue potential over the next five years.
10. Names and phone numbers of potential customers who will tell investors of their intent to buy the product.
11. Size of the company in five years, likelihood of the company going public within three to five years.
12. Pricing of the financing round (percent owned after financing).
13. Who controls the company.
14. Vesting terms of the shares of employees.

Source: Saratoga Venture Finance

---

a startup company's condition and plans in three to five years. Hambrecht & Quist's head of research, Bill Welty, told *Business Week* in the April 20, 1987, issue that his firm looks for these factors to guide its decisions to buy, sell, or hold emerging growth stocks:

- **New Products:** "The company must have on stream new products that will help change the future of the industry it's in. In the case of Genentech and Apple," he said, "we identified such new products early."

- **Leadership:** "The company must be a leader in its particular niche business and face little competition."

- **Price Targets:** "As long as we believe the stock has the potential for a 50 percent climb, we stay with it," said Welty.

- **Unique Knowledge:** When H&Q feels that it no longer has more information about a particular stock than is circulating on Wall Street, it sells the stock.

In May 1986, *Business Week* ran a story entitled "Now High-Tech Moneymen are Picky, Picky, Picky." Its point related to the degree of interest in investing in startup computer companies. Here are a few quotes worth applying to a startup in any industry:

> The difference now is that everyone's a lot more cautious. . . . Whatever the startup, it is more important than ever to have seasoned management that won't lose sight of what the market needs. People don't want more technology—they want solutions to their problems, says Clifford Higgerson, a partner in Hambrecht & Quist Communication Ventures.
>
> Whatever the product, having the right leader is crucial. In the heady days of 1983, eager investors often overlooked management weaknesses when backing startups in hot technology markets. Now stable, seasoned management is prized as highly as innovative products. Investors are willing to pay a premium for an industry veteran launching a second or third new venture.

Closing Deals.   Closing deals is tough work. Many CEOs have celebrated before the cash arrived and later learned that it never would. How does a CEO avoid that? For one thing, by pressing on to the close as if the CEO was the only person doing the work to get to the close. Another is to recall what motivates the VC and to use that knowledge in the negotiations.

If the CEO is a "high techie" and hates to negotiate, he should get a consultant or lawyer who likes to rough and tumble with VCs, someone who is familiar with the notorious "creeping close" phenomenon, someone who can coach the CEO on how to close a deal. It is well worth their fees to use such a consultant to get the best deal possible. Once the deal is done, there is no getting back the excess stock that was needlessly given away.

The CEO must *brush up on negotiating skills,* just as professional ball players brush up on their basic skills. He will never regret doing the best job ever in this phase of the company's life.

As for secondary rounds of capital, a CEO should *plan well in advance, start earlier than he thinks is necessary, and plan for fund-raising to take a lot longer than it seems it should take.* There is nothing less dependable than a venture capitalist's assurances that "We'll get the money, don't worry." What can be done if the VC chooses to string things out until the company starts missing payroll? It takes weeks and months to get alternative VCs interested, and to get them to complete their due diligence on the struggling startup. The best negotiating lever is getting several VCs into competition and to retain plenty of cash in the bank. Meeting key milestones is a strong foundation on which to raise more money. Success attracts success.

Points to Remember.   Here are some key points for CEOs to remember as they go searching for capital:

- The CEO is competing with more than 1000 business plans that the venture firm receives in a given year.

- The VC is looking for a few key things in a CEO and a business plan. Chapter 5 is the guide to follow. Table 9-6 provides a quick checklist.

- Management is worth the most to an investor in today's market, or at least as much as the technology. Without a top leader, a startup will have to be very special to get seed money.

- The CEO will have to be an excellent negotiator to end up with more than 3 percent of the company at IPO time. The CEO can use all the help he can get in this once-in-a-lifetime negotiating event.

- VCs have to make a living too. They take large risks. It is important to respect their need for high ROIs.

- Many VCs have learned a lot and earned a lot. The CEO will benefit by listening.

- The CEO must be deliberate and not rush. In picking the VC firm to lead the financing, the CEO must make the best possible decisions.

- The character of the VC partners is important. The CEO will be dealing with his board member for the next five years. They will be the CEO's new bosses and control the CEO in the rough days ahead.

Examples follow of CEOs who experienced the process of raising funds for their statups. The first case study follows Hans, a determined founder of a software startup, New Software Inc. This case study is—unfortunately—rather typical.

Case Study: New Software Inc.

New Software Inc. was founded by Hans, a scientist with a breakthrough technology in database software. The prototype worked well in the laboratory and had been funded all with his own money. Hans decided it was time to get the real stuff, venture capital, to hire some engineers to convert the lab product into a viable commercial success.

He called up a few VCs he had read about in the newspaper and got quick invitations to visit. Hans did so, clad in his usual tieless attire, equipped with just himself and his ideas.

The VCs listened and were interested. Hans had distinguished himself in past years as a senior engineer of an emerging growth company. They told him, however, that they needed to see a business plan. Could he get started writing one soon? And would he be open to recruiting a strong CEO?

Hans said he would get started right away and drove back to his home, where he worked at night and on weekends on his business plan. The more he worked on it, the more he realized that he needed lots of help, from a general manager to a strong marketing manager and top sales manager. The hardest part was explaining how Hans's database technology would be so much better that people would stop purchasing dBASE and start buying his product.

The more Hans tried to work on the business plan, the more frustrated he became. He did not want to hire a CEO. He really wanted to lead this effort himself and not give up leadership to someone he didn't know. He decided to seek corporate venture funds instead.

After nine months of work, the interest of corporate venture capital managers remained low, so Hans finally gave in to an offer for the seed round from a venture capital firm on the opposite coast. No one in his region would back Hans without an experienced CEO in place.

That seed cash lasted eight months before the company realized it was in trouble. By then, Hans and his skeleton engineering crew were behind schedule, had less than half the software written, and were not close to the speed of performance that they had promised from Hans's technology.

Suddenly aware that he was going to miss the next payroll, Hans dropped all development work, got everyone to help create a nifty demo piece of software, and personally started trying to get corporate venture capital to save his company.

After four nightmarish months of constant worry and eight payroll advances from the seed investor in the form of a loan secured on all rights to the technology, Hans successfully got verbal agreement for $4 million of capital from a Fortune 500 company that wanted full access to Hans's technology. Hans agreed.

But the seed investor vetoed the deal three times until Hans dropped the price per share to a point where the VC suddenly announced he would be investing in 25 percent of that round. The Fortune 500 company refused to go along with such a deal. Meanwhile, the corporate giant had suddenly been shocked to find that its bread-and-butter business had gone flat. All spending was suddenly frozen, including the commitment to invest in Hans's startup.

As it turned out, Hans's engineers quit after missing two payrolls. The seed investor ended up with half-finished technology worth nothing. And Hans' dreams went down the drain. Had Hans instead started by recruiting a strong CEO and together creating a well-thought-out business plan, the company might have succeeded. Instead, Hans had to settle on a VC investor and suffered severe consequences. Hans never prepared a capital-raising plan; rather he just shot from the hip and hoped for the best. The result was failure.

Some CEOs have better results than Hans. In the next case study, the real-life CEO not only got started in better condition than Hans, but has gone on to become the leader of one of America's 500 fastest-growing companies according to a survey by *Inc.* magazine.

Case Study: Devices Corporation

Devices Corporation was founded by two top technologists, Dick and Arthur, with less than ten years of successful experience in business. College friends, they joined a giant, IC Corporation, after graduation from engineering school, and later quit to join the R&D group of an exciting new startup, Oak Micro Technology. Its chairman, the chief scientist, and the CEO were wrangling from the first day the company got started, and after three years of mediocre progress, Dick and Arthur quit to start their own company.

They got $500,000 of venture money from Carl, a businessman who had started a venture capital firm. He was a respected personality in the semiconductor industry. He understood their technology and believed that a large market existed for products that could be built with Dick's and Arthur's new ideas.

However, as a condition to investing, Carl had insisted that a top-flight CEO be found well before the $500,000 of seed money ran out. Dick and Arthur agreed, willingly.

By January of the following year, the three-man board and the two founders had recruited Jim, one of the best marketing and sales leaders in the industry. Jim was just finishing his last year at the startup he had founded seven years earlier and had let Carl know that he was looking for a good startup to lead as CEO.

Jim negotiated a tough package with the venture capitalists, including repricing the seed round because Jim felt the dilution to the founders and employees was excessive. Carl would be board chairman. Jim joined Devices Corporation and immediately launched into upgrading the company's business plan, particularly the strategy and market positioning of the company and its products. Using word processing and laser printers, the new plan was completed in very professional style in five weeks. Jim then sat down with the company's experienced lawyer and the startup consultant Jim had hired. Together they began to plan the strategy and tactics for the next round of capital.

Two weeks later, the search for the second round was started. The goal of the core team was to get $5 million in the bank in three months, including funding from four VCs, the seed round firm and three new ones, one of which must come from the opposite coast.

The deal closed in 71 days. Instead of $5 million, there were offers for $11 million from nine firms. The core team and board of directors decided to accept offers for $6 million from five firms, picking the firms according to their character, experience as operating managers in the company's industry, and their track records as investors.

While the capital was being raised, Dick and Arthur remained focused on product development. As a result, before the second round closed, the engineers had met their key milestones. On the day of closing on the financing, everyone celebrated at dinner.

A careful funding plan was built upon a carefully prepared business plan. A team drew up the plan, lead by a CEO savvy in marketing and strategy. The two founders turned leadership over to a stranger whose efforts contributed to a very successful funding effort. Needless to say, the employees finished this stage of the company's life with smiles on every face.

There is an old saying, "Experience is cheapest second-hand." So why not apply that to your capital-raising campaign? Sure, owning 100 percent of your own company sounds great, but having enough capital to achieve the fullest potential of your company sounds even better to most CEOs.

We recommend that you read the material in Appendix C, which includes the written descriptions provided by three leading VC firms. A careful review of these descriptions will allow you to compare typical differences in what VCs are looking for.

So now that you understand—better than most—how the VC investor thinks and acts, you can plan and negotiate a fair deal, fairer than you would without good preparation.

Now let's go on to look at a popular source of alternative capital, venture leasing.

10

Leasing As a Source of Capital

Smart entrepreneurs quickly learn to protect their precious equity capital. In other words, they soon realize that almost any source of money other than equity is less expensive capital. Leasing is an important source for the high tech startup. In this chapter, we will discuss important additional sources of venture capital, in particular how to raise equity capital in the form of venture leasing.

Entrepreneurs also catch on to how important it is to have financial flexibility—the time and room to maneuver, particularly when the sharks are circling. Sustainable competitive advantages are built on lower costs of capital and quicker speed in responding to freshly perceived opportunities and problems in the marketplace. Leasing can make a valuable contribution to the creation of competitive advantage.

Leasing money is not only cheaper funding—it has also proved reliable. Our research shows that it is found in many balance sheets of IPOs since 1980, providing a valuable source of specialized growth capital for startups and emerging high tech companies.

However, our research also revealed that most CEOs are inexperienced with lease money, and that they consequently often overlooked lease capital, incorrectly priced leasing company offers, and generally underused this significant source of capital. Interviews showed that the CEO needs to know where to look for lease capital, how to price it, and how to negotiate a lease deal.

The two primary sources most commonly found participating in lease deals are the landlord and the equipment lessor; we will discuss their roles in detail, and we will also analyze the terms and conditions of a typical leasing term sheet.

Three case studies illustrate the role of leasing capital in startups. The case study of Chips and Technologies shows how the landlord became a key partner at just the right moment—when the chips were down, one could say. It was a win-win situation and history showed that both parties made out handsomely, particularly in financial terms.

The case study of Tophill Systems is based on an actual startup that successfully negotiated a leaseline that added 23 percent to its capital base immediately after closing its Round 1 venture deal. It is a classic case of a winning CEO who was unfamiliar with sophisticated leasing salespeople, but who learned and ended up in the driver's seat with a fine deal.

The case study of Range Semiconductor is another classic case, that of the startup that had to downsize. It all happened in the Great Electronics Winter of 1983-1986. Faced with a severe shortfall of revenue well below its business plan, this startup company decided to try to buy more time by converting fixed leasing costs to more flexible, stretched-out, monthly payments.

These three case studies provide examples and lessons learned that will help CEOs better plan their financial flexibility.

The Landlord As a Source of Venture Capital

"Rent, don't buy!" was the consistent advice of the CEOs and venture capitalists we talked to. That advice was universally applied to decisions on leasing or buying real estate. Yet that is the opposite of what some of the grand giants of Silicon Valley like National Semiconductor and Intel did. They began to buy land as soon as they could. National bought parcels at below $90,000 an acre in the 1960s and 1970s—land that is now worth over $1 million an acre. Intel began buying out its existing leases as soon as the good times began to flow in the late 1970s. Yet giants still lease a great deal of space. Why? For the same reason that startups rent: to get a lower cost of capital and to retain more strategic flexibility. Many observers of the early 1980s assert that high tech startups should not be in the business of investing in real estate. Considering the 30 million square feet of newly constructed, empty R&D space in Silicon Valley from 1985 to 1990, those counselors proved right.

Landlords thus become venture capitalists. They size up the startup's chances of success, check it out with the venture capitalists, and sign the CEO to a five-year lease.

As the lease document begins to be negotiated, landlords quickly separate into two camps: paper people and deal-makers. Paper people want to put the lease documents in a vault and collect the monthly check without interruption, except for an occasional "How's it all going?" on the phone during periods of slack business. These landlords constitute about 80 percent of those in real estate in Silicon Valley.

The deal-makers are people like Bill Marocco of W. L. Marocco Development Company and John Arrillaga of Peery-Arrillaga, both of Santa Clara, California. They strongly prefer to negotiate without an expensive middleman (a real estate broker). A broker gets about 6 percent of a five-year lease, adding a cost of about $40,000 to $150,000; such brokers or developers have been known to bend corners to get a desirable startup into one of the many local buildings that they personally built and financed.

Freed of the constraints of a middleman, these deal-makers will give a period of free rent and add needed special leasehold improvements in exchange for warrants to buy the startup company's stock. The deal then turns into more of a horsetrading session than the staid negotiation of a boring lease.

For capital-intensive startup companies in businesses like semiconductor manufacturing, cooperation on leasehold improvements can be worth millions of dollars of capital supplied through the facility lease instead of from expensive venture capital. Semiconductor companies are now among the most capital-intensive of the electronics startups; some have even gone into a business partnership with deal-makers in order to extract cash from the vaults of landlords.

Case Study: Chips and Technologies

Chips and Technologies was founded on December 5, 1984, with personal capital from Gordon Campbell, who was soon joined by Gary Martin as CFO. Campbell found to his shock that at that time classic venture funds were nearly impossible to obtain at any price, so he decided to turn to alternative sources. Bill Marocco was already his choice as landlord, based on the rates charged startups at that time, and Campbell started his search for alternative funding with Marocco, who was to play an important role in the life of Chips.

Marocco, a well-known independent industrial real estate developer in Silicon Valley, welcomed Campbell's interest in talking over a deal in person. Campbell was known to Marocco, who had done some discreet checks on Campbell's new business prior to both parties signing the office lease. Marocco's decision was largely based on character references: he sized up Campbell and decided he was a manager worth the risk.

They met in Marocco's office to talk business. Campbell chose to focus Marocco's attention on one single point: getting him to understand Chips's sustainable competitive advantage. He was well prepared from arduous (and unproductive) presentations to more than 40 classic venture capital firms; he kept to a simple agenda and avoided elaborate slides and overhead foils or handouts. Instead, he talked about the vast, untapped market—in the millions of units per month—that awaited the first company to ship the most obviously needed product in the personal computer industry. He patiently presented the skills of Chips' management, the technical team's talent, and the cash flows that could result from a success.

Then he gave Marocco the bottom line: "Bill, I want you to invest $1 million in the next round of financing of Chips."

Most people would blanch at that request. However, deal-makers respond with, "For how much of the company?" Shortly thereafter, in October 1985, Round 1 closed for $1,705,000. The shares went for $0.65 each. Marocco was elected to the Chips board of directors, where he continued to serve for several years. Chips shipped its first products in the fourth quarter ending December 1985.

Based on the business's successes, Round 2 quickly followed, adding $1,528,000 by January 1986. Those shares were sold for $1.00, mainly to four Japanese companies that had contracted with Chips to provide it with manufacturing facilities and services. That further leveraged the seed capital. Thus, Campbell and his team were able to turn near-disaster into sweet victory. By IPO time, the Chips stock sold for $5.00 per share. Campbell, his fellow founders, key managers, and all employees with options collectively owned 63 percent of the company. In contrast, Cypress Semiconductor personnel owned 25 percent of their company.

Equipment Lessors

A second important source of funding is the lessors who invest in startups by leasing equipment to new enterprises. Companies that provide lease capital to startups are a special breed of capitalist. They come in several forms and make their money in several ways. The entrepreneur who understands the differences will be much more likely to successfully attract lease capital at competitive rates.

Who They Are.   Because of the complexity of an equipment lease, there are several types of leasing companies. A leasing deal looks deceptively simple, but it can be a complex collection of elements: parties that provide capital in the form of tax breaks, other parties that collect interest and principal payments, providers of the portion of the lease that is equity, and suppliers of debt in several maturities. There is nothing simple behind the scenes about leasing.

A lessor is either a broker or an institutional investor. Brokers bring together the complex parties—as do institutional sources of funds—but brokers typically do not put their capital at risk in the startup. Examples of each in northern California were often mentioned during our interviews: John Hancock Leasing of Hayward, Meier Mitchell & Company of San Francisco, and Western Technology Investment of San Jose. Each claims a speciality: one claims to be the most experienced warrant-based high tech equipment lessor in the U.S., while another represents low-cost funds for well-secured financings. The point is that all leasing firms are not alike.

To the entrepreneur, the differences among lessors are important if they represent an opportunity to: (1) reduce the cost of funds, and (2) increase the flexibility of the funding.

First, the startup CEO must be sure the lease money *actually* comes in. That turns out to be quite important. Raising capital takes a great deal of time and emotional energy, two resources a startup company lacks. Our research revealed that a high proportion of lease deals are not completed. The lessor often turned out to be unable to get all the parties behind the scenes to sign up to take on the risks of (in essence) loaning long-term money to a shaky, unproven company. The CEO is also sometimes subjected to the dangers of bait-and-switch tactics from the seedier leasing salespeople.

Second, there is a correlation between the higher quality of firms and a lower cost of capital for a lease. Professional, experienced firms like John Hancock, Meier Mitchell, and Western are often found in the final Silicon Valley runoffs, after elimination of other, less experienced bidders.

Finally, each lease deal has terms and conditions that are customized to fit the particular needs of the startup. Experienced players are much more inclined to significantly give and take in their negotiations, and this is true even of the leading electronic lending banks that sometimes enter this market. The large institutional investors tend to avoid the riskier deals, and are more likely to be entering startup financing at later stages than the brokers. Recent entries have, however, tended to be aggressive in their negotiations, but short on valuable venture leasing experience.

Equipment lessors have differing motivations for being in this high-risk financing market. The astute CFO should attempt to uncover the lessor's priorities. Some want to maximize their gain ("upside") through warrants and will take more risk for more warrants. Some are just looking for financing opportunities for their funds and attempt to minimize risk via additional security and shorter maturities.

How They Make Their Money.   Equipment lessors make their money by owning equipment used by startup companies that pay monthly for its use. At the end of a preset term, the startup must either stop using the equipment or purchase it, typically at fair market value, or sign up for a new lease.

Meanwhile, the lessor has typically sold the tax benefits, such as depreciation, which the startup would have had to wait to use until it became profitable several years later. And the lessor also has arranged to restructure and sell packages of the incoming cash flows to be safer to debt participants and riskier to equity participants.

In exchange for the greater risk, the equity partner then asks for warrants from the startup. We found that the broker sometimes takes them all, while at other times deals were made that split the warrants into complex pools of capital.

Cost of Leasing: Cash and Equity.   The combinations of cash flow, tax benefits, equity, warrants and debt, plus the security deposits and fees, all boil down to an offer called "the term sheet." An example of one is contained in Figure 10-1. Below is a composite of actual terms of startup equipment lease deals revealed to Saratoga Venture Finance for deals done in Silicon Valley between 1985 and 1990.

- The after-tax internal rate of return (IRR) for the monthly cash payments was between 16 percent to 30 percent per annum.

- The cost of warrants almost tripled the total cost of capital of the typical startup equipment lease financing, raising the ROI or internal rate of return (IRR) to a range of 36 percent to 46 percent per annum after taxes.

More Than Leasing Money

CEOs should know that so-called leasing companies are also sources of startup capital in special forms. Be aware of this as you open discussions with a leasing company. For instance, Western Technology tells startups to look at them as in the role of "filling the gap between equity financing and traditional bank lending and leasing. These services are offered nationally to companies representing all areas of venture capital investments." Knowing that, the CEO can talk long-term relationship from the first moment on, and can set up for the day when later-stage funding is ripe, ready to go back to the leasing company as a source of midround venture funding.

FIGURE 10-1. Typical Term Sheet of Equipment Lease Financing for a Startup Company

PARTIES TO THE TRANSACTION:
    1. Lessee: XYZ Company ("XYZ")
    2. Lessor: To be arranged by Lease Broker

EQUIPMENT
    1. **Equipment Description:** The equipment to be leased will include test equipment, computer equipment, and furniture and fixtures.
    2. **Total Cost:** Not to exceed $ _____
    3. **Deliveries:** The equipment is expected to be delivered prior to December 31, 199_.

TRANSACTION STRUCTURE: On or before December 31, 199_ , the Lessor will purchase the equipment from the vendor and/or the Lessee and simultaneously lease the equipment to the Lessee. The Lessor will provide 100 percent of the funds necessary to purchase the equipment.

    A true lease document will evidence the agreement between the Lessor and Lessee. It is anticipated that the lease will be a Master Lease with schedules evidencing periodic takedowns.

LEASE INFORMATION
    1. **Delivery and Acceptance:** All equipment delivered and placed in service will be acknowledged and accepted by the Lessee per a written Delivery and Acceptance Certificate.
    2. **Base Lease Term Commencement Date:** There will be a Base Lease Term Commencement Date for the equipment subject to each funding by the Lessor.
    3. **Lease Rate Factors:**
    __ monthly payments each in advance equal to ____% of equipment cost.
    4. **End of Lease Purchase:** At lease expiration the Lessee will have the option of buying the equipment at its then fair market value or renewing the lease at the equipment's then fair rental value.
    5. **Casualty Values (Stipulated Loss Value):** In the event the equipment is destroyed or otherwise rendered permanently unfit for service, the Lessee will pay a Casualty Value. The Casualty Value will be calculated at the outset of the transaction and will dictate the amount of the Lessee's casualty insurance coverage.

OTHER CONSIDERATIONS
    1. **Federal Income Tax:** The Lease Rate Factors quoted herein are based upon the following assumptions:
        a. **Investment Tax Credit:** It is assumed that no investment tax credit (ITC) is available to the Lessor.
        b. **Depreciable Life:** The equipment is expected to be depreciated over five (5) years using the "200 percent double declining balance switching to straight line" schedule as outlined in the Tax Reform Act of 1986.

(Continued)

FIGURE 10-1.   Typical Term Sheet of Equipment Lease Financing for a Startup Company (continued)

2. **Tax Indemnification:** The Lessee will indemnify Lessor for any loss of tax benefits as listed above caused by acts, omissions, or misrepresentations by the Lessee.
3. **Net Lease:** The Lease will be net to the Lessor. Lessee will be responsible for all expenses in connection with the equipment, including taxes (except taxes based on the income of the Lessor), franchise taxes, charges in lieu of taxes, assessments, insurance premiums, all cost of operation, repair, maintenance and rebuilding, and all the charges related to the equipment or its operation.
4. **Expenses:** Any expenses incurred by the parties, including fees and expenses of counsel and/or accountants, are for the account of those parties. Appraisal fees will be for the account of the Lessee.
5. **Stock Warrants:** As an inducement to lease equipment to the Lessee, the Lessor will be granted the option to purchase _____ shares of the Lessee's series X preferred stock at $ ____ per share. This represents a __% coverage ratio. The warrants have an exercise period of _____ years from the final Base Lease Term Commencement Date. The warrants will contain piggyback registration rights similar to those granted to the holders of this series of preferred stock.
6. **Commitment Fee:** A Commitment Fee of $_____ is required by the Lessor to initiate its due diligence review process. The entire Commitment Fee is refundable if the transaction is declined by the Lessor. Should the transaction be approved and the lease line instituted, the fee will be applicable on a pro rata basis to the first period's rental as the line is drawn down. Should the transaction be approved and the Lessee choose not to utilize the lease line, the fee will be retained by the Lessor and treated as compensation for time and effort expended.

Case Study: Tophill Systems

Jim, the CEO of Tophill, had just finished Round 1 for $7 million. The venture capital participants were first class and he was now ready to commit to a three- to five-year lease for a more permanent home for his team, which had been squeezed into rented quarters for the six months between the Seed Round and Round 1. The furniture rental fees were eating the cash supply and the engineers were eager to get their hands on leading-edge computer-aided engineering systems.

Good publicity in the San Jose Mercury News *"Business Monday" section had alerted the leasing community. The phone had been ringing with salespeople seeking a visit to check up on Tophill. Jim had also been given a couple of names of lessors by two of his lead venture capitalists. He called an old CFO friend to check up on the quality of those he had been considering. Although he was a superb negotiator, Jim had no prior contact with leasing people and was not sure of his ability to analyze and make a wise decision. Moreover, some members of his board of directors were strongly in favor of purchasing everything to avoid the cost of paying interest.*

Jim had also decided to scrimp on new hires and had been using part-time help hired at a deep discount from Big Six Accounting, the blue-chip CPA firm. He planned to add a strong CFO at a later date. For now, he would get along with a smart administrative assistant, and he would use Bob, his CFO acquaintance, as a consultant on this project.

After exploring eight proposals, Bob and Jim cut the number of offers to a total of five firms and then put in personal phone calls to each finalist, requesting final written offers. The five selected firms responded in four working days. But the eliminated firms rebid aggressively, anyway!

By Friday of the first week, nine proposals were facing Tophill. Each had different cash flows, terms, warrants, and special conditions. Jim was disappointed that there was no clear-cut winner. (He didn't know that lessors do not go for approval within their own firms until after the lessor is awarded the deal; that is why it is important to have multiple bidders.) When Bob and Jim reviewed the proposals, here's what they found:

- *It was deceiving to use the lowest lease rate factor because the up-front deposit and fee arrangements differed so much.*
- *The warrants were at different costs and lengths of term, with differing IPO conditions.*
- *Each lessor had differing reputations for certainty of getting a deal done.*
- *The cheapest cash flow IRR lessor required the largest security deposit.*
- *The second lowest IRR lessor would not finance software for more than 25 percent of the $1.5 million lease line.*
- *A third would not fund more than $65,000 worth of furniture.*
- *A fifth insisted on attending all board meetings and getting all materials and minutes of the board.*

Jim made his final deal with Bluebird Leasing, based on these decision factors:

1. *No leasing companies in board meetings. Informal meetings were welcome, but not formal sessions with the board.*
2. *He requested written assurance from the lessor's ultimate source of money that the deal had been prescreened. Jim wanted no surprises.*
3. *Two rounds of counteroffers had gotten a top lessor to be the lowest in both the after-tax cash flow IRR and the all-in IRR, although by only the narrowest of margins over the number-two lessor.*
4. *The number-one lessor, Bluebird Leasing, had expressed an early desire to continue funding Tophill through and beyond the IPO.*

Bluebird Leasing got the deal, on terms along the lines of those shown in the term sheet in Figure 10-1.

Case Study: Range Semiconductor

Mike, the new CEO of Range Semiconductor, had just finished looking at the CFO's latest business plan projections. If layoffs could be done as his VPs had agreed, the variable costs would be cut low enough to give Range a chance at survival.

In 1986, after two years of revenue, this four-year-old startup was going through the pain of massive restructuring, including a new president. The new president, brought in by the venture capitalists on the board, was given one goal: save Range.

To keep the technology team in place and to give the marketing leader a chance to build some revenue-building new products, Mike decided he needed more room to maneuver. The only costs left to attack were the fixed ones—the building and equipment leases.

Mike told his CFO to figure out some way to cut the lease cash flow drain and to do so in 90 days. The goal was to get an extra year of cash flow out of the concessions of the leasing participants, including the landlord.

Tim, the CFO, had been with Range since early days; he was employee #16. He had personally arranged the company's four lease lines and its five-year facilities lease. The $8 million of equipment and the facility lease represented about 68 percent of the company's fixed costs.

Eager to get started, Tim launched into action. He called for a gathering, called "an all-hands meeting," to start the ball rolling. He expected an uphill battle, but was confident that much of the $2.5 million in deposits could be freed up and some concessions in monthly payments could be negotiated. After all, he reasoned, "isn't it in everyone's best interests to keep Range alive?"

Over the next seven months, Tim struggled in vain to get his concessions completed. In the end, he was unable to succeed for reasons of "good news": the semiconductor industry began to rebound in 1987, and under Mike's leadership Range's revenues began at last to climb. However, Tim learned the hard way some important lessons on leases:

1. *Stick to just one simple source of equipment lease money. Tim had arranged so many, in such complex deals, with multiple parties head-quartered around the country, that he was never actually able to get all of them around the table for a unified negotiating session. In this case, the quest to get lowest-cost funds ended up being high cost when the going got rough.*

2. *The landlord was indeed willing to negotiate revised terms. But only if he "was not the patsy." The equipment lessors had to give just as much.*

3. *The easiest landlord to negotiate with is one who owns the property. All others must act "as a prudent man" on behalf of the remote, uncaring pension fund whose money has purchased the building.*

4. *Don't believe that security deposits are "free"—that is, that they cost nothing. This becomes clear as soon as the startup gets into trouble. Cash spells life to the startup that is missing payroll.*

5. *Commercial banks are more likely to renegotiate terms in times of trouble than other sources of lease money. Tim believes that there are two reasons for this: banks have much more skill at working out troubled loans, and their goal is to have a long-term relationship with those startups they choose to support with loans and leases.*

6. *Range's sole negotiating lever was the danger of bankruptcy. Private talks with people familiar with SEEQ and other restructured high tech companies showed this to be true. The winners had engaged special bankruptcy legal counsel—rugged, determined types who spearheaded the gathering of all related parties.*

Postscript: As of 1991, Range has turned around and is ready for its IPO.

The Lessons of Leasing. The alert CFO should realize that equipment lessors have different investment objectives from venture capital investors, and in distress situations their interests may be different from those of the company's investors. These differences will become even more apparent as we examine the role for commercial bankers in the next chapter. As for obtaining cash from landlords and venture equipment lessors, the CEO who uses the lessons learned in this chapter's case studies will incur less dilution, obtain greater flexibility, and get closer to achieving the capital-raising plan needed for his or her company to succeed.

11

Bankers and Bootstraps As Funding Sources

The Role of Bankers

The old hands, experienced at starting new enterprises, have found many ways to get the most benefit from a long-term relationship with a banker, even if the bank grants them not a penny to get the company started. In this chapter we will look at what commercial bankers and other funding sources can—and can't—do for a startup.

We will first explore the conventions and practices that currently prevail, indicating what can realistically be expected from a friendly banker. Next we will look at how loans can be used for a startup. We will also suggest other sources of capital such as government money and funds from family and friends, with the goal of relating these alternative sources of capital to venture capital sources. We will consider whether the entrepreneur is wise to mix them, and under what circumstances they might be mixed.

Finally, we have provided insight from our interviews with startup veterans about how they pick and work with a top banker.

Conventions and Practices.   Because of the business economics of today's commercial banker in the United States, a CEO of a startup must be prepared to work with a bank in a very different way than is appropriate with venture capital equity investors.

A commercial bank earns most of its money making loans at interest rates higher than the cost of money it buys to make such loans. It counts on 97 percent to 100 percent of the loaned monies to return as principal, whereas a venture capital firm expects that 30 percent to 60 percent of its invested capital will never return anything. For the commercial banker, interest payments must cover the loan losses—typically under 1 percent of the principal at risk—as well as provide the gross margin needed to pay for operating expenses and profit. The banker considers it a good piece of business when a loan earns at least a 3 percent spread between interest income from the loan and interest expense on the supporting deposits.

Because of this low-risk profile, the commercial banker is not in the business of providing venture capital to startups, many of which may never see success. Furthermore, the bank is usually constrained by U.S. law from taking much in the form of shares as compensation. Therefore, the banker is generally precluded from sharing in the high potential rewards open to the venture capitalist. As a result, banks do not provide equity capital of any kind. The bank expects the entrepreneur to get high-risk capital from other sources.

Some of those sources, however, are often related cousins to the commercial bank. The larger banks are owned by holding companies that can go into other businesses, some of which can help provide startup capital. Banks have equipment leasing subsidiaries. Several have successful venture capital subsidiaries, while others have groups dedicated to making loans to private, emerging growth companies. And small as well as large banks will lend money to a small business if it qualifies for one of the several U.S. government-backed loan guarantee programs. But these are money businesses that are separate from the familiar commercial bank.

Since banks are not a source for startup funding, what good is a commercial banker to a startup?

The Long-term Partner. A startup represents the dream customer to bankers with a long-term view. They have visions of a long relationship, of growing huge along with the next Apple. Accordingly, if the startup passes the banker's screening and due diligence, he or she is willing to begin working with it from the first day of business. The banker will start cautiously, getting to know the CEO, the company, and its investors. He will read your business plan carefully. Because of the banker's long-term importance to the startup, the CEO should cooperate from the beginning and plan each step of the relationship as it progresses. The CEO and CFO should invest time in growing the relationship. It is worth the time. The commercial banker can help add millions of dollars of value to a company.

Business Advisor. A banker should be chosen as carefully as a CPA firm. The advice given in Chapter 5 for selecting a CPA firm can be applied as well to choosing a banker. The banker should be a competent business person, someone familiar with the larger emerging growth companies in high technology businesses. The banker's experience will be valuable for many reasons, including these:

- *The banker will spot soft areas in the business plan.* He has advance knowledge of upcoming capital shortages. The banker can also correct unrealistic assumptions about inventory and accounts payable and receivable, and can explain the magic ratios that bankers' credit analysts will later use to evaluate granting the first request for a working capital loan.
- *The banker's experience can head off unrealistic expectations,* such as an unrealistic rate of projected sales growth, or profit margins much larger than any that have been sustainable by other clients over many years in your industry.
- *Some of the banker's customers may be good customer candidates for the startup.* The banker can provide personal introductions to busy executives who are hard to reach, yet are important to the startup.
- *The banker knows the best venture capitalists in the area* and will help get the CEO in to see them, a very valuable introduction. A CEO will be identified by the venture capitalist according to the company that he keeps.

Credit References. The business plan has probably assumed that the company will be able to get its suppliers to grant credit so the startup can pay its bills in 30 days or so. That is a reasonable assumption and a good goal, but is much harder to achieve than might be expected. Suppliers are wary of a new company, one that does not yet have a track record at anything except spending a dwindling pot of money (and that has not yet shipped its first product).

A loyal banker can help bridge the time period until sales get started and the company earns its Dun and Bradstreet credit rating. By being informed about a company from the beginning, a banker is in a position to be a credit reference, talking with the suppliers who call the bank and telling them why he has confidence in your company.

This will help the startup get needed credit from key suppliers, and get the suppliers started on the right foot and in the habit of granting the company good credit terms. The payoff is that later, when the startup is a large, fast-growing company, the suppliers' credit will add up to millions of dollars of financing that the startup did not have to use precious equity for.

Lease Lines.   The banker may have an equipment leasing subsidiary or good relations with an independent firm. If so, this is one way to start an early credit relationship with the affiliated bank. Chapter 10 supplies leasing details. A banking relationship should be included in any leasing plans and in the decision of which leasing company to do business with.

Loans.   Bankers call loans by various names, depending on their purpose, security, and risk. The type that a startup company will first be eligible for is called a *working capital loan*. It comes in the form of a line of credit, and in the case of a startup, will be intended to finance the cash flow delay between the time the company ships the product and the time it finally collects all the cash from the customer. It is a loan whose amount is limited to some percentage of the total of the accounts receivable (U.S. only) that are outstanding from reliable customers at the end of each month. As the receivables go up and down, so does the principal amount of the loan. The banker can explain the details, and the CEO and CFO should review the business plan with the banker to fit such financing into the startup's long-term plan.

The important thing for the CEO to know is when a company can qualify for such loans. They are a lot cheaper than venture capital. Bankers all use different criteria to test the credit-worthiness of a young company, but a banker familiar with high tech startups will begin by looking for the date the first receivables are booked. That will be the first test. Next, the banker will look at when the startup plans to begin being profitable. And then the banker will look at the startup's ability to repay the loan—from what source the needed repayment cash will be coming. The banker must understand all of this in case the startup experiences adversity that raises the risk level and causes the bank to temporarily disqualify it as a creditworthy customer.

All of this quantified analysis is done on computer models built by the bank. They digest a business plan and produce new data and facts that a banker needs to do his homework. (In fact, the output is still called a spreadsheet and is where the concept for VisiCalc and Lotus started.) By getting the business plan at the beginning of the company's life, the loan officer can quickly determine the degree of realism in the CEO's goal of attaining the working capital loans. For instance, the banker will tell the CEO whether a debt-to-worth ratio of 1.75 to 1.1 is acceptable in the current business climate. The banker will also demonstrate how financial statements are viewed from a banker's conservative perspective.

And behind all of the numbers, the banker will be looking to the CEO as the leader, to be responsible to repay the bank's precious principal, even in the bad times. The more confident the banker is in the CEO and the startup's team of managers, the more likely the company is to get the loan sooner than its competitors. And even more important, the banker will support the startup when it runs into trouble, through the hard times, when capital and business counsel are needed the most. So get the banker in to meet the whole team, on the company's premises. The more the banker knows, the more likely he or she is to provide support through thick and thin.

Payroll and Other Services. As soon as the startup is incorporated it will need a bank account, and the need for a payroll account will quickly follow. The banks are very competitive in services to do payroll and related tax bookkeeping, starting with even the smallest of businesses. These are areas where a business wants the best quality service and the most "free" accounting help it can get. The changing payroll tax legislation is a headache to keep up with, especially when a sales force will be operating in many of the 50 states. And the required reports are a burden on a company's administrative staff. Such services are often provided best by the banker. The bank's references in this area should be compared with the payroll service alternatives such as ADP, but the future and the long-term relationship should be kept in mind when a decision is being made.

Growing Together. A CEO must pick a banker as carefully as the company's investors, and treat the relationship as very long term. As the company succeeds, the commercial banker will help more and more. International subsidiaries will need a local banker, and customs departments of governments and overseas suppliers will require letters of credit. The business between the company and its bank will grow accordingly. It will need services such as trustee and transfer agent when it goes public, and here again the banker will want to help. It is important that the banker and the CEO get to know each other early, and that the banker is kept informed as the company grows.

How does one choose a banker for an emerging company? We found the most interesting answer coming from one of high technology's great veterans, Don Cvietusa, senior vice president of Silicon Valley Bank:

> Choose a banker for a startup *very* carefully. Take some time to select an experienced technology banker who is knowledgeable about emerging companies, one who has excellent venture capital relationships. Approach with a deposit in hand, thereby providing the banker with his "raw material." Build "depositor leverage" and be "bankable" well before you become bankable in a credit sense.

Personal Loans

If the CEO is determined to start the company with his or her own equity capital and does not want classic venture capitalists in the company, the personal loan can be important at the beginning. We found it common for careful founders to self-fund the seed round themselves, get the first product finished, and then go after venture capital. Software startups were typical. But venture capitalists told us that for purposes of flexibility and control, VC firms generally do not want the clutter and complication of commercial loans to the entrepreneur in the capital structure of a company after the VCs have entered the picture.

The entrepreneur who has decided to go on without venture capital backing will find the personal loan to be a limited source of funds for starting a company. In our research we found that loans from commercial banks to individuals were made primarily to the sole proprietorships and closely held companies, but rarely to the high tech startup. And a track record was strongly preferred, with an active, healthy business in operation, and with good customers and their receivables on the books. Home equity loans were often mentioned by the entrepreneurs who told us how they had done it. Bankers always want some security to fall back on to repay their loan in case of trouble.

The Personal Cost.   The entrepreneur must be sure to count the cost before doing any personal borrowing, especially if the family home is put up as security for a bank loan. A spouse may not be able to stand the strain of waiting to see whether you will lose or keep the house, and if you do forfeit the house, the kids would have to relocate in the middle of their school year. This adds to the stress of the already hard job of launching a complex company successfully, and an entrepreneur may not want to add such problems to an already full bag. More than 60 percent of the funded companies go bankrupt, and Dun and Bradstreet says that, according to its extensive records on nearly every business in the United States, small businesses are seldom successful.

Government-Backed Loans

Congress has several active small business loan programs. Any commercial banker can provide details about them. They are intended to reduce the risk to the banker in loaning money to a company. There is however, a big gap between the intent and the practice. To get such a loan, one must go through an ocean of paperwork, forms, and time-consuming work, and the outcome is far from guaranteed.

Because of these conditions, one should be careful about counting on federally backed loans in a financing plan. Venture capital has worked successfully for many good reasons. The commercial banker will have good advice about the tradeoffs in the alternative sources of capital for a company.

Small Business Administration (SBA).   There is a bureaucracy in Washington, D.C. that was created to promote good things for small businesses. We could not find a single use of it in famous startups or in the interviews of companies we have dealt with over the years since this research started in 1981.

However, anyone determined to start on his own should seek all the help available. We did find that the commercial banker was the source most familiar with what help might be obtained from the SBA.

Inc. magazine is full of examples of startups that got going without classic venture capital sources. Every issue makes suggestions on where to go for alternative sources of funds. Such reading is probably much more beneficial than government-generated documents.

SBICs and MESBICs.   These are abbreviations for two organizations that operate under federal legislation to encourage equity capital investments in small companies. The SBA licenses SBICs under state laws. The SBA adds capital to that raised by the owners of the SBIC, which makes equity and loan investments in small companies. It all started in 1958, intended to fill a shortage of capital for small companies. A MESBIC is a cousin to the SBIC.

Some early venture capitalists got started as SBICs and some still exist and are active. We found that most SBICs are affiliated with a commercial bank holding company, so the friendly commercial banker is again the best information source. Several of the guides to venture capital firms list SBICs next to the venture capital firms.

Mom and Dad and Other Friendly Bankers

Many startups got going with cash from Mom and Dad or from relatives; some say that is what really got Microsoft started. After we did some checking, we found that it was the startup classified as a "bootstrap" that used this source of funds most often.

Classic venture capitalists and their lawyers are wary of having to get permission from investors that they view as unsophisticated. The phrase *sophisticated investor* is intended to classify the type of investor who knows what he is doing, has a large net worth, and has invested a lot in a wide variety of companies. In the course of getting a company off the ground, it may be neccessary to make big changes and obtain refinancing, and the small investors who put their money in because of a personal relationship may have trouble dealing with these changes. The laws of each state are restrictive about what the big "sophisticated" investor can do to the so-called widows and children who invested their life savings in the first round of financing; for example, they are prevented from writing down all investors' stock to near zero value, and reinvesting fresh cash in the hope of turning the company around at last. And VCs do not relish having to kick the CEO out in case of trouble and then face the wrath of a few small investors that are the CEO's friends and relatives.

We asked the successful and unsuccessful company CEOs what their advice was in these cases. The consensus was that the entrepreneur should stick to seeking funds from only those investors who can afford to lose all the money invested in the company. In fact, some high tech attorneys insist that such a warning be sent in writing to each potential investor. The entrepreneur must listen to and follow the advice of his attorney in all these cases. Just *mentioning* an investment possibility to an individual starts the meter ticking in many state small investor protection laws. In order to stay out of trouble, the entrepreneur must know what can be said to whom and how often.

It is also important to realistically count the cost: What kind of damage would be done to family relationships if all the savings of one's family and parents were lost because the entrepreneur's company failed? How would a spouse feel? And what about the kid's college expenses?

Bootstraps

A word on bootstraps. These are companies started by a few founders who decided to fund the whole company with their (or other individuals') personal money. They are famous in the folklore of the high tech startup business because they smack of the cowboy in all of us, and have the romance (and revenge) of the rebel who showed the world that the founders could indeed succeed in spite of everyone else's lack of faith in their wild and wonderful idea and themselves.

Bootstraps that make it big in the high tech world are rare. Yet they are yet another case of the great American dream and should not be ruled out as impractical.

Case Study: Dell Computer

As a word of realistic hope, remember Dell Computer of Austin, Texas. According-ing to Business Week, *Michael Dell "launched his business at age 19 from a University of Texas dorm room. His strategy—selling IBM-compatible comput-ers through the mail to customers who were reluctant to pay computer-store prices—was an instant success."*

Dell got started in 1984 as a bootstrap. Only when growth exploded did he sell a portion of his company to later-stage venture sources so that he could grow the company to IPO size. IPO was in 1988.

In 1991 Dell Computer was an international operation, employing 2,100 people and generating 40 percent of its sales overseas. Chairman Dell's 35 per-cent ownership of the stock of the company, which had $500 million in annual sales, was worth $200 million. This is a classic bootstrap, a true example of how a smart CEO saw an opportunity in the market and self-funded his bootstrap to success.

For further bootstrap ideas, get your hands on a September 1991 copy of *Inc.* magazine. It features an article titled: "Great Companies That Were Started with $1,000 or Less: The Secrets of Bootstrapping."

Personal Savings

Without realizing it, most startup founders use a lot of their personal savings to get their company started, even if they do not self-fund a single round of capital themselves.

The founder must first be prepared to finance the time between leav-ing an employer and getting the first paycheck from the funded startup. And he must be prepared to absorb the cost of a cut in pay, particularly if the founder is an upper-level executive of a large corporation. Finally, those first legal expenses and marketing reports often come out of the founders' bank accounts.

And if the founder decides to gamble his savings on the seed round (or more) of the startup, it is necessary to plan on how to deal with the adverse effects of the company's getting into trouble, such as missing payroll for a month or two. The founder must be prepared to lose it all—that's the nature of risk in a startup, no matter how well he or she plans and believes in it.

In the next chapter we will further discuss the role for corporations as venture capitalists and how to raise funds from wealthy individuals. As the 1990s began, large amounts of fresh venture funds were arriving in the United States from Asia. And there was a clear resurgence of funding from wealthy individuals. These and alternative, "small" stock exchanges will be reviewed to show the pros and pitfalls of using such alternatives to fund your startup.

12

Other Sources of Venture Capital

We spoke with a lot of founders whose initial plan was to "get a big company or a few rich guys to finance us, at least for the start." Their goal was to avoid the more sophisticated venture capitalists and thereby retain a higher proportion of ownership of their company.

Our research revealed that the trouble with that plan is that it is very hard to attract such funds in amounts large enough to adequately fund a solid startup. Even worse, according to a few of the CEOs who had to live with these investors, they often proved to be far from naive, and the percentage the founders gave up was often larger than what other conventionally funded, comparably sized companies gave up.

Raising funds from individuals must be done according to strict rules laid down in each state by the government body that controls the issuing of securities. A good attorney is necessary for anyone who decides to go this route.

Let's take a look at various nontraditional sources of funding.

"Old 49ers" Who Struck It Rich

There is one type of individual investor who some startups have found
can be an acceptable source of funds. These are people from the high tech
industry who have made it big in another startup and are actively
searching for a similar company—one they can understand—in which to
invest their earnings.

Three to six such investors can usually fund the seed round; they are
often people who have known each other over several years. These
people are found in very private circles, not in offices or at venture capital firms. They are found by asking the people who are in contact with
such business successes—a friendly banker, your accounting firm, a
startup consultant, and CEOs of other companies.

If this type of private investor investigates the startup and chooses not
to invest, he can often lead you to a favorite venture capital firm where
your work with the individual will accelerate the due diligence process.

Startup veterans tell us they believe such people make good board
members and that they drive just as hard a bargain as the venture
capitalists.

"Angels": Sophisticated Nontech Pools of Money

Worlds of Wonder got started with capital from a pool that is not run by
an investor specializing in high tech investments. Family fortunes made
in Masonite wood products, oil, and paper have funded several new
enterprises. We found numerous examples of such investors seeking out
high tech startups in order to get higher returns on their capital.

The track record for these investors is not public, so we could not determine how likely they will be to stick with a startup as a long-term investor in high tech startups. We suggest that the entrepreneur look for
them at the same time they search for classic venture capital. Try to get a
bit of competition working, and then choose from the best of the lot.

Asian and European Sources

Since 1983, foreign capital has entered the U.S. money markets in huge
quantities. The venture capital industry has seen a regular increase in
funds from Europe and Japan, as well as from the Middle East and
Southeast Asia, particularly Hong Kong and Taiwan.

These funds are mainly entering one of two channels of investment.
The first channel is that of the limited partnerships of the venture capital
firms. VCs spend a lot of time enjoying Europe and lately Asia as part of
their treks to raise more capital.

The second channel is direct investment in startups by the larger foreign corporations. Fortune 500 companies in Europe and Japan have started and continue to make diverse equity investments in U.S. startups. One of the most famous is Chips and Technologies. Over the past five years the trend is for such monies to enter the later stages of funding for a startup.

Foreign investors can be found mainly through personal contacts who work with foreign business people. Trust is required to an even greater degree than when working with American businesses—the trust that comes from working together over long periods of time. Personal introductions help, but we were told in our interviews to warn startup companies to expect little enthusiasm for an unknown American seeking capital for an untested idea.

Foreign companies are active in merger and acquisition activity, especially, in recent years, the Japanese. If, for example, a small startup needs capital to launch a second product family, and the company has already established its position as a producer of high tech products, the CEO will be better able to attract foreign sources of capital than at the seed round. According to the people with whom we spoke, the prices to be paid were fair and the negotiators used U.S. measures of worth.

With the good comes the bad. One case study that we found sobering was that of Tony LaPine. In a *Forbes* article (August 10, 1987) on how LaPine was "lured by the siren song of strategic alliances," the story is told of how corporate investors in the form of Kyocera Corporation and other Japanese firms put up $2 million and built an $8.4 million plant in Japan to make LaPine's disk drives. The strategic alliance was arranged by the lead investor, Prudential-Bache. It started with good intentions, but new product deliveries and investors' payments went sour and so did the deal. It then took an even worse turn when LaPine and all but a handful of his 100 employees were dismissed, leaving the technology in the hands of investors.

Other deals have been very successful, including many quietly acquired companies that did not get up enough steam to get to the IPO stage.

We recommend that any decision to go after foreign capital be tempered with the reality that it is just like other venture capital: there is no free lunch. According to the skeptics, foreign investors can in fact be as dangerous to work with as the nearby venture capitalists. Some experienced CEOs highly endorse the use of foreign capital. We suggest that the CEO be cautious, and not leave out consideration of classic venture capital.

Corporate Venture Capital: Fortune 500 Companies

Many startup CEOs feel strongly that an alliance with a strong corporate giant will help them get ahead of the pack and into a leadership position, and that their startup will be more likely to succeed.

We found many examples of this in the genetic engineering industry, and in a growing number of deals done within the electronics sector. Almost every genetic engineering company has some corporate partner. In electronics, investment deals between high tech startups and domestic giants like IBM, General Motors, Raytheon, and Kodak—as well as foreign companies like Siemens and Olivetti and Nixdorf—have been common over the past decade. More recently, deals have been cut with Japanese, Korean, and Taiwanese conglomerates.

Our sources told us that they have learned a number of lessons over the past years, based on the results from startups that worked with corporate investors. This advice can help the CEO plan a wise strategy for raising capital:

- *Corporations make good operating partners.* They are operations and technology biased; they are not focused on maximizing the ROI of their investment in your company. Their experience at running similar high tech businesses may be of considerable advisory assistance when a startup runs into trouble.

- *Corporate pricing of deals is less expensive.* People interviewed said they believed that corporate venture capitalists often set shares at price levels somewhat below those of the typical venture capitalist. Corporate investors have less pressure to get rich on the startup company because they have more interest in the startup's technology than in its potential wealth.

- *Corporate deals can be dangerous.* Several founders told us they lost their jobs, their technology, and their companies when the corporate investors' bread-and-butter businesses got into trouble, and the investors put a freeze on all funds, including the promised next round for the starving startup.

- *Venture capitalists prefer to invest without corporate venture capital.* VCs prefer to keep corporations out until nearly IPO time or unless a big sales deal can be done between the startup and the corporate investor as part of the investment transaction. Part of the reasoning for this is similar to the VCs' bias against working with the CEO's relatives as investors—their goals are too different. VCs also tend to believe that corporate investors generally underprice a deal.

- *Corporate investors take longer to decide.* Venture capitalists can act much faster because they do not have to wait for the next quarterly board meeting or public shareholders' meeting to call for a vote on the investment.

- *Corporate deals can be very complex.* A sales deal for a thousand systems or to license a company's next technology can sound great, but the legal work may cos~ months of precious time before the deal is concluded. Contingert deals and deals linking equity pricing to units that may—or may not—be purchased by the corporate investor are sophisticated contracts, requiring skilled lawyers who often must travel halfway around the globe in order to get the deal documented and ready to sign.

■ *Corporate partners can greatly increase credibility.* For example, Sun Microsystems learned this lesson quickly when Kodak became a committed buyer and later an equity investor. Another example is Metaphor, which was having a hard time getting going until P&G stepped in; later, IBM appeared with a big technology and money deal.

■ *Corporate board members are more patient than VCs.* Several CEOs strongly held this opnion. Their contention was that corporate representatives are more humane or patient than the VCs are. They translated this to mean that the CEO would probably be allowed to stay on the job longer with corporate investors on the board than when VCs are the sole source of funding.

This advice represents the consensus of those we talked to. Each corporate investor has its own character, just as each VC firm does. The deans of the venture firms are eagerly sought after by experienced startup CEOs. Each investor should be carefully reviewed. The corporate investor must be evaluated as carefully as the VC—don't blindly assume that our advice will hold in every specific corporate situation. The priorities of the corporate investor candidates must be determined so that the CEO can find a good fit with the startup's capital-raising plan. There are pros and cons, but corporate investors may have an important role to play in a startup's capital formation plan. Such a generalization is difficult to substantiate, and was denied by several successful CEOs. Whatever the case, be forewarned.

Securities Registration and Legal Limitations

We strongly advise entrepreneurs not to raise a penny of investment capital from another party until legal counsel experienced in such matters has been consulted. There are carefully created laws governing the process of raising money, because the public has so often been cheated in the past by unscrupulous people.

A good securities attorney will be able to steer the entrepreneur clear of the land mines. It's impossible even to call a few friends up on the phone to solicit their money without falling under some aspect of securities law. Well-intended founders have often created a bag of snakes for a professional attorney and for sophisticated investors by hustling a lot of people for funds, leaving a trail of green investors eager for their "first killing," and a wide-ranging collection of warrants and other contingent securities behind for the newcomers to clean up. That kind of behavior has killed deals with top VC firms.

Stock Exchanges As Sources of Venture Capital

During the 1980s a new interest arose in attempts to use small public stock exchanges to raise venture capital. According to our research, there are several reasons for this:

- Capital raised in a public offering is believed to be cheaper than private capital.
- Larger amounts of capital can be raised from the public than from private pools of capital.
- Members of the board of directors can be selected without including venture capitalists.
- Entrepreneurs have succeeded in using public stock exchanges to raise venture capital.
- Investors seem to remain eager to invest in private deals floated over the exchanges.

The NASDAQ has been used by blue chip venture firms and their genetic engineering companies to raise capital for companies that have not yet become profitable or who have nothing to sell but R&D contracts and licenses. But there are four other public stock exchanges that are more often mentioned as alternatives to venture capital: Denver, Vancouver, London, and lately Taiwan.

Denver Stock Exchange. The very low price per share stocks, called "penny stocks," have occurred on the NASDAQ as IPOs from time to time, but the Denver Stock Exchange is the clear leader in this category, notorious for its flouting of SEC rules and for the many hucksters who have landed in jail and returned to the same business (selling penny stocks) shortly after serving their sentence. *Forbes* magazine regularly warns investors of the scams, as do other watchers of the securities industries. The title of an article in the June 29, 1987, issue of *Forbes* was:

Crime Wave
Yes, the SEC is nailing fat-cat insider traders. But meanwhile, outright crooks, big and small, prey on the investing public almost with impunity. Are the laws inadequate? Or the cops?

The article speaks for itself. In our research, we found no famous startups that used this source of venture capital. We advise you to avoid it.

Vancouver Stock Exchange. Since 1985, there has been a rising interest in the Vancouver, Canada, stock exchange, and investment activity there has grown. A number of stories about the Vancouver Stock Exchange have appeared in popular publications.

Vancouver is an exchange where a startup company can sell shares while it is still in the development stages of life, and have middlemen tout the company's business plan until it gets to the selling stages and beyond. It acts as a kind of stock market for private deals, actively trading on the basis of the uncertainty of a company's realizing some, all, or more of the goals in its five-year plan.

Many small companies have raised millions per issue, and some, including a few high tech startups, have become successful.

However, CEOs are strongly advised to get the best help possible to protect them from running afoul of the law and securities regulations. And it will consume a lot of the CEO's time to answer the new investors' questions on how the startup is coming along.

Most people we spoke to consider Vancouver to be just a step less controversial than the Denver Stock Exchange. Journal articles are sobering in their reviews of the speculation, manipulation, and dangers of Vancouver. We advise alternatives. Anyone who insists on taking a look must proceed with caution, including consultation with one of the better CPA firms and a reputable law firm.

London, Taiwan, and Other Foreign Stock Exchanges. By 1985, the entrepreneurial fever in America had spread to Europe, and London became the leading European stock exchange for IPOs. Learning of the much more lucrative fees charged by Wall Street firms, Europeans began to become less like closed clubs, with the attendant inefficiencies, and started to compete with Wall Street as a source of world-class capital, including capital for startups. European investment bankers were looking for IPO deals as an additional source of income. During the 1980s, this has resulted in several U.S. startups going public *before* they had their U.S. IPO. By 1990, the Taiwan stock exchange was booming, but claimed few high tech IPO success stories.

Opinions about the rationale for this varied a great deal among the observers with whom we have spoken. One venture capitalist who supported the strategy of using London for IPOs argued that investors had learned of the U.S. successes of IPOs, and that demand exceeded the supply; ergo, doing a London IPO would fetch better prices than in the States. We have found no research to either confirm or deny that hypothesis.

One respected Wall Street firm said that the founders of the U.S. company he took public in London were greatly afraid of robbers and kidnappers, believing that an offshore offering that made them wealthy would attract less attention than a U.S. IPO.

As for the rest of Europe and the world, the French and other exchanges in Europe and Asia are making progress in getting up to the level of capability in London. In a few years they may be competing with London for IPO deals.

Other reasons for non-U.S. IPOs included: the startup had large investors headquartered in the region; the startup did considerable business in regional countries; or the founders were born and raised in neighboring countries where investors would possibly be more likely to identify with the founders' original country of birth.

We concluded that an IPO offering on the London Stock Exchange would be a better choice than on other European stock exchanges. London firms did warn us that certain restrictions on IPOs might be required that could be avoided in a U.S. offering. Taiwan remains a hotbed of speculative investing.

Potential Problems and Pitfalls

The personal lust to do the dream startup with clever financing can become both the energy that pulls it off and the cause of doing something very unwise to raise funding. Desperation to succeed can create demands on individuals that result in actions that border on the foolish or even the illegal.

When problems occur between founders and potential investors, we often find that the idea behind the startup was not realistic relative to other startup alternatives that investors had. Competition for money pools exists every day. As every ballplayer has learned, some days it is best to head for the showers and get ready for the next game rather than continue a clearly losing cause.

When there are too many private investors the situation can become unmanageable for a small company. The entrepreneur may find himself spending large amounts of time with investing relatives—way beyond the obligation he imagined when he first thought of ask for their money.

Mixtures of other types of investors may prove unwieldy. We have found that successful investment deals are usually marked by simplicity, and urge the entrepreneur to try for the least complex deal structures possible. Based on the experiences of those we interviewed, we doubt that more than two of the alternative sources of capital we have described here can be successfully mixed.

13

Wall Street and the Initial Public Offering

When it's time for your initial public offering, you—the successful entrepreneur who has made it through all stages of startup funding and of getting your product to market—must look to Wall Street. In this chapter we will look at how investment bankers are ranked for high tech companies, their role in the IPO, what and who motivates them, and how rich they can get from an IPO. You will learn how to choose the best investment banker for your company.

The IPO is explained in detail, particularly how to time it, how to conform to securities laws, and how to price it, including how to apply some financial technology. We'll also look at the question, "What should we do after the IPO?"

The chapter includes lessons from the IPO trenches, specifically from details about the actual Microsoft IPO. Microsoft faced all the key issues that a startup's CEO and CFO must deal with at IPO time.

New Issues and IPOs

"New issue" is the term applied to the first offering of stock of a new company, while IPO stands for "initial public offering." They are two terms from the jargon used in the special investment world that high tech industry observers talk about so often. This world is filled with glamour, glory, and a great deal of work for participants, who plan to make a ton of money when the IPO is completed.

This is the stage at which investment bankers enter the world of the startup. The investment banker is in charge of the process that results in a single transaction that causes a flurry of activity in a startup.

The most significant change for the CEO and the startup company is being in the public limelight. Now the media are interested in the company and its leadership, and they request many time-consuming interviews, which takes up the time of the CEO and his or her staff.

The Wall Street security analysts enter the picture, taking up even more time for interviews than the media.

All this activity has a single objective: to attract and retain the institutional investors who will buy and hold the newly issued shares of the company. The analysts forecast the financial outcomes, the investors listen to their prognostications, place their bets, and wait for the company's results.

Institutional investors are looking for new issues that will get them a higher return than they can get by trading stocks on one of the major stock exchanges: National Association of Securities Dealers Automated Quotations (NASDAQ), Over the Counter (OTC), or the New York Stock Exchange (NYSE). The risk to investors in new issues is high, because the investment jungle is filled with hot speculators and rapidly moving stock prices. The number of shares available for purchase in a company already on the stock exchange is a tiny fraction compared to the number of shares that can be purchased in a new issue startup, which means that the liquidity risk is much higher for an IPO investor. The business risk is also higher, and therefore a higher return is required to attract investors.

Forbes, Business Week, Inc. magazine, and the *Wall Street Journal*—as well as a lot of newsletters for investors who specialize in IPOs—also cover the new issues market, and their articles make for instructive, sobering reading. Annual reviews and regular IPO articles appear in them, including these headlines from our random collection of clippings over the past six years:

> **Stellar performances of companies in *Venture's* Fast-Track 100 chart have Wall Street under a spell.**

> **When the going gets good, the good go public.** But even in a hot IPO market, there are precautions entrepreneurs and investors must take.

Wall Street Goes Public. Last year, we told you investors were looking for proven management and a history of solid performance. Well, they changed their minds.

From Harleys to Teddy Bears, everybody's going public. The explosion of new stocks is astounding—and investors keep snapping them up.

Smart Money. IPOs: It can pay to have second thoughts first.

Hot, hot, plop. Investment bankers set records in the new-issue market. Investors did not do as well.

Stacked Odds. Here's a tip on playing the stocks in the steaming new-issue market boom. But with the investment tip come important caveats.

Over the years we have found that the new issues market takes on fads and fancies, just like other investment markets. There is an enduring interest in high tech companies because of the belief that they have an above-average chance of growing much more rapidly than other corporations. This means that the investors in such companies will become richer than if they had invested in low tech companies. The wisdom of this investment strategy is debated daily in the investment circles of Wall Street institutional investors, who range from endowment managers at universities to pension and mutual fund managers.

All this interest in an IPO puts the pricing of one share of stock into a new zone of financial estimation, scrutiny, techniques, and limits. Publicly traded stocks are compared with the recent IPO's stock to get relative pricing comparisons. Techniques for placing a price on a share of the IPO company's stock range from very crude to very sophisticated, and all this methodology receives the cold test of reality in the real world of stocks that are bought and sold every minute. This is a far cry from the much more private world of the startup.

At times investors lose most of their money and become angry, believing they were misled by the company and its IPO helpers. The result is a lawsuit. Some companies associated with these legal actions are well known to media readers. In the August 10, 1987, issue of Business Monday, the *San Jose Mercury News* reported on 14 Silicon Valley companies whose shareholders hit them with lawsuits alleging that investors were misled during stock offerings in the 1982-1983 bull stock market. Four of the defendants made settlements that totaled $50.3 million. In early 1990 several very successful high tech darlings "hit the wall," slowed their growth unexpectedly, and their stock prices crashed. Oracle and a half dozen others were quickly sued by lawyers specializing in such lawsuits. Most of these legal actions were against established companies, ones that had gone public long ago. But the message is clear: Do not try to get public money if bad news is just around the corner. It is dangerous to try to raise money just before bad news becomes public.

The underlying, fundamental problem is the danger of investing in a "shooting star"—a company that gets going well, goes public, but has no staying power and sinks into mediocre financial performance shortly after IPO. It is no wonder that veterans of IPOs with whom we spoke talked a lot about "juryproof prospectuses" and "D&O" (directors and officers) insurance.

Now let's turn to the process of going public, starting with the investment bankers.

The Role of the Investment Banker

The investment banker will take the central leadership role at the time a company decides to do its first public offering of stock. It is the investment banker and his firm that will gather the lawyers, the analysts, and the many others who are needed to do the work for the IPO. The documents must comply with sophisticated securities laws. The behind-the-scenes workload is enormous and very time-consuming, requiring intense amounts of effort from a lot of people inside and outside the company. The process is complicated and must be done well. The investment banker is hired and paid a very large sum of money as a fee to ensure that the deal is done successfully by all the individuals involved. This job is akin to that of a shepherd herding a flock of sheep to market.

How Investment Bankers Are Organized.   Robertson Stephens & Company is a San Francisco-based Wall Street firm that began its successful rise by helping high tech startups go public. An examination of its organization demonstrates what the investment banker really does. The organization consists roughly of the following kinds of people:

- *A pool of new business employees* who call on private companies to screen them and discuss their interest in taking the company public. These specialized sales people ("new business" managers) are usually the CEO's first contacts with the investment banking firm.

- *The corporate finance staff* of the investment banker. This group stands prepared to arrive at the startup to do the work required after the CEO chooses their firm to do the IPO.

- The *research staff*, people who investigate the startup once the firm is chosen. They give an independent opinion of the company's quality, and the risk and potential of good financial results over the next year or so.

- The *syndication staff*, which assembles a group of other Wall Street firms to insure (underwrite) the IPO so that the risk of the deal can be diversified. Each member signs up to share in supplying capital to back the deal. That group is called the "underwriters."

■ The *sales department*, which consists of stockbrokers who offer the new stock to investors, mainly institutional investors. These people are called "institutional sales people."

■ The *traders* are those who make a market for the stock by trading it, buying and selling shares in various quantities each minute of the day.

All together, all the people mentioned above make up the organization called an investment banking firm. They are also known as stockbrokers and Wall Street firms.

There are many variations of this organizational structure, depending on the various securities that a firm decides to try to make a profit on. For instance, Montgomery Securities has its own venture capital business that invests along with the classic venture capitalists. Other firms have merger and acquisition departments or departments that make markets in stocks of much larger companies. The giants of Wall Street, such as Goldman Sachs, are full-service organizations that offer virtually any security-related service to investors.

Investment banking firms make money in various ways, including charging fees equal to a percentage of the money raised for an IPO. In a good year, the owners of these firms make many millions of dollars per person, and exceed even the league of riches that venture capitalists range in.

This is a service industry, and the competition is fierce and intense. There is much drama in the behind-the-scenes power plays and politics among Wall Street firms, venture capitalists, and members of the boards of directors of startup companies. On the other hand, investment bankers try never to miss a chance to do an attractive deal and are therefore rarely confrontational. As one observer told us, "They are always trying to be very polite to everybody."

Differentiating Investment Banking Firms. Investment bankers are like venture capitalists: each person has a distinctive character, and collectively these people make up a firm's unique approach to the business. There are several distinctions that are important to you and your company. The most important is the firm's track record with new issues, as distinct from its experience in raising capital for much larger, more mature companies. We have assembled lists of investment bankers based on those we found most often mentioned as participating in IPO stock offerings of high tech companies. Table 13-1 lists those firms that have done a lot of IPO business over the years; they are presented in rank order, based upon several selection criteria, mainly volume and

TABLE 13-1.   Ranking of Investment Bankers for Emerging Companies

(Based on interviews of CEOs and CFOs of new high tech enterprises and the number and size of IPO deals done in 1985 through 1990)

1.   Goldman, Sachs & Co.
2.   Morgan Stanley
3.   Robertson Stephens & Company
4.   Alex Brown & Sons
5.   Hambrecht & Quist
6.   Montgomery Securities
7.   Merrill Lynch
8.   Kidder Peabody
9.   Paine Webber
10. Cowen & Company

Source: Saratoga Venture Finance

reputation as quality high tech IPO investment bankers. And *Forbes* frequently notes that the following regional firms have often done IPOs that outperformed those done by the bigger firms:

Keefe, Bruyette & Woods

Piper Jaffray Hopwood

Robinson Humphrey(division of Shearson Lehman)

Dain Bosworth

Morgan Keegan

Some distinctions are worth noting:

■ *Rising stock prices do not necessarily mean a good investment banker did the deal.* A big rise in the stock price after the IPO was finished does not necessarily mean the offering was a success. If the rise is too large, the underwriter badly misjudged the market and cost the company millions of dollars that was given away to new investors at the expense of the startup's employees and private round investors.

■ *Smaller, regional firms should not be ruled out.* They often have better track records than the larger high tech specialists or the giants of Wall Street.

■ *Competition and the movement of professionals from one firm to another have caused changes in the leadership of the firms that do a lot of IPOs.* In the 1970s, the most often mentioned IPO firms for high tech companies consisted of the venerable Hambrecht & Quist, Alex Brown of Baltimore, Robertson Colman & Stephens of San Francisco, and L. F. Rothschild, Unterberg and Tobin. The arrival in the early 1980s of

Goldman Sachs, Morgan Stanley, and other big names from Wall Street increased the competition for IPOs, and the rankings have since shifted considerably.

- Choosing an investment banker for a firm should be done carefully, using several criteria, only one of which is the rankings shown in Table 13-1.

How Investment Bankers Make Money

A CEO can do a better job of negotiating and managing the investment bankers if he or she understands how the investment banking firm makes its money on taking a company public. The "fee" that is charged by the investment banking firm is actually not one fee, but a collection of fees granted to various members of the syndicate that team up to take a company public. The name or names on the front cover of the prospectus share the "management fee" for what is called "running the books." This is more than a policeman or accountant type of duty. Those investment bankers have worked hard to get accepted as the lead underwriters and have agreed to be held responsible for the degree of success of the offering. They grant the rest of the syndicate the privilege of participating in sharing the fee.

The number one position is granted to the firm whose name appears on the left side of the prospectus cover. Although the management fee is often equally shared by the two or three firms on the cover that choose to co-manage the deal, the left-hand position gains reputation and prestige for that firm, particularly for influencing the next IPO candidate company's CEO with respect to how capable the firm is.

The underwriting fee, which in the case of Microsoft, for example, was $732,290, is shared by the long list of firms that have put up a portion of their firm's capital as a sort of guarantee to back the deal. The fee is split in proportion to the amount of capital the firm agrees to put up to back the deal. This is the least profitable of the investment banking activities, because it is used to cover expenses and is involved in stabilizing the price of the stock in its first days of trading. Bankers regularly spend more than this fee covers.

The best way for the syndicate to make a great deal of money is to sell as much of the stock as possible. Aggression is extreme among the sales staffs of the firms. The goal is to outsell everyone, regardless of size, and to capture as much of the selling fee—which equals about 60 percent of the whole fee—as is possible. The bankers we interviewed told us that some pretty wild dealing takes place when shares allocated to one firm that cannot sell all of its shares are offered to other firms that have obtained orders for more than their allotments.

Greenshoe. Greenshoe is an option (to buy stock at a fixed price), which is given by the IPO company to the investment bankers doing the IPO. For instance, Sun Microsystems granted a 30-day option to their investment bankers, co-led by Robertson Stephens & Company, to purchase up to 600,000 shares at the IPO price.

Unlike the underwriting contract for the IPO shares, which obligates the underwriters to buy all the IPO shares at the IPO price, there is no obligation to the investment bankers to purchase any of these additional shares.

In effect, this is a "bonus" to the underwriters, because if the aftermarket price rises to above the IPO price within 30 days, then the underwriters may purchase the extra shares at the lower IPO price, sell them to investors at the higher market price, and pocket the difference as a profit. For instance, the Sun shares were offered at $16.00 each. A 20 percent increase in 30 days to $19.25 would mean $1,950,000 in additional profit for the underwriters, in addition to their fee of $3,920,000—a 50 percent boost!

Greenshoe economics clarify some of the reasons that investment bankers try to price IPO shares so that their price increases quickly by a significant amount in the aftermarket.

The Cost of Doing an IPO

Investment bankers first sign a company to an exclusive contract to do the IPO. The contract includes charging the company for certain of the expenses they incur in doing the deal, plus a percentage of the total capital raised. The expenses can easily be $500,000 for a $25 million offering. The "underwriters' commission" or "investment banker's fee" is in the vicinity of 6 percent to 12 percent of the total offering, including any capital sold in the IPO by selling shareholders.

These expenses are probably the most costly a startup ever incurs because, under federal and state tax laws, none of them are tax deductible. Thus, if the combined tax rate were 42 percent for a company, an 8 percent fee (including expenses) would be the equivalent of 14 percent pretax cost of money!

The fee is negotiated between the company and the investment banking firm. It includes many subsets of fees, each composing a pool for many participants doing many tasks. They are broken down into two main groups: the fee of the investment banker and all the other expenses. These are discussed in detail below.

Details of IPO Expenses. To start with, assume a startup chooses to raise $10 million in a small IPO, with all the capital going to the company and no selling shareholders. The costs for such an offering would be about 9 percent to 12 percent of the $10 million raised. The exact amount of expenses depends on three factors:

1. The *size of the deal*. The larger deals have the lower percentage costs, but the absolute dollars of expenses get very substantial.

2. The *degree of work* that lawyers and auditors must go through to clean up the books and records of the company and to convert them into a satisfactory prospectus.

3. The *amount of competition* between the investment bankers desiring to do an IPO and degree of difficulty they anticipate in selling investors on buying the stock offered by the company.

Table 13-2 contains a list of expenses for a new issue. It was compiled by an investment industry group that sought to issue a list of "typical costs" of going public. It is for a very small underwriting, $10 million.

IPO costs—as a percentage of the value of all the shares sold in the IPO—rise rapidly as the deal gets smaller. This occurs because the amount of work to raise $10 million is about the same as the amount of work to

TABLE 13-2. Typical Cost of a $10 Million IPO in 1987

Underwriters' commission		$850,000 (8.5%)
Other Expenses:		
Legal fees	$120,000	
Printing the prospectus	$90,000	
Accounting firm's fee	$80,000	
State registration (Blue Sky) expense	$20,000	
Stock transfer agent	$4,000	
SEC registration fee	$2,000	
National Association of Securities Dealers fee	$1,000	
All other expenses	$15,000	
Total Other Expenses		$332,000 (3.3%)
Total All Expenses		$1,182,000 (11.8%)
Total Capital Raised		$10,000,000 (100%)

Source: Grant Thornton, Capital Markets Group

raise $25 million. The top investment bankers will strongly advise a startup to raise as much as possible, in the region of $25 million. Of course this also increases the absolute dollars of fee or "commission" for the investment banker and syndicate.

The percentage represented by "Other Expenses" shown in Table 13-2 is larger than in most of the actual IPOs for the period 1985-1990 that we analyzed; this is largely because the IPOs we examined were mostly in the region of $25 million. It was not unusual for Other Expenses in the prospectuses we examined to total $500,000 or more, or about 2 percent of the capital raised. This was more consistent than we anticipated. We had hypothesized that these expenses were rather fixed, and not dependent on the amount of capital raised. But while our sample was small, our findings suggest that the participants— especially lawyers and accountants—may incur and bill their fees as some implicit percentage of the capital offered, just as the investment bankers do.

CEOs who have done IPOs recommend that a first-timer CEO should set and adhere to a budget for each item on the Other Expenses list, using the same level of judgment as for any other service supplied to a company. The amount of cash that could be saved by the company appears to be considerable, perhaps lowering the costs by as much as 20 percent.

Microsoft IPO.   Table 13-3 contains our estimates of the details of what made up the fee charged in one of the most famous IPOs in recent time, the Microsoft offering of March 13, 1986. IPOs since then, including those

TABLE 13-3. Economics of an Initial Offering: The Microsoft IPO

Size of Microsoft IPO	$58,695,000		
×			
Total fee of whole investment banking group	× 6.24%		6.240%
Total financing fee =	$ 3,661,450		
Total financing fee	$ 3,661,450		
×			
Proportion for the managers who are "running the books"; "Names on the front cover of the prospectus"	× 20%	=	1.248%
Management fee (Often split equally between the managers) =	$ 732,290 /2	=	$366,145/mgr

(Continued)

TABLE 13-3.   Economics of an Initial Offering: The Microsoft IPO (continued)

Total financing fee	$ 3,661,450			
×				
Underwriting fee for syndicate of underwriters		× 20%	=	1.248%
Underwriters' fee	$ 732,290			
×				
Proportion for each underwriter set by number of shares underwritten; Share for lead firm =	440,500 shares/2,795,000 all shares		=	15.76%
Lead firm's share of underwriters' fee	$ 115,409			

Total financing fee	$ 3,661,450			
×				
Fee for selling stock		× 60%	=	3.744%
Selling commission =	$ 2,196,870			
×				
Proportion for lead firm: Assume they sold 20% of the Microsoft IPO shares		× 20%		
Selling commission for lead firm =	$ 439,374			

SUMMARY

Total Fee		Lead Firm's Share (Estimated)
Managers		
$ 732,290	1.25%	$ 366,145
Underwriters		
$ 732,290	1.25%	$ 115,409
Sales		
$2,196,870	3.74%	$ 439,374
Total financing fee		
$ 3,661,450	6.24%	$ 920,928

Source: Saratoga Venture Finance

in 1990, show that similar results prevail today. The Microsoft deal shows the magnitude of one of the largest offerings seen in some time. In terms of percentages, it is therefore a good measure of the efficiency of the costs charged to a company going public. We would expect that a less famous company will have to pay higher percentages for an IPO fee (based on the Saratoga Venture Finance database, which contains information on the economics of IPOs).

Table 13-3 uses the Microsoft IPO as a basis for estimating the approximate fees received by each member of the investment banking group. Because the actual details are private, the data in the table is an estimate of the approximate compensation earned by one of the co-lead bankers, Goldman Sachs. Goldman is considered by most to be number one in equity deals in the world, and a firm of unequaled high character. The estimate is based on discussions with underwriters who were not in that deal, but that compete with one another for IPOs. The exact numbers are less important than the reader's appreciation for what motivates the investment banking group to behave as it does to earn the larger portion of the overall fee.

An analysis of the costs charged Microsoft reveal the following:

- The $58.7 million offering in this IPO is about double the size of the offerings of most other highly successful companies that went public during the same period of 1986. This suggests that the efficiency of the cash cost per dollar raised by the IPO company will go up as the size of the deal rises (if one uses percentages to measure efficiency).

- The fee of 6.24 percent was consistent with the range of fees charged in similar size offerings (Table 13-4). The split of the Microsoft fee shown in Table 13-3 is estimated. Actual fees, splits, and amounts are uniquely negotiated by participants in each deal, depending on several factors, mainly size of the IPO capital to be raised. A fee closer to 7 percent or higher would be more typical for a $25 million IPO.

- Fees can be negotiated downward some distance below any so-called normal range. The data in Table 13-4 support this contention, as do

TABLE 13-4. Fees Charged for Five High Tech IPOs

IPO	Capital Raised	Fee Charged Percent	Fee Charged $Millions
Alliant	$26.5M	6.9%	$1.8M
Convex	$23.5M	6.4%	$1.5M
Network Equipment	$40.0M	7.0%	$2.8M
Cypress Semiconductor	$67.5M	6.2%	$4.2M
Sun Microsystems	$64.0M	6.1%	$3.9M

data shown us by the investment bankers themselves. Competition works well in such negotiating situations. The CEO should set the target low and get agreement to it before signing the underwriting contract. In fact, it may be desirable to make the fee a primary determinant in choosing an investment banker.

- Not shown in Table 13-3 is a category called Other Expenses, which are in addition to the investment bankers' fee. For Microsoft, the total Other Expenses (for CPA firm, lawyers, and special prospectus printer) were $541,000, or 0.92 percent of capital raised.

- In the case of the Microsoft deal, we do not know exactly what the final fee was for everyone. But we believe we are pretty close in estimating that Goldman Sachs made about $1,000,000 on that offering. At the end of the day, everyone we spoke to said that they could appreciate how hard Goldman Sachs worked to earn its share of the fee.

- As for profit, it is much less than the calculated $3,661,450. Usually all of the portion called the underwriters' fee is used to pay expenses of doing the deal, supporting the trading in the stock, and the end is often a small loss on this portion of the deal. The selling commission requires paying for the costs of the personnel doing the work as well as their related overheads, as does the fee for running the books. The pretax bottom line for the deal was probably about $2 million, about half the gross fee of $3.7 million.

The Role of Institutional Investors

The power brokers in the world of publicly traded securities are institutional investors. That is also true for the IPO deals. Wealthy individuals are somewhat of a factor, but the giants are as dominant here as in the NASDAQ and New York stock exchanges.

Investment bankers work hard to be the firm that gets to place the purchase orders for the institutions that buy shares in a new issue. Salespeople told us that the competition for sales and trading commissions is fierce. Investment bankers are eager for the buying customer to make a gain on the IPO stock. Several individuals said they believed this desire causes a strong bias against overpricing the opening trading price of the stock of a new issue. The necessary role of the investment banker is to delicately balance a nice increase in the price of the stock of the new issue on the one hand against the danger of being embarrassed because of a wild upward surge in the stock's price in the aftermarket. Too much run-up and the selling company will be upset because it had to sell too many shares to get the funds it wanted; too little rise in the price and the buying institutions will be upset because they want to count on a solid price increase.

Although the company is paying the fee and expenses, the investment bankers are not really working for the company doing the IPO. Over the years they have changed to become oriented to very short-term transactions and not to long-term relationships. Many years ago, the investment banker sat on a company's board forever and advised it on financing strategies. Today the economic forces at work cause these bankers to race from deal to deal, concerned about how to make as much money as possible for their customers—the institutional investors who have billions to invest every day. Although the bankers try to retain and nurture long-term relationships, one can really expect most investment bankers interest in a company to be limited to the next deal that they can do for it. The competition in their business is fierce, and they must be on their way, chasing the next deal as soon as the current one is done. They have a short attention span. Some venture capitalists compared such behavior to that of used car salespeople and real estate brokers. We consider this remark unfair to the quality investment banker. Startups need strong Wall Street firms. This controversial situation presents additional problems in post-IPO relations with Wall Street, which we will discuss later in this chapter.

Together, the investment banker and the institutional investors are very powerful, and they can make a lot of money. *Financial World* magazine estimates that the 10 most highly paid Wall Street professionals—investment bankers or institutional money managers—earned an average of $68.8 million per person in 1986, and in 1991 we read of Wall Street partners earning in excess of $20 million per year. Such people represent a group that must be respected, one that must be incorporated into plans for a company's capital formation.

Choosing an Investment Banker

Choosing an investment banker is exciting. The choice involves making selections that are not black and white, but the right choice is important. The consensus of startup CEOs is that a good choice can make a large positive difference, while a poor choice can compromise a company's future well-being.

While a company is still private, the CEO will receive a few phone calls from new business professionals of investment banking firms. They are checking to see whether the company should be on their list of target accounts.

Once a company is on an investment banker's list, the CEO can expect to receive a lot of flattering attention, as will the members of its board of directors. The goal of the banker is to lock up the lead position, to become the designated manager who runs the books and thus earns a nice IPO fee. Because there is intense competition between firms for the handful of top IPOs each year, a CEO of a promising startup has an excellent starting point from which to begin the selection process.

For the company ready for an IPO, any of the top 20 Wall Street firms could get the job done. But just getting the money in the bank is not enough. After the IPO, someone has to help make a good market for the stock. The degree of attention by Wall Street investors is a direct function of the amount and quality of research reports written about a company by the underwriting firm's analysts. Furthermore, some firms have business reputations that a CEO would prefer to associate with or avoid. And board members will also have various opinions on which firm to choose.

Here is the advice of experienced high tech CEOs on choosing an investment banking firm:

- *Start by finding the best research analyst, one who understands the industry and technology.* This is the person who will interpret a technology and its business applications for the salespeople pushing the stock. It is also the person who will go on the "road show" with the CEO, when the CEO stands up before institutional investors to tout the company's good future. It is the analyst who will take precious time to write long reports about the company's chances of success and its products. A company's customers and employees will read those reports. Never pick an investment banker who lacks a top research analyst—one who is familiar with and respected as an analyst of the company's technology and who favors that industry. A CEO can easily identify the top analysts by conferring with an experienced CFO of a large public company in the same industry.

- *Pick a firm known for its integrity.* This is very important because of the abuses and poor service that some technologically astute but financially naïve companies have had over the past years. Most well-known firms have retained high reputations, but some have grown tarnished over the past four years. Presidents of some IPO companies have told us in strictest confidence of shockingly unethical misdeeds of the bankers who led their underwriting. The CEOs complained that their companies had suffered from the misuse of information and that post-IPO support dwindled to near zero. They also complained of questionable stock trades by bankers that they soon grew to mistrust. We concluded that the best check on investment bankers is to talk privately with the CEOs and CFOs who have done IPOs in bad times as well as good times. One can learn as much from the reasons a firm was *not* picked—or would not be picked for the next offering—as from the reasons it was chosen. Such work should be treated as seriously as a reference check of a key candidate for a vice presidency in the company.

- *Look for managers who are businesslike, people whom it would be desirable to work and be associated with.* As with picking an accounting firm, the CEO should be looking for character as well as competence. It is important to be methodical and thoughtful and to avoid being distracted by flattery. You want the best the company can attract. CEOs unfamiliar with the Wall Street crowd should start with the person who will manage the deal. It is important to look for characteristics that indicate the presence of a good businessperson, someone who can negotiate well on the founders' behalf, someone who can be trusted. One good way to find this person is to attend the many meetings and mini-conventions put on by investment bankers to expose the newest in high tech companies to institutional investors. Dinners and lunches over a period of a year or so are also advised. This is an important decision and should not be made in haste.

- *Compare statistics on IPO success and failures.* The post-IPO facts are important, as well as how many and how much capital was raised. The CEO should look for the bias of the banker; some have stronger retail and mutual fund customers than wholesale or institutional. The bankers themselves will each supply data, and the CEO can compare the facts presented by each firm. *Forbes* magazine and other publications also closely scrutinize IPO performance.

- *Be sure to check out how thoroughly the banker's research analyst followed and wrote about the IPOs that the firm took public.* Some CEOs told us of poor post-IPO service and were bitter about the "greediness" and "grab and run" attitudes of their bankers. CEOs with recent IPO experience can be helpful. The startup CEO should talk to them about their experiences with (or without) the finalists on the list for investment banker to the startup company. Note that analysts quite often move between firms; the analyst who did a good job for banker A may now work for banker B.

The importance of the analyst in selection of an investment banker is noted by Raymond Moran, Director of Research of Cowen and Company. Cowen regularly ranks in the top of the research lists of high tech institutional investors. Moran's comment reflects our findings as we spoke with CEOs who went through the IPO process:

> A research analyst with superior understanding of a client's business and needs improves the ability to better position the company and communicate its long-term value in a highly credible manner.

And here is the suggestion of one of the grand veterans of high tech IPOs, Sandy Robertson of Robertson Stevens in San Francisco:

> I recommend that CEOs looking for an IPO investment banker should seek a firm where everyone in the organization understands the company's

industry and business. This is especially important because an IPO is a chain of events—each critical to the success of the delicate IPO. Each person in the investment banking firm—corporate finance, research analyst, syndicate, sales, trading, and 144 stock administration—has to be successful when it is their time to carry the ball. To have a single expert in your high tech industry just won't get the job done. An IPO is too important to be left up to generalists or an individual. Everyone must be competent, experienced with high tech IPOs, able to team up, and do their part and do it well for the IPO to be a success. That is what to look for when picking your investment banker.

And finally, here is the advice of Goldman, Sachs & Co. to a CEO selecting an investment banker.

> The selection of an investment banker involves both near-term and long-term criteria. For the purposes of executing a successful IPO, the investment bank should be actively involved in leading a significant number of equity offerings of high-quality technology companies. The investment bank should have a strong research presence in technology in general and in the company's business in particular, and should provide active trading markets and significant distribution capabilites. Since the choice of an investment banker represents a commitment to a longer-term relationship as well, the banker's capabilities should also be able to accommodate a company's anticipated growing and changing needs. The firm should project a global presence that provides its clients with access to capital markets and other opportunities throughout the world. The investment bank should have capabilities, experience, and dedicated resources in the areas of mergers, acquisitions, joint ventures, and strategic alliances. In addition, the bank should be able to provide advice and expertise in areas that will likely become important over time, such as real estate/headquarters financing and foreign exchange. Finally, but very importantly, a CEO should feel comfortable with the members of the prospective investment banking team and its firm's long-standing commitment to technolgy and its clients.

The Initial Public Offering—The Holy Grail

A CEO will be better equipped to run a company while it is private if he or she understands how important the IPO event is to each participant in the IPO process. This perspective helps the CEO get the company tuned up and in good shape as it approaches the magic IPO date. This is an important part of planning, because the CEO may have to halt R&D expansion for a while or put on an extra heavy sales staff to boost revenues. The toughest decisions for the CEO will be to consider doing something that would be good in the short term for the IPO, but could be bad for the success of the company three years or so later.

Employees. Psychological research reveals that every one of us wants to belong to a group, preferably a successful one. The IPO creates just that situation, as well as creating a pool of wealth that employees can share in. In reality, only a few people make a financial killing as an employee, except in unusual conditions such as with Apple and the personal computer revolution. In fact, behavioral scientists note that, rather than actual wealth, the primary stimulant to people on payroll is the association of belonging to a company that is an observable winner.

These people want to believe: in themselves, in their leaders, and in the whole company as winners. This success orientation was borne out by our talks with doctors, psychologists, and family counselors at hospitals and clinics in Silicon Valley.

When a company finally goes public, the CEO is fully exposed and must live in the spotlight, explaining disappointments as well as achievements to a vast audience that tends to be highly critical of the company and its leadership. "The press seem to be looking for the negative more than the good results," lamented one CEO.

The management of employees goes a lot better when the stock price continues to rise; no one sells his or her stock then. But eventually the price will drop. Then the party comes to an end, and the reality of hard work returns. CEOs warned: "Too much IPO fever is like too much alcohol—it produces hangovers." When Microsoft got to IPO, Bill Gates was concerned that having the company's stock public would adversely distract employees.

Finally, the CEO should keep in mind that missing an IPO window can be very demoralizing to employees. It is hard to avoid building up expectations, but keeping the IPO dreams farther away than nearer is better than having to deal with a tired crew that has just had its balloon pop.

Founders. To the original core team, the IPO means a lot—especially as the reality sinks in and the bank account begins to grow in riches. Lives change. Families change. People change.

Some told us that the reward is having recognition and fame at last. To others it was the arrival at a peer level with some role model in the high tech world. Some people frankly said that it was pleasant to get revenge of sorts on the venture firms and business colleagues that turned them down or said that they would never succeed.

In cases we have observed firsthand, founders exhibited an enormous zeal to get to IPO time, some willing to pay almost any price—to their friends or their families. This appeared especially evident as the company came within a year or so of the first IPO date. Loyalties appeared to shift to the faction that favored an earlier IPO date. Pressure mounted to "get public while we can." And we also detected a tendency for founders to believe that "after the IPO, things will get back to normal."

Investors.   Venture capitalists view the IPO as the date to get liquid. They told us that they work hard to get this far, enduring great risks, disappointments, and hard times. At last the day comes when they can begin to distribute shares to limited partners, rack up another high ROI in their portfolios, and seek out fresh money to manage, based on the latest successes.

The pressure on a VC to get his companies public is enormous. The VC does not run the operation of the startups; that must be left to much less experienced people with questionable track records. The possibility of a rising star turning into a fading star is always there, as history shows. Markets can turn against the startup while it is still private. IBM or some other giant can make (and more than once *has* made) a surprise move that ruins the tiny company's bright prospects.

Stock markets cannot be counted on. They move up and down, with little the CEO can do but watch. IPO stocks move in and out of fashion. When the new issues market is dull or dead, the VC must risk more capital and invest to keep the private company alive, further draining funds intended for investment in other new enterprises. When the new issues market is hot, as it was in 1982-1983 or 1985-1987, the VC can sleep better at night because the windows of liquidation opportunity are wide and unlikely to close in a day or so. Dave Anderson of Sutter Hill noted that 1986-1987 conditions were outstanding, but that as soon as the stock market's success flattens or turns down, the venture capital community gets much less euphoric. This happened after October 19, 1987. But by early February, 1988, the first IPOs reappeared with more rumored to be forthcoming soon. The long window that opened in 1990 has been good to startups. And good days in the stock market make for great prices per share in each IPO. More IPO successes mean more fresh money for VCs, and they are happy.

Because of these factors, the VC is not friendly to anyone who would hinder one of his private companies from going public. This includes founders that logically argue for waiting because the changes to the company plan might reduce its long-term potential.

The Process of Going Public

Vast numbers of books and articles have been written to educate the CEO on the process of going public. A selection of these are listed in the bibliography at the end of this book. There are many other fine publications available from the top accounting firms and from all the specialized printers of prospectuses. They are updated often, and most are free—just call one of their local offices for a copy.

The value in these documents is that they serve as discussion pieces for planning sessions with the company's staff, lawyers, and accountants prior to going public. The real education comes in actually doing an IPO. When searching for the right VP of finance, the CEO should look for someone who has some experience with an IPO.

Timing Is Everything.   Nothing is so disheartening as missing the boat. "Get the IPO done when it can be done," said several veteran board members of startups.

A close second to missing the IPO (for another year or so) is selling a new issue into a softening market, going out at $6 a share instead of $16—only to see the market rebound and the price rise to $19 per share two months later.

Treasurers are specialists in timing successful financings, but few have yet to become CFOs of high tech companies. Occasionally the original CFO is very experienced at picking the timing of the IPO, but that is not common, and the necessary judgment and wisdom is commonly defaulted to the VCs on the board of the company.

Investment bankers are skilled at sensing the opportunity for good timing of a new issue. They are eager to do deals and will sense even the tightest window available to squeeze the deal through. They do not want a slow-selling deal because that means they get stuck with "inventory," stock that remains unsold because not enough buyers could be found on the day the IPO was sold. The underwriting firms can lose millions on a bad day if the stock market plunges and the new issue price follows the drop. Thus the banker does not want to overprice a deal and will instead underprice the stock a bit to cover the risk. The banker would prefer to sell into a rising stock market than into a flat or declining one. The banker will also know when the road show has produced enough over-subscription and will call it off and close the deal while it is hot. A good example of the use of this tactic is the Network Equipment Technology IPO. The NET management cut the road show short when the orders far exceeded the supply of shares.

The short-term timing of an IPO should be left up to the lead invest-ment banker. CEO thinking should be concentrated on getting into a financial condition that will give the company the flexibility and luxury of choosing the best date to go public. Financial flexibility is worth a lot. Table 13-5 lists six ranked reasons most often cited by the participants for going public. Another factor that sometimes plays a part is the number of stockholders. Securities and Exchange Commission regulations require the shares of a private company to be registered when the number of shareholders reaches 500. For example, Microsoft (founded in 1975) went public in 1986, just as the number of shareholders was approaching 500.

TABLE 13-5. Ranked Factors in the Timing of Going Public

1. *Capital Needed.* The startup needs capital in such a large amount that a private placement would be difficult.

2. *Cheapest Cost.* The IPO costs less than another round of venture capital.

3. *Cashing In Chips.* Everyone wants to get liquid, particularly the venture capitalists.

4. *Large Enough.* The startup is now large enough (in sales) and profitable enough to take public.

5. *Hot Stock Market.* The stock market is hot and hungry for IPOs of new high tech companies.

6. *Prestige.* Management, employees, the board of directors, and the venture capitalists want the fame and glory of being associated with a successful high tech company.

Source: Saratoga Venture Finance

Participants, Practices, and Principles. The group that is assembled to do the company's IPO will work together very closely over a short, intense period of weeks. Their first focus will be to get the prospectus written, along with the related SEC registration documents. Here is what IPO veterans say about the participants in an IPO:

- *Lawyers.* There will be two law firms, one representing the company, the other the investment banker. They should send partners to do the work; no one else can make the necessary on-the-spot decisions that are needed to keep the work progressing quickly over the inevitable hurdles.

  The job of the legal people is to keep their client from getting too exposed in the written documents. They will fight each other over tradeoffs between who should be more or less exposed, the company or the underwriters. Both law firms are trying to write a document that fully complies with securities law, tells an exciting story about the company, and, in case of lawsuit, is easily defensible, or "juryproof."

  These high tech-experienced lawyers are very expensive and scarce. Picking carefully can save expenses. The rules of thumb are: the farther from New York City the better; the farther from major cities the cheaper. Many smaller law firms familiar with high tech startups are very experienced in public securities law. They are familiar with the startup company and can do an excellent job. The investment banker's counsel should be from a firm as close to the company's location as possible and familiar with high tech deals; the CEO should insist on this. The costs are likely to be lower because the hourly rate will be cheaper and understanding of the business, industry, and technology will be there in depth.

■ *Accountants.* The CPA firms will be trying to get the company's books to balance for all of the past five years, and to comply 100 percent with GAAP (Generally Accepted Accounting Principles). If the books have been kept up to date from the beginning, the accountants will be preparing the company for the IPO date and there should be no surprises. The recent trend toward using microcomputer accounting systems for even the earliest stages of a startup is also helping get the books ready for public offering time without as much cleanup work as in the past. The partners of accounting firms are very aware of the many lawsuits that arose from the 1982-1983 IPO boom, such as the Osborne Computer lawsuit against auditor Arthur Young by venture capitalists. Before the partner signs the formal CPA firm's opinion that a company's books are clean, it is the partner's job to be sure that all the numbers have been checked many times over.

The accounting fee for the IPO is expensive, but it is not as large as it seems because the IPO-related work carries over to the annual audit, which uses much of the IPO accounting work. The IPO does, however, begin a new era of life for the company. Rates charged by the auditor for a fledgling startup company no longer apply. The company will also be required to file SEC documents each year and will be charged additional auditing fees for the new SEC filings such as 10-Qs and 10-Ks.

■ *Investment Bankers.* The lead investment bankers' teams must include the top high tech partner in at least a couple of the meetings, and a senior corporate finance veteran in all the sessions. The firms will be sure to have several very young people doing a lot of the detailed, grubby work, chasing down facts and figures, fetching the needed materials from the company's accounting and other staffs. The bankers must make the prospectus sound at least interesting, if not a bit exciting, without increasing the risk of lawsuits. The partners will be extremely busy, typically simultaneously doing several other deals. One sign of this is that they constantly leave the working room to make phone calls during the drafting of your prospectus.

Most of all, the lead investment banker wants the SEC papers prepared and filed as soon as possible to avoid missing any window of opportunity to get the deal out and finished.

■ *Printers.* There are specialist printing companies whose sole job is to print, in strictest confidence, 100 percent-accurate securities documents such as prospectuses in large quantities, at any time of day or night, and distribute them in hours to virtually any location of the world.

These printers are very expensive as printers go, and charge for every edit and change. Their bills are usually far over the budget they submitted in their bid for the job. They will be able to document every charge to the penny, attributing every change to instructions from the prospectus team. The key to keeping the bills lower is to submit only the final—or nearly final—draft to the printer and to use all the electronic tools possible to cut down manual labor in these mostly union shops.

Practices and Principles. The lead investor is the controller of the IPO working group, and is held responsible for adhering to the agreed-upon schedule.

The attorneys will be expected to compromise along the way and still produce a jury-proof prospectus. The attorneys will try to eliminate the typical claims made by the company's marketing staff in its aggressive efforts to sell to customers and to the industry media.

The "due diligence" work is the double-checking done by the underwriters and the CPA firm. They will carefully check the facts claimed in the prospectus by the company. The investment banker has the freedom to challenge any figure or claim made.

"Get it done" is the slogan of the whole IPO team, especially as the second week of work proceeds. Life can get pretty agonizing as draft after draft follows change after change. To quote an investment banker who was one of the Microsoft IPO working group, "As usual, it was like the Bataan death march."

Writing the Prospectus. The key to understanding a prospectus is to know that it is never used to sell the company's stock. That is the job of the investment bankers' sales staffs and is the reason the road show is so important.

The prospectus is a foundation document that marks a point in the life of the company. It is like a written business plan—its importance diminishes quickly as time passes.

As a result, things said by management to potential investors become more important than things written. At this point, practices that were acceptable for a private company must begin to be more disciplined. This applies particularly to statements by company officers about forecasts of sales or profits. Officers used to telling customers or employees about the company's planned results must be trained to restrain themselves after the IPO date, because such projections have fueled lawsuits.

Pricing the Shares

Alex Brown's head of corporate finance Dick Franyo says, "I let the market tell us the price of each IPO." He feels that his firm's job is to fairly present the company to potential buyers and let them make up their minds on the price at which to sell the shares.

That is the reason the research analyst's opinion is so important and the road show is taken so seriously. The road show is a trip organized by the investment banker. It takes the CEO and the company's top management to the big money-market cities. Over a week or more of whirlwind meetings, the CEO's team endures countless breakfasts, lunches, and dinners, then, in the mornings and afternoons, making presentations to selected institutional investors who have expressed interest in buying shares of the company.

The IPO share prices are determined by the market makers in much the same way that they set prices for the stocks of larger companies with longer track records. The most obvious difference is in the strong emphasis on the future—especially the growth in earnings and magnitude of return on invested capital of the new company, which is less than five years old. Special attention is given to the likelihood that the company will have excellent results over the next 12 months. In addition, the "uniqueness" of the company is closely examined. Managers are looked squarely in the eyes so that investors can decide whether the (usually) young management can continue to keep the company on the road to success.

Institutional salespeople from investment bankers are looking for "a good story"—their term for the company that has the best prospects for explosive success but that has not yet been discovered by the larger investment community. They try to find good stories, get their customers into the stock, and then turn their find over to the "herd," hopefully to get the demand for the limited supply of stock to drive the price up. Weekly meetings with the research and corporate staffs of investment bankers focus on the details of the outlook for companies that the investment banker is close to, including the IPOs. The salespeople grill their counterparts to test the suggestions and investment opinions presented, then proceed to their phones and round up orders from clients around the globe, from Tokyo and Singapore to London and Paris, as well as throughout the United States.

While all of this activity is going on, the traders in the syndicate are testing the market with their colleagues in the firm. They must decide how to handle oversubscriptions if the stock gets hot and demand exceeds supply. Similarly, they must be prepared to act if interest in the stock dwindles and the inventory of shares that the underwriters bought from the company is in danger of remaining unsold. If the expectations for preliminary demand for the stock are not met, the company may change its mind on the number of new shares to be offered, as well as on any amounts of shares to be sold by selling shareholders. This in turn will influence the price.

By the time the IPO is ready to go public, the whole focus is on setting the "strike price,"or the exact price at which shares will be sold to the investment banker (who will immediately sell them to waiting investors). The size of the order book and the ratio of orders to available stock will influence the final decision to increase or decrease the number of shares offered, or to change the intended price. In the end, the judgment of the investment banker will be relied upon to set the exact price. The agreed-upon price is then fixed, checks are exchanged, and the shares become the property of the underwriters. They, of course, hope to hold the shares for only a few minutes, selling the whole lot and the greenshoe as quickly as possible.

Comparables.   Investment bankers rely heavily upon comparables to price an IPO. They prefer to look for companies in the same or a related business and use those companies as a guide to pricing the new issue. The more unusual the company, the more the bankers run into difficulty using this technique. The startup's bankers will prepare such data for its deal and the CEO will be able to see and review the data with them. The CEO can also request that the investment banker prepare similar data on any company with which the CEO wants to compare his company.

Ratios.   Comparables still do not answer the question, "What numbers do the investors look at to make a pricing decision?" That is the subject of hot debate among investors worldwide, but it has been well researched over the past 25 years. The truth is that a few leaders set the prices and the herd follows. The numbers that the leaders look at most are future expectations (not history) of cash flow (not profits) and operating earnings tax adjusted (not net income), and return on invested capital (not earnings per share). The more important figures and ratios used are shown in Table 13-6. These primary factors are then converted into traditional financial statements in projected form and translated to price per share and multiples of revenue.

The CEO can forecast the numbers for his own company and apply the ratios used by research analysts, thereby reaching a decision on what the stock price should be. This will help in dissecting the reasoning the investment banker uses in setting the stock offering price. It will also help the CEO decide whether to hold off and wait for a better stock market or go now for a sure deal but at a lower price.

What Constitutes a Successful IPO?

Deciding what constitutes success in an IPO is worth thinking about, because the difference between a good and a bad IPO is worth millions in value to the company.

TABLE 13-6.   Quantitative Factors Used By Leaders to Set Stock Prices

- **Cash Flow from Operations.**   This is the sum of the cash in and out of the business—before considering the effect of cash from sources of financing.

- **Growth Rate of Business Profits.**   This is the rate of growth of the operating profit, not the "bottom line," which is distorted by interest income (surplus cash) and expenses (capital structure).

- **Return on Invested Capital.**   This measures return as the operating profit adjusted for taxes divided by capital. Capital equals the total of all capital (interest-bearing plus equity) already invested in the company. The higher the return, the higher the worth of the company (per share).

- **Likely ROI from Capital That Has Yet to Be Put to Work.**   This measures the possible return over extended future periods from the company's invest- ing fresh money in new projects such as R&D on new technology and new products.

- **Requirement for Fresh Capital Needed to Run the Business.** This determines the "cash flow" requirement of the company, measuring the amount of fresh capital needed each year to support the company's planned growth.

- **Financial Structure.**   This measures the proportion of total capital that will be in the form of interest-bearing capital the company intends to use. This is then converted to a measure of risk. Too much debt per dollar of total capital will increase risk and reduce the worth of the company (per share). However, debt is cheaper than equity because of the tax deductibility of interest ex- penses. Thus, more debt reduces the company's cost of capital. This increases the worth of the company (per share).

Source: Saratoga Venture Finance

Potential Problems and Pitfalls.   The central problem is picking the timing of the IPO. Waiting can be risky if business slips away from the company, but waiting can mean higher sales and greater value per share. There are also legal pitfalls linked to the post-IPO business performance of the company. The dangers of a lawsuit are quite real. Gene Amdahl personally had to pay $2.4 million in one lawsuit. Legal actions are pending on many more millions of dollars for companies whose stock prices plunged after their IPO.

On the other hand, missing the window can be very costly. There is an old treasurers' saying: Take your money while you can get it. There are companies that have been waiting for a good part of a decade because they missed their chance while an industry boom was on, such as in 1982–1983. When the industry went into a slump in 1984, they had to wait for a recovery. Only in 1987 were their financial statements beginning once again to qualify them for a public offering. In the period beginning 1990, IPOs were holding their values well, indicating that there has been less wild pricing of IPOs recently.

IPO investors are very picky about the companies in which they choose to invest. In the October 1987 issue of *Venture* magazine, Kenton Wood, president of D. H. Blair & Co., a company familiar with IPOs, said this about what his people look for: "Comparables are less important. We look at the uniqueness of their concept, barriers to entry, size of their market, management quality, and the downside risks."

The post-IPO price of the stock is of intense concern to everyone. The consensus is that the price per share should rise a lot, quickly; to most commentators that spells success. But if the rise is too sharp, it means the selling company has lost: it has sold more shares and its investors sold a larger percentage of the company than was necessary. A better solution would have been to sell at the price where the shares do not move in price after the IPO until an increase is due to a change in the perceived performance of the company's future or to improved actual results that pleased investors.

It is very costly to pick an investment banker who does a poor job. This can and does happen when an IPO gets second-class attention or when the investment bankers are inept at IPOs. This is most likely in hot markets, when alternative deals are vying for the attention of over-worked corporate finance staffs at the banks. The solution is for the CEO to manage and oversee the IPO, relying heavily on the CFO to ensure that the deal gets its "unfair share of attention." Close scrutiny will also pressure sales staffs of the investment bankers to control information leaks better and to more carefully manage trading in the shares.

The company is put into a very dangerous situation when there are no Wall Street security analysts following and writing about the company after the IPO. This possibility is very real. Jerry Anderson, a cofounder and former chairman of the computer-aided engineering company Valid Logic of San Jose, California, lamented that one of his two lead bankers promised but never wrote more than a short introductory piece on Valid within the two years after the banking firm got its fee for the IPO. *The Wall Street Journal* wrote a lead article about the problem in the August 12, 1987, issue of the newspaper. The headline read as follows:

Feeling Neglected
High Tech Companies Say Wall Street Firms Are Abandoning Them After Initial Stock Offerings,
Some Entrepreneurs Say, Bankers' Attention Wanes
Paying for the Prestige Factor

How to address and correct this post-IPO problem is discussed in the next section.

After the IPO

A successful conclusion to the IPO does not end when the IPO deal closes. It continues to the point at which the company is understood with reasonable accuracy by the investment community, and the company's strategy, competitive advantage, and future prospects are being reasonably recommunicated by the Wall Street research community.

How do you achieve this desired result in a multi-trillion dollar global stock market that trades hundreds of millions of shares daily, has tens of thousands of stocks of companies to invest in—let alone bonds, government bills, mortgages, real estate, gold, paintings, and so on? A fledgling company with less than two million shares sold to the public is not of much interest to most of the giant investors. Furthermore, each high tech company must compete with other hot IPOs that are much more easily understood, such as consumer products companies that have huge upside potential in the large consumer markets. Getting regular attention is difficult and requires a lot of planning, strategy, and hard work, day after day after day.

The following sections reflect the advice of high tech company CEOs and CFOs whom we have interviewed since 1982. We're providing a consensus of their comments, but their opinions about what to do were wide-ranging.

Managing Shareholder Relations.   Shareholder management or "investor relations" is the process of controlling information released to the public while remaining in compliance with the law, so that expectations about the company's future are kept in line with reality.

This process must be actively managed, because experience has shown that, left on their own, the investment community and general public media will gradually create distorted stories about a company, its products, financial health, and managerial competence. Such distortions increase the difficulty of managing the business, especially when large Fortune 500 customers begin to believe that the tiny company is in serious financial difficulty.

To do the job properly, the company must create a careful investor relations plan that is designed with the same thoroughness as a marketing plan for a product line. This requires skill and experience, such as that of a CFO who has done it before, a PR firm that offers such services, or an investor relations consultant who specializes in this area.

The company will need one person whose primary daily task is to disseminate and control the release of information to Wall Street research analysts and institutional investors. This person must be intimate with the policies and strategies of top management; in other words, he or she must know what is going on behind the closed doors of the CEO's office. Surprises are unforgivable to Wall Street. Trust and discretion are two of the working skills of the investor relations manager.

Firefighting is a regular task of the investor relations manager. It occurs all too frequently: all companies hit a quarter when business is suddenly going to be shockingly below last week's forecast; or the industry starts to sink and everyone starts layoffs; or a company's newest, highly touted wonder product suddenly cannot be finished on schedule by its engineering department; or when a company's latest product release turns out to be full of software bugs and customers are screaming murder!

The nature of investor relations is that of ferocious intensity. When trouble sets in, the CEO and his staff must drop all tasks until a tactical plan is created to deal with the latest rumors, good or bad, on Wall Street. The phones start ringing madly and will not stop until management provides satisfying answers to questions from the local business news editors, irate investors, and worried research analysts.

Honesty and integrity are very important. Once burned, analysts are like elephants: they do not forget. "Burning an analyst" consists of surprising him or her, and a good surprise is as undesirable as a bad surprise. Any surprise prevents the analyst from being able to get the story—good or bad—out to favored institutional investors, complete with advice on what to do about it. Analysts are often burned, and therefore are experienced doubters, capable of detecting—from tone changes and intimations on the phone—any deliberate withholding of information about significant current or upcoming events.

Consistency is important. Once a CEO starts to give out numbers, he must not stop during the embarrassing times. For instance, some companies openly talk about order backlog when it is strongly rising but stop when it gets bad. Good analysts have learned to read the situation exactly that way, and no one is fooled. Inconsistency makes the research analyst's job more difficult. The analyst has built a spreadsheet model to forecast the financial statements of your company, using the parameters that the CEO has been giving out. If the CEO stops giving out the information, more uncertainty will be introduced into the analyst's forecast; the CEO may then read of negative reports by the formerly favorable analyst, who is now explaining to his investing clientele why the new forecast and report on a company have changed so much.

Potential Problems and Pitfalls.   Investor relations must be deliberately managed—as actively and deliberately as any other aspect of a business.

Here are some of the problems the fledgling public company may face:

- *Time Consumption.*   A CEO should count on the same percentage of time needed for managing investor relations as was required while the company was private. Regis McKenna and Intel committed Intel's top management to spending at least 10 percent and sometimes 20 percent of their time on each business trip with the media and Wall Street analysts.

- *What Is Said.*   There is a large difference between what one says to insiders such as employees and venture capitalists and what one says to outsiders such as the top research analysts for Cowen or Merrill Lynch. Some CEOs have found this hard to learn, particularly those who have been heads of divisions of large corporations and have become CEO of a company for the first time in their lives. Inability to adjust has cost several CEOs their jobs, according to some we spoke to who have experienced this problem first-hand.

- *Control.*   Frustration of CEOs rises as they learn how independent the outside media reporters and research analysts are. It is difficult to adjust to the reality that those people can say whatever they want about a company—and do. Trying to "fix" and "correct" their opinions is often a time- and emotion-consuming effort that is wasted.

- *Consistency.*   A company's Wall Street positioning must be consistent with its business marketing positioning. Its customers will seek out and read the written Wall Street reports about its successes, failures, and expected future. Such reports must be considered an important part of a company's marketing communications program. Wall Street will not regurgitate an exciting story about your company if that company's marketing positioning statement is not crisply defined and in place. Analysts are very astute at poking holes in strategies, uncovering "me-too" plans, and they are good at detecting lack of sustainable competitive advantage and distinctive competence.

A company can get special help from veterans of such investor relations activities by attending local chapter meetings of the National Investor Relations Institute. Here is a short list of the key principles that investor relations veteran Carol Abrahamson presented to members of the National Investor Relations Institute:

- Stocks are sold, not bought.
- Financial markets are strongly influenced by supply and demand factors.
- Information moves Wall Street as it builds expectations leading to assessment of the value of the stock of a company.
- Investors come in many types, some more appropriate for a company than others.

- Every company has unique investor relations needs that change over time.
- Every different type of investor has different information needs.
- Companies must fiercely compete to be noticed by investors.

Investor relations specialists can help a CEO build an investor relations program that is customized for a company's special needs, whether it went public a year ago and is now frustrated at dwindling interest by Wall Street, is recently public, or has an IPO coming up in a few months and wants to plan ahead of time. The consultants feel their work will help a company reap appropriate benefits: consistent demand for its shares, fair valuing of its stock, and orderly trading of its shares.

Participants and the Role of the Securities Analyst. There is a collection of people who will regularly team up in the investor relations program for a company. Experts can get a company started quickly and methodically. In addition, there are special roles for each of the other participants:

- *Lead Spokesperson.* This is the person designated to directly answer the numerous daily phone calls from investors and others inquiring about the company's stock and prospects. New IPO companies usually designate the CFO for this job. Others choose the CEO. It is a time-consuming assignment and is rarely delegated to the investor relations manager.

- *Investor Relations Manager.* This person must handle the administration and details of the newly public company. This includes taking the first calls from Wall Street analysts who will be requesting personal telephone interviews with the CEO and CFO, as well as visits to the company. This manager will be very influential in how well Wall Street regards the quality of communication with the investment community. It is a demanding job, one for people who are very good at being discreet, who are absolutely trustworthy, and who are good at articulating the company's positioning statement and strategy.

- *The CFO.* The investor relations manager is usually responsible to the chief financial officer. This arrangement is a consequence of the need to comply with SEC regulations and the CFO's familiarity with the financial community. The VP of marketing usually cooperates with the CFO, but focuses more time on communicating with customers than with investors. The CFO is considered a close second in importance to the CEO as far as communicating with research analysts is concerned. That responsibility can be daunting to a financial leader who has come up the ladder as a controller or auditor. This is one reason so many VCs hesitate to automatically grant CFO status to VPs of finance in companies about to go public. This is evidenced by the frequent number of times a startup adds a CFO "heavy" shortly before it goes public.

■ *Lawyer.* The chief counsel to the company, usually an outsider in a private law firm that helped the company go public, assists in several ways. He or she reviews and advises on 10-Qs and other SEC submissions read by analysts. This attorney counsels on press releases affecting investors, especially those involving responses to wild trading in the company's stock, bad news such as layoffs, or unexpectedly bad financial results. The attorney provides practical advice on what to tell analysts in difficult circumstances, based on firsthand experience. In the end, however, the CEO, not the chief counsel, is responsible for what is said. The objective is to give the law firm an opportunity to review special news intended to be sent to Wall Street and the press, so that the company can benefit from a legal professional's advice and avoid unnecessary legal mistakes in communications with analysts and reporters.

■ *Board Members.* Especially important news is almost always previewed in confidence with those members of the board of directors who are active in the company. Quarterly earnings and bad news are most often discussed before release, typically on the phone or after the nearly final draft of the related press release is faxed *in confidence* to the secretary of the board member. This enables the CEO to keep everyone together, keeps communication consistent, and enables the CEO to benefit from the experience and judgment of board members, who often have been through similar situations in the past. The spate of shareholder suits in the 1990s demonstrate the importance of this practice.

■ *Public Relations Firm.* The company's public relations firm often helps implement the investor relations program. Even if it does not, it must be kept informed of important events so it can keep up with the company's media communications, in which it is closely involved. The most common mistake made, according to veterans like Paul Franson of Franson & Associates of San Jose, California, is to tell the PR firm after the fact. Close cooperation between investor relations and public relations will keep the two programs consistent.

■ *National Investor Relations Institute.* This and local clubs of investor relations people are where the tactics and skills of investor relations are learned and new ideas are openly discussed.

■ *Research Analysts.* These are the people employed by the investment community to investigate and report on companies. They differ in their role and relations with a company. Analysts work for one of the two sides on Wall Street: the sell side, consisting of the famous brokerage and investment banking firms on Wall Street like Goldman Sachs and Kidder Peabody, as well as the specialized high tech firms like Cowen and Alex Brown; or the buy side, consisting of the institutional investors such as the diversified financial services firm of The Capital Group of Los Angeles, managers of mutual funds like T. Rowe Price of Baltimore, and hired money managers such as Rosenberg Capital Management of San Francisco. They specialize in technologies and industries. Sell-side analysts consistently earn over $100,000 a year, the top ones several times that in a great year. It is rare to see reports written by buy-side analysts, but that does not make the buy-side analyst any less important to spend time with than the sell-side analyst.

The toughest job is to keep the analyst's expectations in line with reality without forecasting a company's financial results for the next quarter or year. This requires experience and very careful communication in order to avoid legal trouble.

The Speaking Forums.   There is a regular circuit of meetings at which officers of a new issue can speak. These are arranged by high tech business firms so that institutional investors can hear CEOs present their companies. The American Electronics Association holds several forums each year on the west and east coasts of the United States as well as in Europe. Each of the high tech investment banking firms like Cowen, Hambrecht and Quist, Montgomery Securities, and Robertson Stephens & Company put together investor meetings that focus on technologies such as life sciences and electronics. Participation is by invitation, but invitations are not too difficult to obtain. The lead investment banking firm should help the company plan its year of meetings.

Investors come to these meetings as one method of efficiently looking at live managers of the exciting new companies they have heard about. Both analysts and portfolio managers attend. They attend the daily meetings where the CEO tells the company's story; they also spend dinners and lunches talking in small groups with a company's representatives.

Case Study: Microsoft Goes Public

In closing, we wish to suggest that you spend time reading an unusually well-written case study of a real IPO—Bro Uttal's "fly-on-the-wall" inside look at the Microsoft IPO process, published in the July 21, 1986 *Fortune* magazine. It is worth studying; it is rare that such detail is documented so well. The article accurately depicts other IPOs, based on our interviews and personal experiences in the past with the IPO events.

It is also worthwhile using the Microsoft prospectus to calculate one's own forecast of the offering price of the Microsoft IPO because the stock shot up so strongly after the public offering. CEO Bill Gates' strong desires and goals for the IPO should be compared to what actually happened. The reader should stand in Gates' shoes on the timing, pricing, and management of the pre- and post-offering events and then reconsider plans to get his own startup public.

14

Corporate Sources of Venture Capital

There are three corporate sources of capital for high tech startups: merger or acquisition by another company, creation of an internal startup, and venturing with large corporate funds. Each source has unique requirements and considerations for the CEO of the high tech startup, and each has proved successful as a viable source of funds for a new enterprise. In this chapter we will describe the pros and cons of each approach.

Mergers and Acquisitions

Venture capitalists of the pre-1970 era used to look to mergers and acquisitions (M&A) as the most likely means by which to cash in their investments. Today, the emphasis is on getting to an initial public offering. However, more companies are still acquired than go public.

In 1987, the *San Jose Mercury News* researched the fates of 43 companies that had received venture capital funding during the previous five years in Silicon Valley. Of the 43, only 9 made it to a public offering. The 34 others included bankruptcies as well as several, such as American Cardiovascular, that were acquired.

Since the venture boom days of the early 1980s, mergers have been taking place at a faster pace as consolidation of startups becomes a harsher reality. All types of companies are involved: electronics, hardware, software, life sciences, and environmental. There have also been several private purchases of U.S. startups by Japanese, Taiwanese, European, and other non-U.S. corporations of considerably larger size.

Several venture capitalists noted that during the 1990s they expected even more M&A activity to take place because the overheated stock markets of the 1980s had cooled off and reduced high valuations and easy money. In the absence of a startup IPO market, M&A activity increases. The stock market crash of October 19, 1987, made stocks of smaller companies bargains in the eyes of established corporations. And October 1990 scared investors again. Unfriendly takeovers have also occurred, but remain fewer and farther between than in lower tech industries.

How and Where to Start.   Let's look at this from the viewpoint of the corporate executive who would like to acquire a startup or access its technology. When asked how the M&A teams of Fortune 500 corporations should approach a high tech startup acquisition, the VCs uniformly responded by saying, "Start with a board member who can be quietly approached to test the waters." Investors suggested approaching a member of a venture firm because such contacts can often lead to additional opportunities for acquisition of technology and businesses. But when the executive has a specific company in mind, the early discussions with the venture capitalist can help the suitor better understand the degree of sensitivity that the managers of the startup may have to being approached by a buyer. If the suitor is acceptable, the proper introductions will be made and the talks can get off on the right foot. VCs noted that few high tech CEOs have any first-hand experience with an acquisition and its repercussions, whereas the VCs are most likely to have such know-how and be more astute in handling the more sophisticated aspects of acquiring a high tech corporation without causing the core team to depart.

Pricing.   Pricing an acquisition of a private startup will follow the same techniques and methodology described in earlier chapters. The Saratoga Venture Tables can be used to help determine the cost of a proposed acquisition. A number of consulting firms offer services that include valuing private companies. It is important to understand the venture capitalists—their motivations, techniques for pricing, target ROIs, and current portfolio condition. The last item is especially important to know for each VC investor. The VC firm whose other portfolio companies are in trouble will be more likely to support and urge the sale of one of its startups because the resulting ROI will increase the overall performance of the sagging portfolio.

Management Thinness.   One should be especially careful of the thinness of management in any startup. Even the most experienced CEO has little support or backup, and rarely enough to get all the job done every day. The corporate buyer may be dismayed to find that a large part of the expected profits went to just adding badly overdue managerial support to the struggling startup.

Business or Just Technology?   One should be especially thorough in separating a startup's exciting technology from any problems it may have in sustaining a viable business. The methods for detecting and analyzing this problem are discussed in detail in Chapter 5, following practices familiar to large public corporations and the guidelines of Peter Drucker and McKinsey & Company research.

Learn the Venture Capital Formation Process.   It is important to respect the process of capital formation in the high tech startup. Chapter 3 uncovers the phases of the process, step by step. This process is described from the viewpoint of the startup's CEO, but it includes the important issues that the potential acquirer will encounter along the way in considering the acquisition. It will keep the acquirer from stepping out of line and from bumbling along like a newcomer trying to get along in the very private, very strange world of high tech startups.

Respect the Soul and Spirit of the Startup.   High tech companies have an intense soul and spirit in their cultures that the acquirer must respect. To win over the core of the company's people is a must. The technology team will be especially skittish about any outsider taking over control. Even in a troubled company, the high tech artists are an independent lot. Anything the newcomer does that puts water on the flame of a company's spirit is very dangerous. Ben Rosen, who backed Lotus and Compaq, was asked how he rekindled the flame of a startup once it was extinguished and he replied, "I really do not know of a formula for doing that; it is extremely difficult to accomplish." Winning over the entrepreneurial hearts of the employees is critical to the successful acquisition of a startup, or else the buyer will see that enterprise dwindle to a fraction of its promised potential.

Our first case study is about how the president of National Semiconductor reacted to the painful situation of vulnerability to takeover. It can help the merger and acquisition specialist of a large corporation who is looking at M&A as a way of investing in technology or increasing revenue and profits. It is also a good example of how jealous a high tech CEO can feel about his company, particularly about an outside corporation coming in to take a position of authority in the company he has founded.

The second case study, American Cardiovascular, illustrates an acquisition that was a success for both the acquiring company and its investors as well as the startup.

Case Study: National Semiconductor

In 1976, Charles E. "Charlie" Sporck, president of National Semiconductor Corporation of Santa Clara, California, was faced with a serious problem. The stock of his company had rocketed ever since he had left Fairchild to lead the creation of what had become National, the wonderchild of the semiconductor industry in the decade of the 70s. But after setting record after record for financial performance, Sporck saw the dream turn into a nightmare as sudden internal problems caused earnings to first slow and then sharply reverse their former upward path. The stock plunged from highs of the mid-fifties to the low teens in 1976. Wall Street rumors spread like wildfire, and soon there were stories of raiders looking at National. The stock market value of the company hit a low of $62 million.

Sporck was angry that anyone even mentioned a possible merger with another company. He got even angrier at the mention of a possible raider buying the company. He had seen firsthand at Fairchild Camera and Instrument Corporation what an established eastern U.S.-based management had done to the western-based fledgling transistor and integrated circuit operations of Fairchild. "They never understood the business," he would frequently comment. "They didn't know what they were doing." It was that concern—of an outsider coming in and wrecking National because strangers didn't understand the semiconductor business—that disturbed him so much.

Sporck also had a very heavy emotional attachment to National. He recalled the years of loyal employees. Long-time employees told of the end of one quarter when his wife and children showed up at the factory in Santa Clara to help employees box semiconductors for shipment to customers—so that the company would have enough cash flow from collecting the receivables to meet the next quarter's payroll. Employees fondly retold such stories to visitors; the company had a very intimate character to its culture. In 1976, as the takeover rumors continued, the employees grew openly angry at the idea of someone other than Charlie running National. They rallied to support him and his leadership.

Sporck listened to the wide-ranging advice people offered on what to do in the threatening situation. While Sporck's people were working around the clock from Connecticut to Bangkok to Santa Clara to fix the internal problems, world-famous law firms and Wall Street investment bankers flew to headquarters to meet Sporck, each proposing some tactical plan designed to ward off a raider or exact the highest price if the raid were successful. The fees for attorneys and Wall Street bankers would represent a substantial payoff in either scenario. They would get their fees if National won against a raider, but would also get their fees if National lost against the raider. It was the latter scenario that made Sporck furious.

Finally Sporck made his decision: "Tell the press that National will leave a 'scorched earth' if any raider tries to make a pass at us," were Sporck's instructions to his staff. After considering the myriad of possible solutions, Charlie decided that there was only one worthwhile way of dealing with the problem: he would personally resign from National if a raider tried to take control of even a portion of the stock of the company. Even a single seat for the suitor on the board of directors of National was too much. Sporck could leave and be instantly employed by a competitor of National's in minutes. Sporck did not manage under a non-compete contract; in fact he hated management contracts and refused to use them in his company. And people in large numbers pledged that they would follow him from National—especially key top and middle managers who deeply respected Sporck—as well as the intensely loyal R&D staff and hourly employees. A raider would be left with an empty shell: not only the brains and know-how would be gone, but the company's soul as well.

As it turned out, Sporck retained control of his company, solved the internal problems, and later went on to acquire several businesses for National in friendly transactions. These were merged into the National culture, some becoming the foundation for what became the Systems Division of National, which represented over half the revenue and even proportionally more of the profits when the semi-conductor industry was in the depths of a major recession in 1985 to 1986.

The final irony came in 1987: National acquired Fairchild from its parent, Schlumberger. This was made possible by circumstances as well as by management. After the 1976 National takeover rumors had died out, new ones arose of several other possible unfriendly takeovers. Eventually Gould Inc. came after Fairchild. Wilfred Corrigan and his managers at Fairchild fought back with lawyers and investment bankers, but eventually had to give up by selling out to a 'white knight,' the French oil equipment supplier Schlumberger. A highly successful company, Schlumberger was expected by many analysts in the Wall Street community to quickly turn Fairchild around in a display of management brilliance that would dazzle the home-grown methods of the current crop of high tech managers of Silicon Valley companies.

Rebuffed but undaunted, Gould made a second attempt, this time at the much smaller but technology-rich Texas company, Mostek. Feisty L. J. Sevin and his loyal Texan management fought back, but they too ended up in the arms of a white knight, United Technology.

Less than three years after those acquisitions, the companies' leaders left and so did their key technologists. Corrigan left to found LSI Logic, a gate array ASIC (application-specific integrated circuits) startup company that went public successfully. Sevin left and teamed up with Ben Rosen to start their own venture capital firm that later was the lead investor in Lotus and Compaq. The Fairchild and Mostek technologists landed in semiconductor companies all over the United States, including many new enterprises.

United later shut down Mostek and sold off its assets.

Schlumberger finally put Fairchild up for sale in 1987 after losing vast sums of money in the operation. The final buyer was Charlie Sporck, who had been the general manager of Fairchild's semiconductor operations just before he left to lead National.

Case Study: American Cardiovascular

This successful startup was funded by a team of venture investors led by Ray Williams, a very quiet, successful, hands-on investor in high tech early-stage companies, and eventually sold to Eli Lilly in 1986.

Williams says he often prefers to sell to large corporations after a successful startup finds it is ready to cash in the chips. In this case, the customers of American Cardiovascular were in the medical profession, where the channels of distribution are dominated by the selling staffs of the large pharmaceutical companies. The American products were a natural fit in the strategy of the buyer. The selling founders and employees exchanged private stock for instantly registered public shares, without the hassle of having to fight for post-IPO attention in crowded Wall Street.

Williams noted that he strongly prefers to begin without corporate venture capital, however. He feels corporations involved in the earliest stages hinder management from realizing the fullest potential of the technology, and can often slow the company's reaction to the market and to overcoming the many troubles that a startup encounters. After the birth pangs are over, however, Williams believes that acquisition by a large public corporation makes a very attractive way for the startup to get public while adding further strength to the new company.

This friendly acquisition has been considered a successful marriage by both parties. The change of leadership was done in an orderly fashion. Williams had been CEO for a long time and had increasingly turned over daily management tasks to operating managers; he quietly bowed out. The American Cardiovascular company remained intact, and the buyer, Lilly, gained entry into the new business it was seeking. Employees got career paths in a well-run corporation, some with the opportunity to become technology "fellows" of a corporation where R&D is a revered discipline with vast sums of money and resources at its disposal.

Internal Startups

During the past five years, a new form has arisen for creating and financing a high tech company. We call it an "internal startup." It is a novel approach—an evolution of the lessons learned by independent and successful new enterprises—and it has advantages over a merger or acquisition. We provide two case studies that illustrate successful internal startups.

The internal startup is a separate business entity of an operating high tech company. It may or may not be a subsidiary. The parent company wants to keep its management and employees focused on its bread-and-butter business while simultaneously creating and entering a related business run by carefully chosen personnel. Those personnel are motivated like startup entrepreneurs and receive founders' shares, which are eventually bought out by the parent corporation in accord with some prearranged valuation method.

Potential Problems and Pitfalls. As with new children, there are a number of special things to watch out for when doing an internal startup. One should have the patience to work them out, because we found that there is a very high success rate for internal startups, far greater (one tenth of the failure rate, according to our estimates) than in classically funded venture startups. It is an area of pioneering, and it offers the entrepreneur a large degree of creativity; it also requires substantial work to construct the legal and financial aspects of the new enterprise.

Incentive Compensation. The internal startup pays competitive wages and adds an equity incentive package. The wages often include a cash bonus program in addition to base wages. Cash bonuses are uncommon in startups. Such compensation reflects the large company corporate involvement of the emerging growth parent companies, which have been pioneers of the internal startup. The equity incentive is in the form of options to buy stock, usually in the form of a standard incentive stock option package with four-year vesting. The rest of the option structure can get quite creative; some alternatives are discussed below.

Tax Benefits. The parent company can reduce the cash cost of its investment in the internal startup if it can qualify for a write-off of the capital invested in the startup. To do so, several companies have purchased at least 80 percent of the startup at the beginning of its existence. Thus a $4 million capital investment would be reduced by the approximate combined federal and state tax rate (about 40 percent).

Other structures have included starting with an R&D partnership that gained the benefits of tax write-off of the first expenses of the startup.

Accounting.   One of the greatest problems of an internal startup is that of accounting for a buyout of the minority shareholders (who are the founders, management, and employees) of the internal startup. The American Institute of Certified Public Accountants (AICPA) and its theoreticians have forced its member CPA firms to require that under most conditions any buyout of minority shareholders must be recorded as an acquired asset that must be depreciated over the economic life of the asset. Translated to business terms, this means that a $4 million investment that creates a new enterprise that is owned 80 percent by the parent and that becomes worth $50 million in five years requires the buyer of the remaining 20 percent, worth $10 million, to write off the high tech asset against the combined earnings of the acquiring parent. Since the life of the technology at the moment of acquisition could be argued by the CPA firm to be short, a five-year life or $2 million of non-tax-reduced paper expense would be charged against earnings for five or fewer years. That is enough to wipe out the profit from the consolidated internal startup in many cases.

CFOs and CEOs we spoke with feel this is irrelevant nonsense created by accounting theoreticians. The combined entity has no less or greater cash flow than on the day before the two were combined. A company doing an IPO does not record its increased worth and charge it against its own earnings. In fact, the buyer of the internal startup adds value by consolidating 100 percent of the startup for tax purposes.

We found some creative efforts under way to circumvent the accounting problem. One was to aim from the beginning at letting the internal startup do an IPO, to be set free at some time from the parent. Claris Corp., a subsidiary of Apple Computer, is one recent example. The proponents of such a startup argue that this kind of internal startup was created because of an "incompatibility" problem within the parent company, and an IPO is a fine way for the parent to reap the rewards of its investment and hard work. Yet Claris was "reacquired" by Apple after all the dust settled.

Another creative method is for the eventual cashing in of the chips to take place immediately. This structure has the parent immediately putting a future value on the shares owned by management and employees, buying 100 percent of the startup from day one, and vesting the shares over four years, contingent on reaching revenue and profit goals of the business plan.

Some corporations are using R&D equity partnerships. Classical in form, they allow special tax benefits to be created and thus reduce the cost of the startup to the investor. The buyout accounting issues remain, but not if the startup does an IPO and goes off to operate independently of the parent.

Valuation.   Valuing an internal startup is no more difficult than valuing a company going public or one selling shares in a private round of financing. Several companies used a combination of hired help—a consultant, an investment banker, a CPA firm—and their own financial staffs to reach a value for the buyout of the company. Fear of the valuation issues should not prohibit anyone from considering an internal startup.

Expert Help.   The same caliber of professional help is needed for this new variety of startup as for the classical kind. An internal entrepreneur can benefit from the experience of a good startup consultant, startup lawyer, or high tech CPA firm, as well as the professional investment banker familiar with high tech startups. Such help will be needed because of the pioneering nature of an internal startup.

Case Study: Quantum and Plus

Quantum Corporation of Milpitas, California, successfully used an internal startup to solve a business dilemma that prosperity had created for the company. The company had reached IPO as an original equipment supplier of large disk drives to systems corporations. Quantum's technology then enabled them to create a skinny disk drive that fit a slot in personal computers. Market tests showed that the potential was very large. But management—ranked one of the top 10 percent of well managed companies by several electronic publishers' polls—was concerned that the retail computer store focus of the new business opportunity would confuse the parent company, distracting from the heart of the company's success as an OEM supplier.

Management decided to solve their problem by creating an internal startup. Its name was Plus. A separate corporate structure was created, complete with separate building, its own business plan, and dedicated personnel. Compensation was arranged in a confidential manner, with an incentive package of stock for the risk-taking employees that was competitive with other startups.

Plus quickly leaped to the head of its served market, becoming the industry standard. Revenue and profits rolled in. Plus and Quantum won. So did the risk-taking employees of Plus.

Since this success, other companies, including Cypress Semiconductor, have taken this idea and have advanced it further.

Case Study: Chips and Technologies

Chips and Technologies, one of the most quickly successful startups in recent years, found that its success rapidly attracted new business opportunities that called for the application of its computer systems, computer-aided engineering, and semiconductor designing technologies to several markets that its first cus-tomer base, the IBM clone manufacturers, did not necessarily match. At times there was some overlap; at other times there was no direct relation to the original business.

Gordon Campbell and his management studied the situation and decided that the best solution was to create a series of startup-like businesses. They began by using a combination of internal divisions while also creating new outside corpo-rations. The new enterprises are headed by successful managers, first choice being given to current employees, followed by outside recruiting of successful startup entrepreneurs. For businesses that are found not to be directly related, Chips has agreed to assist and or fund several as independent startups. Equity has been provided by venture sources, including both monies from founders of Chips itself as well as other private venturing individuals. In some cases, Chips has provided services and charged for them at arms-length prices so that both parties can benefit.

The result is a continuous stimulation to new business ideas, a rapid process of screening and evaluation of opportunities, and a prompt startup mechanism that immediately gets to work to get the new enterprise in business. Both Chips and the new enterprise benefit. Individuals receive incentive packages that are consistent with the risks taken by the employees.

Corporate Venture Capital

The larger public companies are active in the venture capital business. Pools of big-company money are invested in startups. This presents a number of opportunities for the entrepreneur, and many have proven successful. We will focus here on the mechanics of dealing with such sources of capital.

Finding Corporate Venture Capital.   Some Fortune 500 companies have created subsidiaries to enter the venture capital market. Others simply invest as part of the strategy of business development units. Usually run by a corporate officer of the parent, these operations are chartered to seek out and recommend areas for new investment. One choice is to fund new enterprises that are in fields of technology and business to which the parent corporation is eager to gain access. The way to locate such personnel is to contact the large company's office of the CEO or CFO and ask whether they might be interested in what the startup company has to offer. Startup CEOs told us that they found that their cold calls were answered, as were calls that followed carefully arranged personal introductions.

ROI Versus Technology.   Corporate venture capitalists are less inter-ested in turning a high ROI on their portfolio of company investments than they are in helping the parent company gain access to the desired technology or business. This is very clear in many of the prospectuses of IPOs that describe the extensive arrangements between the startup and the investing corporate giant.

Pricing. The cost of capital from corporate sources has usually been lower than when a classic venture capitalist is the investor. This is for a combination of reasons, mainly because there is less competitive pressure to perform as a portfolio manager. Other CEOs told us that the greed factor was much lower, and there was a refreshingly lower drive for financial success at all cost. In other cases, we found corporations charging the same cost of capital as VCs. We found it very difficult to get sufficient data on this phenomena, especially on the magnitude of the reduced cost of capital. However, the patterns in our data suggested that corporations grant a modest percent reduction below the cost of classic corporate venture capital, depending heavily upon the technology contract between the startup and big corporation. No CEO of a startup told us he had to pay *more* for capital from corporate venture capitalists than from classic venture capitalists.

Business Deals and Documentation. Corporate venture deals are almost always accompanied by some form of additional legal documentation that formalizes the related business deal that accompanies the investment. The deals range from large-quantity purchases by Kodak of workstations supplied by Sun Microsystems, to technology licenses linked to software and hardware purchases, such as the OEM deal between Nixdorf (big company/reseller) and Pyramid (startup/supplier). The degree of creativity is almost unlimited.

It is mandatory that the entrepreneur gets experienced legal help in structuring and documenting such deals. International deals are especially complex and tricky.

View of Classic Venture Capitalists. There are differing and often conflicting objectives and goals when corporate and classical venture capitalists are compared. The former tend to be long-term in their thinking, whereas the latter are shorter term. The corporate investor seeks more than the maximum ROI, whereas that is the fixation of the classical VC. Corporate investors are deliberate and methodical, whereas fast decisions and immediate reaction to changes in events mark the habits of the classical venture investor. CEOs of startups clearly believe that the corporate investor is less likely to fire the founders than are the classical venture capitalists.

As a result, classical venture capitalists are sometimes reluctant to invest on the same terms as corporate venture capitalists. And in extreme cases, some VC firms will not invest at all in private companies that have already been funded by corporate venture capital. We did not, however, find that the top VC firms are reluctant to join a deal with corporate venture capitalists. Instead, they seem to be simply wanting to be extra careful that the corporate investor and any related business deals made good business sense for the startup.

Foreign Corporate Capital

We must specially address the issue of foreign venture capital in U.S. startups. The trend for foreign investment in startups has been growing along with the cheaper dollar. The French and Germans were very active in the 1982-1985 years, with the Japanese continuing since then to become the major player that often acquires troubled startups and thus gains full access to all their technology. Since 1985, the Koreans have become very visible, and lately large sums of capital have become available from Taiwan, Hong Kong, and Singapore.

We expect these trends to continue. They represent another alternative for the startup CEO to go to for capital, another way to increase competition for the deal. To date, the pricing of deals with foreign sources of capital has appeared to follow the pricing of the American corporate venture capitalist. One special characteristic, however, is the degree of accompanying business dealing; foreign investors virtually insist that any investment include both full access to all the startup's technology and some form of commitment to manufacture in the country supplying the capital. And most of the money goes to later-stage deals, rarely to seed startups.

Corporate Opportunities

Corporate venture funds are available and actively looking for good startups and their technology. The sources are from very large companies in North America, Europe, and Asia. Every deal looks for access to the startup's technology. The cost of capital is equal to or slightly less than a classic VC charges. Internal startups continue to proliferate in creative companies. They require buyout formulas and special management techniques. CEOs of startups should not look for seed-round money from corporations, but rather for mid- and later-round funding. If all goes well, the CEO should also expect to be considered for buyout (instead of an IPO) by the big corporate partner.

Appendices

A: Saratoga Venture Tables

B: Resources for the Entrepreneur

C: Three Venture Capital Firms
   Describe Themselves

A: Saratoga Venture Tables

SARATOGA VENTURE FINANCE EQUITY TABLE™
WAGES AND STOCK OWNERSHIP AT INITIAL PUBLIC OFFERING (IPO)

This is a portion of a Table

TITLE	(4) COMPENSATION	(3),(6),(7) MGT & EMPS OWNERSHIP
f = Founder		
f Chair,CEO,Pres	$121,000	3.1%
f VP Engineering		4.6%
VP Mktg & Sls	$82,000	0.0%
VP Mfg	$72,450	0.0%
f VP R&D-Left	$73,886	0.5%
OTHER	Avg. = $63,667	1.4%
OFFICERS & EXECUTIVES		9.6%
ALL OTHER		15.1%
TOTAL COMMON BEFORE OPTIONS		24.7%
OPTIONS-Outstanding		1.4%
OPTIONS-Available		7.9%
OPTIONS-Total		9.3%
COMMON-Total		34.0%
Major Venture Capital		32.9%
OTHER		21.3%
VENTURE Total		54.2%
PRE-IPO: sum of all stock		88.2%
IPO shares		11.8%
TOTAL OUTSTANDING		100.0%

LABELS & EXPLANATIONS

The Tables contain summaries and approximations. For actual data, see the prospectus.

- # = See list below for footnote explanations
- MGT & EMPS = Management and employees
- Blank compensation occurs when data is not available.
- Zeros for shares occur when data is not available (see averages for approximations).
- Left = Shows executive left company before IPO.
- Avg. = Arithmetic average is used for data given for a group.
- ALL OTHER = Usually shares purchased by exercising granted options.
- Major Ven. Cap. = Includes largest venture investors
- OTHER = All investors, including strategic partners
- VENTURE Total = May include some cash of founders.

FOOTNOTES TO HEADERS

(1) As reported to SEC in prospectus, including Option Plan grants net of repurchases.
(2) Equals (1) plus all option plan shares: granted plus available, net of options exercised for common.
(3) Original shares purchased by executives, net of repurchases from resigned employees, and other private transactions.
(3B) Includes some granted options as well as purchased stock.
(4) As reported to Securities and Exchange Commmission in prospectus for recent fiscal year.
(5) Shows average for earnings of executives for periods subsequent to the last 12 months.
(6) Uses entire option pool: outstanding plus available shares.

ABBREVIATIONS OF JOB TITLES

CEO	Chief Executive Officer
COO	Chief Operating Officer
EVP	Executive Vice President
SVP	Senior Vice President
VP	Vice President
CFO	Chief Financial Officer
CSO	Chief Scientific Officer
Pres	President
BisDev	Business Development
EUR	Europe
F&A or FIN	Finance and Administration
HR	Human Resources
HW	Hardware
INT	International
MFG	Manufacturing
MKT	Marketing
MS	Marketing and Sales
NA	North American or Not Available
OPS	Operations
PROD DEVEL	Product Development
QR	Quality and Reliability
SLS	Sales
SW	Software
TECH	Technology

SARATOGA VENTURE FINANCE EQUITY TABLE™
WAGES AND STOCK OWNERSHIP AT INITIAL PUBLIC OFFERING (IPO)

Apple Computer, Inc.

IPO DATE: 12 December 1980
$22.00 Price per Share

Microcomputers
Inception: 3 January 1977
Cupertino, California

TITLE (f = Founder)	(4) COMPENSATION	(3B) OFFICERS OWNERSHIP	(3),(6),(7) MGT & EMPS OWNERSHIP	(1) PRE IPO OWNERSHIP	(2) POST IPO OWNERSHIP	(3B) OFFICERS OWNERSHIP	(3),(6),(7) MGT & EMPS OWNERSHIP	(1) PRE IPO OWNERSHIP	(2) POST IPO OWNERSHIP	IPO VALUE $22.00 Per Share
Chairman,EVP	$135,182	25.8%	15.4%	12.6%	11.2%	7,029,448	7,029,448	7,029,448	7,029,448	$154,647,856
f V.Chairman,VP		27.7%	16.5%	13.5%	12.0%	7,542,448	7,542,448	7,542,448	7,542,448	$165,933,856
President,CEO		14.0%	8.3%	6.8%	6.1%	2,810,232	2,810,232	2,810,232	2,810,232	$61,825,104
f VP		14.7%	8.7%	7.1%	6.4%	3,989,231	3,989,231	3,989,231	3,989,231	$87,763,082
All Others = 7		21.5%	12.8%	10.5%	9.3%	5,853,312	5,853,312	5,853,312	5,853,312	$128,772,864
OFFICERS & EXECUTIVES		100.0%	59.5%	48.7%	43.4%	27,224,671	27,224,671	27,224,671	27,224,671	$598,942,762
ALL OTHER			28.1%	23.0%	20.5%		12,860,963	12,860,963	12,860,963	$282,941,186
TOTAL COMMON BEFORE OPTIONS			87.6%	71.8%	63.9%		40,085,634	40,085,634	40,085,634	$881,883,948
OPTIONS-Outstanding			12.4%	10.1%	9.0%		5,652,600	5,652,600	5,652,600	$124,357,200
OPTIONS-Available			0.0%	0.0%	4.5%		0	0	2,852,600	$62,757,200
OPTIONS-Total			12.4%	10.1%	13.6%		5,652,600	5,652,600	8,505,200	$187,114,400
COMMON-Total			100.0%	81.9%	77.5%		45,738,234	45,738,234	48,590,834	$1,068,998,348
Major Venture Capital				7.8%	7.0%			4,375,816	4,375,816	$96,267,952
OTHER				10.3%	9.2%			5,753,882	5,753,882	$126,585,404
VENTURE-Total				18.1%	16.2%			10,129,698	10,129,698	$222,853,356
PRE-IPO: sum of all stock				100.0%	93.6%			55,867,932	58,720,532	$1,291,851,704
IPO-shares					6.4%				4,000,000	$88,000,000
TOTAL-OUTSTANDING					100.0%				62,720,532	$1,379,851,704

(7) Vesting for Stock Option Plans is usually 4 years, with six month waiting period, 1/48 per mo thereafter and FMV at time of grant.

Lead Underwriters: Morgan Stanley + Hambrecht & Quist

$101,200,000		IPO TOTAL CASH RAISED BEFORE FEES AND EXPENSES
$5,980,000	5.91%	IPO fee for underwriters
$661,600	0.65%	Estimated expenses of IPO
$94,558,400	93.44%	NET TO COMPANY

4,000,000 nr shares sold by company
600,000 nr shares sold by selling shareholders

Average $1.8M

REVENUE $M	REVENUE $M
Last 12 mos	Last Qtr
$117.9	$41.5
Growth/Year	Growth/Year
146.0%	109.0%
	Nr. employees: 1,015

SARATOGA VENTURE FINANCE EQUITY TABLE ™
WAGES AND STOCK OWNERSHIP AT INITIAL PUBLIC OFFERING (IPO)

Business Land

IPO DATE: 14 December, 1983
$10.00 Price per Share

Chain of retail microcomputer stores
Inception: 30 March 1982
San Jose, California

TITLE f = Founder	(4) COMPENSATION	(3B) OFFICERS OWNERSHIP	(3),(6),(7) MGT & EMPS OWNERSHIP	(1) PRE IPO OWNERSHIP	(2) POST IPO OWNERSHIP	(3B) OFFICERS OWNERSHIP	(3),(6),(7) MGT & EMPS OWNERSHIP	(1) PRE IPO OWNERSHIP	(2) POST IPO OWNERSHIP	IPO VALUE $10.00 Per Share
f CEO	$75,000	43.1%	34.7%	12.0%	9.1%	2,153,336	2,153,336	2,153,336	2,153,336	$21,533,360
f VP-MKTG	$75,000	14.0%	11.3%	3.9%	3.0%	700,000	700,000	700,000	700,000	$7,000,000
VP-OPS	$70,000	0.0%	0.0%	0.0%	0.0%	0	0	0	0	$0 *
VP-STORES	*	0.0%	0.0%	0.0%	0.0%	0	0	0	0	$0 *
VP-BIS DEVL	*	0.0%	0.0%	0.0%	0.0%	0	0	0	0	$0 *
VP-FINANCE	*	0.0%	0.0%	0.0%	0.0%	0	0	0	0	$0 *
OTHER = 4	*Avg. = $31,667	42.9%	23.3%	8.1%	6.1%	2,143,088	1,443,088	1,443,088	1,443,088	$14,430,880 *
OFFICERS & EXECUTIVES		100.0%	69.3%	24.0%	18.2%	4,996,424	4,296,424	4,296,424	4,296,424	$42,964,240
ALL OTHER			13.2%	4.6%	3.5%		818,756	818,756	818,756	$8,187,560
TOTAL COMMON BEFORE OPTIONS			82.5%	28.6%	21.7%		5,115,180	5,115,180	5,115,180	$51,151,800
OPTIONS-Outstanding			17.5%	6.1%	4.6%		1,088,650	1,088,650	1,088,650	$10,886,500
OPTIONS-Available			0.0%	0.0%	3.0%		0	0	701,350	$7,013,500
OPTIONS-Total			17.5%	6.1%	7.6%		1,088,650	1,088,650	1,790,000	$17,900,000
COMMON-Total			100.0%	34.7%	29.3%		6,203,830	6,203,830	6,905,180	$69,051,800
Major Venture Capital				30.1%	22.8%			5,392,476	5,392,476	$53,924,760
OTHER				35.2%	26.7%			6,304,848	6,304,848	$63,048,480
VENTURE Total				65.3%	49.6%			11,697,324	11,697,324	$116,973,240
PRE-IPO: sum of all stock				100.0%	78.8%			17,901,154	18,602,504	$186,025,040
IPO shares					21.2%				5,000,000	$50,000,000
TOTAL OUTSTANDING					100.0%				23,602,504	$236,025,040

Average $3.6M *

REVENUE $M	REVENUE $M
Last 12 mos	Prior Quarter
$10.1	$13.6
Growth/Year	Growth/Year
Not meaningful	Not meaningful
	Nr of employes: 341

(7) Vesting for Stock Option Plans is usually 4 years, with six month waiting period, 1/48 per mo thereafter and fair market value at time of grant.
Lead Underwriters: Rothschild + Lehman

5,000,000 nr shares sold by company	$50,000,000	IPO TOTAL CASH RAISED BEFORE FEES AND EXPENSES
0 nr shares sold by selling shareholders	$2,900,000	5.80% IPO fee for underwriters
	$475,000	0.95% Estimated expenses of IPO
5,000,000 IPO TOTAL	$46,625,000	93.25% NET TO COMPANY

SARATOGA VENTURE FINANCE EQUITY TABLE ™
WAGES AND STOCK OWNERSHIP AT INITIAL PUBLIC OFFERING (IPO)

Chips and Technologies, Inc.

IPO DATE: 8 December, 1986
$5.00　Price per Share

Semiconductors
Inception: 5 December 1984
San Jose, California

TITLE f = Founder	(4) COMPENSATION	(3B) OFFICERS OWNERSHIP	(3),(6),(7) MGT & EMPS OWNERSHIP	(1) PRE IPO OWNERSHIP	(2) POST IPO OWNERSHIP	(3B) OFFICERS OWNERSHIP	(3),(6),(7) MGT & EMPS OWNERSHIP	(1) PRE IPO OWNERSHIP	(2) POST IPO OWNERSHIP	IPO VALUE $5.00 Per Share
f CEO	$125,400	55.7%	43.1%	27.0%	23.3%	3,001,962	3,001,962	3,001,962	3,001,962	$15,009,810
f VP-SALES	$137,500	3.7%	2.9%	1.8%	1.6%	200,000	200,000	200,000	200,000	$1,000,000
f VP-MKTG	$93,300	7.4%	5.7%	3.6%	3.1%	400,000	400,000	400,000	400,000	$2,000,000
VP-OPS	$93,300	5.6%	4.3%	2.7%	2.3%	300,000	300,000	300,000	300,000	$1,500,000
f VP-ENG	$106,909	11.1%	8.6%	5.4%	4.7%	600,000	600,000	600,000	600,000	$3,000,000
f VP-CAE		9.3%	7.2%	4.5%	3.9%	500,000	500,000	500,000	500,000	$2,500,000
VP-FIN		4.3%	3.3%	2.1%	1.8%	232,269	232,269	232,269	232,269	$1,161,345
OTHER	$92,500	2.9%	2.2%	1.4%	1.2%	153,846	153,846	153,846	153,846	$769,230
OFFICERS & EXECUTIVES		100.0%	77.4%	48.5%	41.9%	5,388,077	5,388,077	5,388,077	5,388,077	$26,940,385
ALL OTHER			19.5%	12.2%	10.5%		1,354,665	1,354,665	1,354,665	$6,773,325
TOTAL COMMON BEFORE OPTIONS			96.9%	60.7%	52.4%		6,742,742	6,742,742	6,742,742	$33,713,710
OPTIONS-Outstanding			3.1%	2.0%	1.7%		217,000	217,000	217,000	$1,085,000
OPTIONS-Available			0.0%	0.0%	0.0%		0	0	0	$0
OPTIONS-Total			3.1%	2.0%	1.7%		217,000	217,000	217,000	$1,085,000
COMMON-Total			100.0%	62.6%	54.1%		6,959,742	6,959,742	6,959,742	$34,798,710
Major Venture Capital				23.6%	20.4%			2,623,077	2,623,077	$13,115,385
OTHER				13.8%	11.9%			1,528,000	1,528,000	$7,640,000
VENTURE Total				37.4%	32.3%			4,151,077	4,151,077	$20,755,385
PRE-IPO: sum of all stock				100.0%	86.4%			11,110,819	11,110,819	$55,554,095
IPO-shrs					13.6%				1,750,000	$8,750,000
TOTAL OUTSTANDING					100.0%				12,860,819	$64,304,095

(7) Vesting for Stock Option Plans is usually 4 years, with six month waiting period, 1/48 per month thereafter and fair market value at time of grant.

Lead Underwriters: Shearson + Hutton

1,750,000	nr shares sold by company	$10,000,000	IPO TOTAL CASH RAISED BEFORE FEES AND EXP.
250,000	nr shares sold by selling shareholders	$740,000　7.40%	IPO fee for underwriters
		$424,000　4.24%	Estimated expenses of IPO
		$8,836,000　88.36%	NET TO COMPANY

REVENUE $M	REVENUE $M
Last 12 mos	Last Quarter
$12.7	$7.1
Growth/Year	Growth/Year
Not meaningful	Not meaningful
Nr of employes: 63	

SARATOGA VENTURE FINANCE EQUITY TABLE ™
WAGES AND STOCK OWNERSHIP AT INITIAL PUBLIC OFFERING (IPO)

Cirrus Logic

IPO DATE: 8 June 1989
$10.00   Price per Share

Semiconductors
Inception: November 1984
Milpitas, California

TITLE 1 = Founder	(4) COMPENSATION	(3B) OFFICERS OWNERSHIP	(3),(6),(7) MGT & EMPS OWNERSHIP	(1) PRE IPO OWNERSHIP	(2) POST IPO OWNERSHIP	(3B) OFFICERS OWNERSHIP	(3),(6),(7) MGT & EMPS OWNERSHIP	(1) PRE IPO OWNERSHIP	(2) POST IPO OWNERSHIP	IPO VALUE $10.00 Per Share
f CEO	$213,087	24.8%	13.5%	2.6%	2.1%	328,857	328,857	328,857	328,857	$3,288,570
f VP-R&D	$127,131	36.4%	19.8%	3.8%	3.1%	483,554	483,554	483,554	483,554	$4,835,540
f Employee		8.8%	4.8%	0.9%	0.8%	117,000	117,000	117,000	117,000	$1,170,000
f Employee		8.4%	4.5%	0.9%	0.7%	111,000	111,000	111,000	111,000	$1,110,000
VP-Mfg	$134,083	6.8%	3.7%	0.7%	0.6%	90,000	90,000	90,000	90,000	$900,000
VP-Eng.	$132,830	0.0%	0.0%	0.0%	0.0%	0	0	0	0	$0 *
VP-Mktg	$123,904	0.0%	0.0%	0.0%	0.0%	0	0	0	0	$0 *
f Employee		0.0%	0.0%	0.0%	0.0%	0	0	0	0	$0 *
VP-Strategic Development-Left		0.0%	0.0%	0.0%	0.0%	0	0	0	0	$0
OTHER Avg. of 5 = $94,649		14.9%	8.1%	1.5%	1.3%	198,000	198,000	198,000	198,000	$1,980,000
OFFICERS & EXECUTIVES		100.0%	54.3%	10.3%	8.6%	1,328,411	1,328,411	1,328,411	1,328,411	$13,284,110
ALL OTHER			14.0%	2.7%	2.2%		343,342	343,342	343,342	$3,433,420
TOTAL COMMON BEFORE OPTIONS			68.4%	13.0%	10.8%		1,671,753	1,671,753	1,671,753	$16,717,530
OPTIONS-Outstanding			31.6%	6.0%	5.0%		772,990	772,990	772,990	$7,729,900
OPTIONS-Available			0.0%	0.0%	3.0%		0	0	470,882	$4,708,820
OPTIONS-Total			31.6%	6.0%	8.0%		772,990	772,990	1,243,872	$12,438,720
COMMON-Total			100.0%	19.0%	18.8%		2,444,743	2,444,743	2,915,625	$29,156,250
Major Venture Capital				64.8%	53.9%			8,340,200	8,340,200	$83,402,000
OTHER				16.1%	13.4%			2,076,236	2,076,236	$20,762,360
VENTURE Total				81.0%	67.3%			10,416,436	10,416,436	$104,164,360
PRE-IPO: sum of all stock				100.0%	86.1%			12,861,179	13,332,061	$133,320,610
IPO shares					13.9%				2,150,000	$21,500,000
TOTAL OUTSTANDING					100.0%				15,482,061	$154,820,610

Avg. of 4 = $495K *

REVENUE $M	REVENUE $M
Last 12 mos	Prior Quarter
$36.9	$12.1
Growth/Year	Growth/Year
299.5%	NA
	Nr of employes: 178

(7) Vesting for Stock Option Plans is usually 4 years, with 25% at end of a one year waiting period, 1/48th per month thereafter and fair market value at time of grant.

Lead Underwriters: Goldman Sachs + Alex. Brown + Robertson

	IPO TOTAL CASH RAISED BEFORE FEES AND EXPENSES		
2,150,000 nr shares sold by company	$33,400,000		IPO TOTAL CASH RAISED BEFORE FEES AND EXPENSES
1,190,000 nr shares sold by selling shareholders	$2,338,000	7.00%	IPO fee for underwriters
3,340,000 IPO TOTAL	$660,000	1.98%	Estimated expenses of IPO
	$30,402,000	91.02%	NET TO COMPANY

SARATOGA VENTURE FINANCE EQUITY TABLE ™
WAGES AND STOCK OWNERSHIP AT INITIAL PUBLIC OFFERING (IPO)

Conner Peripherals, Inc.

IPO DATE: 12 April 1988
$8.00   Price per Share

Disk drives
Inception: 18 June 1985
San Jose, California

TITLE f = Founder	(4) COMPENSATION	(3B) OFFICERS OWNERSHIP	(3),(6),(7) MGT & EMPS OWNERSHIP	(1) PRE IPO OWNERSHIP	(2) POST IPO OWNERSHIP	(3B) OFFICERS OWNERSHIP	(3),(6),(7) MGT & EMPS OWNERSHIP	(1) PRE IPO OWNERSHIP	(2) POST IPO OWNERSHIP	IPO VALUE $8.00 Per Share
f Chair,CEO	$189,518	40.0%	24.4%	9.2%	8.0%	3,000,000	3,000,000	3,000,000	3,000,000	$24,000,000
Pres,COO	$160,396	2.5%	1.5%	0.6%	0.5%	187,500	187,500	187,500	187,500	$1,500,000
EVP R&D	$148,857	26.6%	16.3%	6.2%	5.3%	2,000,000	2,000,000	2,000,000	2,000,000	$16,000,000
EVP Sls&Mktg	$130,190	0.0%	0.0%	0.0%	0.0%	0	0	0	0	$0 *
SVP, CFO		0.0%	0.0%	0.0%	0.0%	0	0	0	0	$0 *
VP Sales	$109,611	0.0%	0.0%	0.0%	0.0%	0	0	0	0	$0 *
OTHER = 3	$99,427	4.1%	2.5%	1.0%	0.8%	310,627	310,627	310,627	310,627	$2,485,016
Not an exec Left company		26.8%	16.3%	6.2%	5.4%	2,009,020	2,009,020	2,009,020	2,009,020	$16,072,160
OFFICERS & EXECUTIVES		100.0%	61.1%	23.1%	20.0%	7,507,147	7,507,147	7,507,147	7,507,147	$60,057,176
ALL OTHER			6.3%	2.4%	2.1%		770,110	770,110	770,110	$6,160,880
TOTAL COMMON BEFORE OPTIONS			67.4%	25.5%	22.1%		8,277,257	8,277,257	8,277,257	$66,218,056
OPTIONS-Outstanding			20.2%	7.7%	6.6%		2,486,939	2,486,939	2,486,939	$19,895,512
OPTIONS-Available			12.4%	4.7%	4.1%		1,523,834	1,523,834	1,523,834	$12,190,672
OPTIONS-Total			32.6%	12.4%	10.7%		4,010,773	4,010,773	4,010,773	$32,086,184
COMMON-Total			100.0%	37.8%	32.8%		12,288,030	12,288,030	12,288,030	$98,304,240
Major Venture Capital				19.5%	16.9%			6,330,070	6,330,070	$50,640,560
Other: Compaq Computer Corporation				42.7%	37.0%			13,854,524	13,854,524	$110,836,192
INVESTORS-Total Holdings				62.2%	53.9%			20,184,594	20,184,594	$161,476,752
PRE-IPO: sum of all stock				100.0%	86.7%			32,472,624	32,472,624	$259,780,992
IPO shares					13.3%				5,000,000	$40,000,000
TOTAL OUTSTANDING					100.0%				37,472,624	$299,780,992

(7) Vesting for Incentive Stock Option Plans is usually over 4 years, vesting at 1/48th per month.

Lead Underwriters: Sherson + Montgomery

5,000,000	Shares sold by company
0	Shares sold by selling shareholders

$40,000,000		IPO TOTAL CASH RAISED BEFORE FEES AND EXPENSES
$2,800,000	7.00%	IPO fee for underwriters
$685,000	1.71%	Estimated expenses of IPO
$36,515,000	91.29%	NET TO COMPANY

Average $414K

REVENUE $M	REVENUE $M
Last 12 mos	Recent Qtr
$113.2	$51.2
Growth/Year Not meaningful	Growth/Year Not meaningful

Nr of employees: 1,286

SARATOGA VENTURE FINANCE EQUITY TABLE ™
WAGES AND STOCK OWNERSHIP AT INITIAL PUBLIC OFFERING (IPO)

Convex
IPO DATE: 17 October 1986
$7.50 Price per Share

Minisupercomputers
Inception: 8 September 1982
Richardson, Texas

TITLE f = Founder	(4) COMPENSATION	(3B) OFFICERS OWNERSHIP	(3),(6),(7) MGT & EMPS OWNERSHIP	(1) PRE IPO OWNERSHIP	(2) POST IPO OWNERSHIP	(3B) OFFICERS OWNERSHIP	(3),(6),(7) MGT & EMPS OWNERSHIP	(1) PRE IPO OWNERSHIP	(2) POST IPO OWNERSHIP	IPO VALUE $7.50 Per Share
f CEO	$86,500	28.8%	19.1%	5.5%	4.3%	750,000	750,000	750,000	750,000	$5,625,000
f VP-TECH	$86,500	28.8%	19.1%	5.5%	4.3%	750,000	750,000	750,000	750,000	$5,625,000
VP-DEVEL	$82,308	10.7%	7.1%	2.1%	1.6%	280,000	280,000	280,000	280,000	$2,100,000
VP-INT OPS	$77,846	9.6%	6.4%	1.8%	1.4%	250,000	250,000	250,000	250,000	$1,875,000
VP-FINANCE	$77,846	0.0%	0.0%	0.0%	0.0%	0	0	0	0	$0 *
VP-SALES	*	0.0%	0.0%	0.0%	0.0%	0	0	0	0	$0 *
VP-OPS	*	0.0%	0.0%	0.0%	0.0%	0	0	0	0	$0 *
VP-HR	*	0.0%	0.0%	0.0%	0.0%	0	0	0	0	$0 *
VP-SW	*	0.0%	0.0%	0.0%	0.0%	0	0	0	0	$0 *
CONTROLLER		0.0%	0.0%	0.0%	0.0%					$0 *
OTHER=Avg*	$69,552	0.0%	14.7%	4.3%	3.3%	577,000	577,000	577,000	577,000	$4,327,500
OFFICERS & EXECUTIVES		100.0%	66.4%	19.3%	14.9%	2,607,000	2,607,000	2,607,000	2,607,000	$19,552,500
ALL OTHER			30.9%	9.0%	7.0%		1,213,735	1,213,735	1,213,735	$9,103,013
TOTAL COMMON BEFORE OPTIONS			97.4%	28.2%	21.9%		3,820,735	3,820,735	3,820,735	$28,655,513
OPTIONS-Outstanding			2.6%	0.8%	0.6%		103,024	103,024	103,024	$772,680
OPTIONS-Available			0.0%	0.0%	5.2%		0		913,162	$6,848,715
OPTIONS-Total			2.6%	0.8%	5.8%		103,024	103,024	1,016,186	$7,621,395
COMMON-Total			100.0%	29.0%	27.7%		3,923,759	3,923,759	4,836,921	$36,276,908
Major Venture Capital				52.0%	40.4%			7,039,942	7,039,942	$52,799,565
OTHER				19.0%	14.7%			2,565,508	2,565,508	$19,241,310
VENTURE Total				71.0%	55.1%			9,605,450	9,605,450	$72,040,875
PRE-IPO: sum of all stock				100.0%	82.8%			13,529,209	14,442,371	$108,317,783
IPO shares					17.2%				3,000,000	$22,500,000
TOTAL OUTSTANDING					100.0%				17,442,371	$130,817,783

Average $721K *

(7) Vesting for Stock Option Plans is usually 4 years, with 1/4 at the end of each of the first two years, 1/48 per mo thereafter; fair market value at time of grant.

Lead Underwriters: Goldman Sachs + Robertson

3,000,000 nr shares sold by company	$23,512,500	IPO TOTAL CASH RAISED BEFORE FEES AND EXPENSES	
135,000 nr shares sold by selling shareholders	$1,504,800	IPO fee for underwriters	6.40%
3,135,000	$479,400	Estimated expenses of IPO	2.04%
	$21,528,300	NET TO COMPANY	91.56%

REVENUE $M	REVENUE $M
Last 12 mos	Recent Qtr
$13.5	$9.1
Growth/Year	Growth/Year
Not meaningful	356.3%
Nr of employes: 272	

SARATOGA VENTURE FINANCE EQUITY TABLE ™
WAGES AND STOCK OWNERSHIP AT INITIAL PUBLIC OFFERING (IPO)

Cygnus Therapeutic Systems

IPO DATE: 31 January 1991
$9.00 Price per Share

Transdermal drug delivery systems
Inception: April 1985
Redwood City, California

TITLE f = Founder	(4) COMPENSATION	(3B) OFFICERS OWNERSHIP	(3),(6),(7) MGT & EMPS OWNERSHIP	(1) PRE IPO OWNERSHIP	(2) POST IPO OWNERSHIP	(3B) OFFICERS OWNERSHIP	(3),(6),(7) MGT & EMPS OWNERSHIP	(1) PRE IPO OWNERSHIP	(2) POST IPO OWNERSHIP	IPO VALUE $9.00 Per Share
f Chair.,SVP-R&D	$135,519	55.5%	35.8%	22.9%	16.6%	2,042,115	2,042,115	2,042,115	2,042,115	$18,379,035
Pres.,CEO	$136,519	9.8%	6.3%	4.0%	2.9%	359,580	359,580	359,580	359,580	$3,236,220
VP-Mktg	$115,315	0.0%	0.0%	0.0%	0.0%	0	0	0	0	$0
VP-Ops	$88,062	0.0%	0.0%	0.0%	0.0%	0	0	0	0	$0
OTHER Avg. of 2 = $89,875		34.7%	22.4%	14.3%	10.4%	1,277,196	1,277,196	1,277,196	1,277,196	$11,494,764 *
OFFICERS & EXECUTIVES		100.0%	64.5%	41.3%	30.0%	3,678,891	3,678,891	3,678,891	3,678,891	$33,110,019
ALL OTHER			13.5%	8.6%	6.3%		771,188	771,188	771,188	$6,940,692
TOTAL COMMON BEFORE OPTIONS			78.0%	49.9%	36.2%		4,450,079	4,450,079	4,450,079	$40,050,711
OPTIONS-Outstanding			22.0%	14.1%	10.2%		1,255,788	1,255,788	1,255,788	$11,302,092
OPTIONS-Available			0.0%	0.0%	2.9%		0	0	360,597	$3,245,373
OPTIONS-Total			22.0%	14.1%	13.2%		1,255,788	1,255,788	1,616,385	$14,547,465
COMMON-Total			100.0%	64.0%	49.4%		5,705,867	5,705,867	6,066,464	$54,598,176
Major Venture Capital				24.2%	17.6%			2,155,560	2,155,560	$19,400,040
OTHER				11.8%	8.6%			1,055,748	1,055,748	$9,501,732
VENTURE Total				36.0%	26.2%			3,211,308	3,211,308	$28,901,772
PRE-IPO: sum of all stock				100.0%	75.6%			8,917,175	9,277,772	$83,499,948
IPO shares					24.4%				3,000,000	$27,000,000
TOTAL OUTSTANDING					100.0%				12,277,772	$110,499,948

Avg. of 3 = $3.8M *

(7) Vesting for Stock Option Plans is usually 4 years, with 25% at end of a one year waiting period, 1/48th per month thereafter and fair market value at time of grant.
Lead Underwriters: Hambrecht & Quist + Robertson

3,000,000 nr shares sold by company	$27,000,000		IPO TOTAL CASH RAISED BEFORE FEES AND EXPENSES
0 nr shares sold by selling shareholders	$1,890,000	7.00%	IPO fee for underwriters
3,000,000 IPO TOTAL	$500,000	1.85%	Estimated expenses of IPO
	$24,610,000	91.15%	NET TO COMPANY

REVENUE $M	REVENUE $M
Last 12 mos	Prior Quarter
$3.2	NA
Growth/Year	Growth/Year
26.8%	NA
Nr of employes: 58	

SARATOGA VENTURE FINANCE EQUITY TABLE ™
WAGES AND STOCK OWNERSHIP AT INITIAL PUBLIC OFFERING (IPO)

Cypress Semiconductor

IPO DATE: 29 May 1986
$9.00 Price per Share

Semiconductors
Inception: December 1982
San Jose, California

TITLE f = Founder	(5) COMPENSATION	(3B) OFFICERS OWNERSHIP	(1) PRE IPO OWNERSHIP	(2) POST IPO OWNERSHIP	(3),(6),(7) MGT & EMPS OWNERSHIP	(3B) OFFICERS OWNERSHIP	(3),(6),(7) MGT & EMPS OWNERSHIP	(1) PRE IPO OWNERSHIP	(2) POST IPO OWNERSHIP	IPO VALUE $9.00 Per Share
f President, CEO	$150,000	27.9%	2.9%	2.1%	11.3%	754,666	754,666	754,666	754,666	$6,791,994
f VP-Mktg&Sales	$106,866	11.1%	1.1%	0.9%	4.5%	300,000	300,000	300,000	300,000	$2,700,000
f VP-Mfg	$105,918	11.1%	1.1%	0.9%	4.5%	300,000	300,000	300,000	300,000	$2,700,000
f VP-Fabrication	$101,909	11.1%	1.1%	0.9%	4.5%	300,000	300,000	300,000	300,000	$2,700,000
f VP-R&D	$103,553	11.1%	1.1%	0.9%	4.5%	300,000	300,000	300,000	300,000	$2,700,000
f VP-Engineering		11.1%	1.1%	0.9%	4.5%	300,000	300,000	300,000	300,000	$2,700,000
VP-F&A, CFO		5.8%	0.6%	0.4%	2.3%	155,625	155,625	155,625	155,625	$1,400,625
Others		10.7%	1.1%	0.8%	4.3%	290,132	290,132	290,132	290,132	$2,611,188
OFFICERS & EXECUTIVES		100.0%	10.3%	7.7%	40.3%	2,700,423	2,700,423	2,700,423	2,700,423	$24,303,807
ALL OTHER			6.7%	5.0%	26.5%		1,774,992	1,774,992	1,774,992	$15,974,928
TOTAL COMPANY BEFORE OPTIONS			17.0%	12.7%	66.8%		4,475,415	4,475,415	4,475,415	$40,278,735
Options-Granted			8.5%	6.3%	33.2%		2,225,415	2,225,415	2,225,415	$20,028,735
Options-Available			0.0%	4.2%	0.0%		0	0	1,474,585	$13,271,265
OPTIONS-Total			8.5%	10.5%	33.2%		2,225,415	2,225,415	3,700,000	$33,300,000
COMMON-Total			25.5%	23.2%	100.0%		6,700,830	6,700,830	8,175,415	$73,578,735
Major Venture Capitalists			54.2%	40.4%			14,265,444	14,265,444	14,265,444	$128,388,996
Monolithic Memories, Inc.			2.9%	2.1%			750,000	750,000	750,000	$6,750,000
Other Preferred Investors			17.4%	13.0%			4,590,067	4,590,067	4,590,067	$41,310,603
Preferred-Total			74.5%	55.6%				19,605,511	19,605,511	$176,449,599
PRE-IPO: sum of all stock			100.0%	78.7%				26,306,341	27,780,926	$250,028,334
IPO-shares				21.3%					7,500,000	$67,500,000
TOTAL OUTSTANDING				100.0%					35,280,926	$317,528,334

(7) Vesting for Stock Option Plans is usually 4 years, with a one year waiting period, 1/48 per mo thereafter and fair market value at time of grant.

Lead Underwriters: Morgan Stanley + Robertson

7,500,000 nr shares sold by company	$67,500,000 IPO TOTAL CASH RAISED BEFORE FEES AND EXPENSES	
0 nr shares sold by selling shareholders	$4,200,000 IPO fee for underwriters	6.22%
	$500,000 Estimated expenses of IPO	0.74%
	$62,800,000 NET TO COMPANY	93.04%

REVENUE $M	REVENUE $M
Last 12 mos	Prior Quarter
$16.6	$8.9
Growth/Year	Growth/Year
412.9%	218.2%
Nr of employes: 340	

SARATOGA VENTURE FINANCE EQUITY TABLE ™
WAGES AND STOCK OWNERSHIP AT INITIAL PUBLIC OFFERING (IPO)

Linear Technology Corporation

IPO DATE: 28 May 1986
$8.00   Price per Share

Analog semiconductors
Inception: 10 September 1981
Milpitas, California

TITLE f = Founder	(4) COMPENSATION	(3B) OFFICERS OWNERSHIP	(3),(6),(7) MGT & EMPS OWNERSHIP	(1) PRE IPO OWNERSHIP	(2) POST IPO OWNERSHIP	(3B) OFFICERS OWNERSHIP	(3),(6),(7) MGT & EMPS OWNERSHIP	(1) PRE IPO OWNERSHIP	(2) POST IPO OWNERSHIP	IPO VALUE $8.00 Per Share
f UEO	$135,231	27.3%	12.6%	5.4%	4.6%	950,000	950,000	848,106	848,106	$6,784,848
f VP-MS-Left	$95,163	19.1%	8.8%	1.6%	1.4%	665,000	605,000	254,004	254,004	$2,032,032
VP-MKT	$100,173	2.0%	0.9%	0.4%	0.4%	70,000	70,000	70,000	70,000	$560,000
VP-SLS-Left	$101,173	2.0%	0.9%	0.1%	0.1%	70,000	70,000	21,001	21,001	$168,008
f VP-OPS		19.1%	8.8%	3.8%	3.3%	665,000	665,000	600,000	600,000	$4,800,000
VP-QR		2.2%	1.0%	0.5%	0.4%	75,000	75,000	75,000	75,000	$600,000
f VP-ENG	$101,173	19.1%	8.8%	3.8%	3.3%	665,000	665,000	605,754	605,754	$4,846,032
VP-FA		1.9%	0.9%	0.4%	0.4%	65,000	65,000	65,000	65,000	$520,000
f OTHERS	Avg = $89,191	19.1%	3.3%	1.6%	1.4%	251,751	251,751	251,751	251,751	$2,014,008
OFFICERS & EXECUTIVES		100.0%	46.0%	17.6%	15.3%	3,476,751	3,476,751	2,790,616	2,790,616	$22,324,928
ALL OTHER			25.0%	11.9%	10.3%		1,887,818	1,887,818	1,887,818	$15,102,544
TOTAL COMMON BEFORE OPTIONS			71.0%	29.6%	25.6%		5,364,569	4,678,434	4,678,434	$37,427,472
OPTIONS-Outstanding			29.0%	13.9%	12.0%		2,195,530	2,195,530	2,195,530	$17,564,240
OPTIONS-Available			0.0%	0.0%	2.4%		0	0	429,470	$3,435,760
OPTIONS-Total			29.0%	13.9%	14.4%		2,195,530	2,195,530	2,625,000	$21,000,000
COMMON-Total			100.0%	43.4%	40.0%		7,560,099	6,873,964	7,303,434	$58,427,472
Major Venture Capital				21.4%	18.5%			3,386,000	3,386,000	$27,088,000
OTHER				35.2%	30.5%			5,571,469	5,571,469	$44,571,752
VENTURE Total				56.6%	49.0%			8,957,469	8,957,469	$71,659,752
PRE-IPO: sum of all stock				100.0%	89.0%			15,831,433	16,260,903	$130,087,224
IPO shares					11.0%				2,014,000	$16,112,000
TOTAL OUTSTANDING					100.0%				18,274,903	$146,199,224

REVENUE $M	REVENUE $M
Last 12 mos	Prior Quarter
$17.1	$6.0
Growth/Year	Growth/Year
136.9%	33.8%

Nr of employes: 232

(7) Vesting is usually 5 years and fair market value at time of grant.
Lead Underwriters: Morgan Stanley + Hambrecht & Quist

2,014,000 nr shares sold by company	$21,200,000		IPO TOTAL CASH RAISED BEFORE FEES AND EXPENSES
636,000 nr shares sold by selling shareholders	$1,484,000	7.00%	IPO fee for underwriters
	$550,000	2.59%	Estimated expenses of IPO
	$19,166,000	90.41%	NET TO COMPANY

SARATOGA VENTURE FINANCE EQUITY TABLE ™
WAGES AND STOCK OWNERSHIP AT INITIAL PUBLIC OFFERING (IPO)

Microsoft Corporation

IPO DATE: 13 March 1986
$21.00   Price per Share

Microcomputer software
Inception: 1975
Redmond, Washington

TITLE f = Founder	(4) COMP.	(3B) OFFICERS OWNERSHIP	(3),(6),(7) MGT & EMPS OWNERSHIP	(2) POST IPO OWNERSHIP	(1) PRE IPO OWNERSHIP	(3B) OFFICERS OWNERSHIP	(3),(6),(7) MGT & EMPS OWNERSHIP	(1) PRE IPO OWNERSHIP	(2) POST IPO OWNERSHIP	IPO VALUE $21.00 Per Share
f CEO	$133,000	56.4%	46.8%	40.2%	44.2%	11,222,000	11,222,000	11,222,000	11,222,000	$235,662,000
f EVP-Left		32.1%	26.6%	22.9%	25.2%	6,390,000	6,390,000	6,390,000	6,390,000	$134,190,000
VP-SysSW	$88,000	8.6%	7.1%	6.1%	6.7%	1,710,001	1,710,001	1,710,001	1,710,001	$35,910,021
COO	$228,000	2.0%	1.7%	1.4%	1.6%	400,000	400,000	400,000	400,000	$8,400,000
VP-ApsSW ; VP-OEM SLS		0.0%	0.0%	0.0%	0.0%	0	0	0	0	$0 *
VP-CDROM SW;VP-RtlSLS		0.0%	0.0%	0.0%	0.0%	0	0	0	0	$0 *
VP-INTL; VP-LEGAL		0.0%	0.0%	0.0%	0.0%	0	0	0	0	$0 *
VP-COM		0.0%	0.0%	0.0%	0.0%	0	0	0	0	$0 *
VP-HW DEVL	$96,000	0.0%	0.0%	0.0%	0.0%	0	0	0	0	$0 *
CFO	$109,000	0.0%	0.0%	0.0%	0.0%	0	0	0	0	$0 *
OTHER=Avg of 6	$67,571	0.8%	0.7%	0.6%	0.6%	158,001	158,001	158,001	158,001	$3,318,021
OFFICERS & EXECUTIVES		100.0%	82.8%	71.2%	78.3%	19,880,002	19,880,002	19,880,002	19,880,002	$417,480,042
ALL OTHER			6.0%	5.1%	5.7%		1,435,111	1,435,111	1,435,111	$30,137,331
TOTAL COMMON BEFORE OPTIONS			88.8%	76.3%	83.9%		21,315,113	21,315,113	21,315,113	$447,617,373
OPTIONS-Outstanding			11.2%	9.6%	10.6%		2,681,457	2,681,457	2,681,457	$56,310,597
OPTIONS-Available			0.0%	1.9%	0.0%		0	0	539,896	$11,337,816
OPTIONS-Total			11.2%	11.5%	10.6%		2,681,457	2,681,457	3,221,353	$67,648,413
COMMON-Total			100.0%	87.8%	94.5%		23,996,570	23,996,570	24,536,466	$515,265,786
Major Venture Capital				4.9%	5.4%			1,378,901	1,378,901	$28,956,921
OTHER				0.1%	0.1%			21,099	21,099	$443,079
VENTURE Total				5.0%	5.5%			1,400,000	1,400,000	$29,400,000
PRE-IPO: sum of all stock				92.8%	100.0%			25,396,570	25,936,466	$544,665,786
IPO shares				7.2%					2,000,000	$42,000,000
TOTAL OUTSTANDING				100.0%					27,936,466	$586,665,786

(7) Vesting not disclosed in prospectus, typically over five years.

Lead Underwriters: Goldman + Alex. Brown

2,000,000   nr shares sold by company
795,000   nr shares sold by selling shareholders

$58,695,000		IPO TOTAL CASH RAISED BEFORE FEES AND EXPENSES
$3,661,450	6.24%	IPO fee for underwriters
$541,000	0.92%	Estimated expenses of IPO
$54,492,550	92.84%	NET TO COMPANY

REVENUE $M	REVENUE $M
Last 12 mos	Prior Quarter
$140.4	$49.9
Growth/Year	Growth/Year
44.0%	35.6%
	Nr of employes: 998

Average $553K

SARATOGA VENTURE FINANCE EQUITY TABLE ™
WAGES AND STOCK OWNERSHIP AT INITIAL PUBLIC OFFERING (IPO)

MIPS Computer Systems, Inc.

IPO DATE: 21 December, 1989
$17.50   Price Per Share

RISC computers
Inception: 24 August 1984
Sunnyvale, California

TITLE f=Founder	(4) COMPENSATION	(3B) OFFICERS OWNERSHIP	(3),(6),(7) MGT & EMPS OWNERSHIP	(1) PRE IPO OWNERSHIP	(2) POST IPO OWNERSHIP	(3B) OFFICERS OWNERSHIP	(3),(6),(7) MGT & EMPS OWNERSHIP	(1) PRE IPO OWNERSHIP	(2) POST IPO OWNERSHIP	IPO VALUE $17.50 Per Share
f Chair., Pres, CEO	$311,863	10.9%	2.6%	1.5%	1.2%	295,654	295,654	295,654	295,654	$5,173,945
f Chief Scientist	Consultant	14.8%	3.5%	2.0%	1.6%	400,000	400,000	400,000	400,000	$7,000,000
f VP Dev. Programs		14.8%	3.5%	2.0%	1.6%	400,000	400,000	400,000	400,000	$7,000,000
f VP VLSI Devel-Left		14.8%	3.5%	2.0%	1.6%	400,000	400,000	400,000	400,000	$7,000,000
f Director		6.5%	0.0%	0.0%	0.0%	176,338	0	0	0	$0 *
EVP Field Ops	$564,086	4.7%	0.0%	0.0%	0.0%	127,000	0	0	0	$0 *
SVP Eng & Mfg	$211,277	3.5%	0.0%	0.0%	0.0%	94,000	0	0	0	$0 *
VP International	$215,949	1.2%	0.0%	0.0%	0.0%	31,250	0	0	0	$0 *
VP Legal	$131,331	0.9%	0.0%	0.0%	0.0%	25,200	0	0	0	$0 *
Others = 5	Avg = $118,147	27.8%	6.6%	3.7%	3.0%	750,625	750,625	750,625	750,625	$13,135,938
OFFICERS & EXECUTIVES		100.0%	19.8%	11.1%	9.0%	2,700,067	2,246,279	2,246,279	2,246,279	$39,309,883
ALL OTHER			43.5%	24.3%	19.8%		4,934,951	4,934,951	4,934,951	$86,361,643
TOTAL COMMON BEFORE OPTIONS			63.3%	35.3%	28.8%		7,181,230	7,181,230	7,181,230	$125,671,525
OPTIONS-Outstanding			36.7%	20.5%	16.7%		4,163,147	4,163,147	4,163,147	$72,855,073
OPTIONS-Available			0.0%	0.0%	2.5%		0	0	628,565	$10,999,888
OPTIONS-Total			36.7%	20.5%	19.2%		4,163,147	4,163,147	4,791,712	$83,854,960
COMMON-Total			100.0%	55.8%	48.1%		11,344,377	11,344,377	11,972,942	$209,526,485
Major Venture Capital				23.1%	18.9%			4,696,531	4,696,531	$82,189,293
OTHER: Kubota, DEC, Investors				21.1%	17.2%			4,278,304	4,278,304	$74,870,320
VENTURE Total				44.2%	36.0%			8,974,835	8,974,835	$157,059,613
PRE-IPO: sum of all stock				100.0%	84.1%			20,319,212	20,947,777	$366,586,098
IPO shares					15.9%				3,950,000	$69,125,000
TOTAL OUTSTANDING					100.0%				24,897,777	$435,711,098

Average of 8–$1.6M *

REVENUE $M	REVENUE $M
Last 12 mos	Prior Quarter
$39.4	$17.5
Growth/Year	Growth/Year
183.3%	141.1%

Nr of employes: 592

Lead Underwriters: Morgan Stanley + Cowen

3,950,000	nr shares sold by company	$80,500,000	IPO TOTAL CASH RAISED BEFORE FEES AND EXPENSES
650,000	nr shares sold by selling shareholders	$5,198,000	6.46% IPO fee for underwriters
4,600,000	IPO TOTAL	$900,000	1.12% Estimated expenses of IPO
		$74,402,000	92.42% NET TO COMPANY

(7) Vesting for Stock Option Plans is usually 25% for the first year and 6.25% per quarter over 5 years and fair market value at time of grant.

SARATOGA VENTURE FINANCE EQUITY TABLE ™
WAGES AND STOCK OWNERSHIP AT INITIAL PUBLIC OFFERING (IPO)

Nellcor Incorporated

IPO DATE: 19 May 1987
$16.00 Price per Share

Medical electronic instruments
Inception: 7 October 1981
Hayward, California

TITLE f = Founder	(4) COMPENSATION	(3B) OFFICERS OWNERSHIP	(3),(6),(7) MGT & EMPS OWNERSHIP	(1) PRE IPO OWNERSHIP	(2) POST IPO OWNERSHIP	(3B) OFFICERS OWNERSHIP	(3),(6),(7) MGT & EMPS OWNERSHIP	(1) PRE IPO OWNERSHIP	(2) POST IPO OWNERSHIP	IPO VALUE $16.00 Per Share
f Chairman	$151,946	28.6%	19.6%	7.8%	6.6%	1,024,440	1,024,440	1,024,440	1,024,440	$16,391,040
f President	$169,279	29.3%	20.1%	8.1%	6.8%	1,051,280	1,051,280	1,051,280	1,051,280	$16,820,480
f VP, CFO	$159,278	10.7%	7.4%	2.9%	2.5%	384,360	384,360	384,360	384,360	$6,149,760
f VP Engineering		8.5%	5.8%	2.3%	2.0%	303,920	303,920	303,920	303,920	$4,862,720
VP Human Res.		0.0%	0.0%	0.0%	0.0%	0	0	0	0	$0 *
All Others*	Avg of 6 = $113,959	22.9%	15.7%	6.3%	5.3%	821,469	821,469	821,469	821,469	$13,143,504 *
OFFICERS & EXECUTIVES		100.0%	68.6%	27.5%	23.1%	3,585,469	3,585,469	3,585,469	3,585,469	$57,367,504
ALL OTHER			8.7%	3.5%	2.9%		453,913	453,913	453,913	$7,262,608
TOTAL COMMON BEFORE OPTIONS			77.3%	30.9%	26.0%		4,039,382	4,039,382	4,039,382	$64,630,112
OPTIONS-Outstanding			22.7%	9.1%	7.7%		1,189,098	1,189,098	1,189,098	$19,025,568
OPTIONS-Available			0.0%	0.0%	5.5%		0	0	850,542	$13,608,672
OPTIONS-Total			22.7%	9.1%	13.2%		1,189,098	1,189,098	2,039,640	$32,634,240
COMMON-Total			100.0%	40.0%	39.2%		5,228,480	5,228,480	6,079,022	$97,264,352
Major Venture Capital				60.0%	50.5%			7,830,454	7,830,454	$125,287,264
OTHER				0.0%	0.0%			0	0	$0
VENTURE Total				60.0%	50.5%			7,830,454	7,830,454	$125,287,264
PRE-IPO: sum of all stock				100.0%	89.7%			13,058,934	13,909,476	$222,551,616
IPO shares					10.3%				1,600,000	$25,600,000
TOTAL OUTSTANDING					100.0%				15,509,476	$248,151,616

(7) Vesting for Stock Option Plans is usually 4 years, with one year waiting period for 25%, 6.25% per quarter thereafter and fair market value at time of grant.

Lead Underwriters: Goldman Sachs + Robertson + Cowen

1,600,000 nr shares sold by company	$38,400,000		IPO TOTAL CASH RAISED BEFORE FEES AND EXPENSES
800,000 nr shares sold by selling shareholders	$2,688,000	7.00%	IPO fee for underwriters
2,400,000 IPO TOTAL	$480,000	1.25%	Estimated expenses of IPO
	$35,232,000	91.75%	NET TO COMPANY

Average of 7 = $1.8M *

REVENUE $M	REVENUE $M	REVENUE $M
Last 12 mos	Prior Quarter	Prior Year
$46.2	$21.5	
Growth/Year	Growth/Year	
250.9%	59.6%	
	Nr of employes: 634	

SARATOGA VENTURE FINANCE EQUITY TABLE ™
WAGES AND STOCK OWNERSHIP AT INITIAL PUBLIC OFFERING (IPO)

Network Equipment Technologies

IPO DATE: 23 January 1987
$16.00 Price per Share

Telecommunications systems
Inception: 27 May 1983
Redwood City, California

TITLE f = Founder	(4) COMPENSATION	(3B) OFFICERS OWNERSHIP	(3),(6),(7) MGT & EMPS OWNERSHIP	(1) PRE IPO OWNERSHIP	(2) POST IPO OWNERSHIP	(3B) OFFICERS OWNERSHIP	(3),(6),(7) MGT & EMPS OWNERSHIP	(1) PRE IPO OWNERSHIP	(2) POST IPO OWNERSHIP	IPO VALUE $16.00 Per Share
f CEO,President	$113,279	40.3%	13.1%	4.4%	3.9%	534,513	534,513	534,513	534,513	$8,552,208
f VP-CNC	$82,114	26.4%	8.6%	2.9%	2.5%	350,070	350,070	350,070	350,070	$5,601,120
VP-SLS	$103,154	11.4%	3.7%	1.3%	1.1%	151,141	151,141	151,141	151,141	$2,418,256
VP-MKTG	$74,193	9.2%	3.0%	1.0%	0.9%	122,070	122,070	122,070	122,070	$1,953,120
VP-OPS	$75,847	11.4%	3.7%	1.3%	1.1%	0	0	0	0	$0 *
VP-FIN	$81,239	0.0%	0.0%	0.0%	0.0%	0	0	0	0	$0 *
OTHER		12.8%	4.2%	1.4%	1.2%	169,761	169,761	169,761	169,761	$2,716,176
OFFICERS & EXECUTIVES		100.0%	32.6%	11.0%	9.6%	1,327,555	1,327,555	1,327,555	1,327,555	$21,240,880
ALL OTHER			43.0%	14.5%	12.6%		1,749,432	1,749,432	1,749,432	$27,990,912
TOTAL COMMON BEFORE OPTIONS			75.6%	25.5%	22.2%		3,076,987	3,076,987	3,076,987	$49,231,792
OPTIONS-Outstanding			24.4%	8.2%	7.2%		993,555	993,555	993,555	$15,896,880
OPTIONS-Available			0.0%	0.0%	2.1%		0	0	294,033	$4,704,528
OPTIONS-Total			24.4%	8.2%	9.3%		993,555	993,555	1,287,588	$20,601,408
COMMON-Total			100.0%	33.7%	31.5%		4,070,542	4,070,542	4,364,575	$69,833,200
Major Venture Capital				34.7%	30.2%			4,185,025	4,185,025	$66,960,400
OTHER				31.6%	27.5%			3,806,975	3,806,975	$60,911,600
VENTURE Total				66.3%	57.7%			7,992,000	7,992,000	$127,872,000
PRE-IPO: sum of all stock				100.0%	89.2%			12,062,542	12,356,575	$197,705,200
IPO shares					10.8%				1,500,000	$24,000,000
TOTAL OUTSTANDING					100.0%				13,856,575	$221,705,200

	REVENUE $M	REVENUE $M
Avg of 2 = $912K *	Last 12 mos	Prior Quarter
	$8.7	$10.7
	Growth/Year	Growth/Year
	Not meaningful	Not meaningful
	Nr of employes: 429	

(7) Vesting for Stock Option Plans is usually 5 years, with a one year waiting period, 1/60 per mo thereafter and fair market value at time of grant.
Lead Underwriters: Morgan Stanley & Alex. Brown

1,500,000	nr shares sold by company	$40,000,000	IPO TOTAL CASH RAISED BEFORE FEES AND EXPENSES
1,000,000	nr shares sold by selling shareholders	$2,800,000	7.00% IPO fee for underwriters
2,500,000	IPO TOTAL	$680,000	1.70% Estimated expenses of IPO
		$36,520,000	91.30% NET TO COMPANY

SARATOGA VENTURE FINANCE EQUITY TABLE ™
WAGES AND STOCK OWNERSHIP AT INITIAL PUBLIC OFFERING (IPO)

Oracle Systems Corporation

IPO DATE: 12 March 1986
$15.00   Price per Share

Database software
Inception: June 1977
Belmont, California

TITLE f = Founder	(4) COMPENSATION	(3B) OFFICERS OWNERSHIP	(3),(6),(7) MGT & EMPS OWNERSHIP	(1) PRE IPO OWNERSHIP	(2) POST IPO OWNERSHIP	(3B) OFFICERS OWNERSHIP	(3),(6),(7) MGT & EMPS OWNERSHIP	(1) PRE IPO OWNERSHIP	(2) POST IPO OWNERSHIP	IPO VALUE $15.00 Per Share
f Pres,CEO	$212,513	57.4%	33.4%	30.6%	27.5%	4,608,750	4,608,750	4,608,750	4,608,750	$69,131,250
f SVP Devel.	$122,551	28.0%	16.3%	14.9%	13.4%	2,246,668	2,246,668	2,246,668	2,246,668	$33,700,020
VP Sales Intl		4.1%	2.4%	2.2%	1.9%	326,000	326,000	326,000	326,000	$4,890,000
Employee		2.8%	1.6%	1.5%	1.4%	227,222	227,222	227,222	227,222	$3,408,330
Employee		2.7%	1.6%	1.5%	1.3%	220,000	220,000	220,000	220,000	$3,300,000
VP F&A,CFO	$111,524	1.7%	1.0%	1.5%	1.3%	140,000	140,000	140,000	140,000	$2,100,000
All Others		3.2%	1.9%	1.7%	1.6%	260,000	260,000	260,000	260,000	$3,900,000
OFFICERS & EXECUTIVES		100.0%	58.2%	53.4%	47.9%	8,028,640	8,028,640	8,028,640	8,028,640	$120,429,600
ALL OTHER			19.5%	17.9%	16.1%		2,690,804	2,690,804	2,690,804	$40,362,060
TOTAL COMMON BEFORE OPTIONS			77.7%	71.2%	64.0%		10,719,444	10,719,444	10,719,444	$160,791,660
OPTIONS-Outstanding			22.3%	20.5%	18.4%		3,082,863	3,082,863	3,082,863	$46,242,945
OPTIONS-Available			0.0%	0.0%	4.2%		0	0	707,841	$10,617,615
OPTIONS-Total			22.3%	20.5%	22.6%		3,082,863	3,082,863	3,790,704	$56,860,560
COMMON-Total			100.0%	91.7%	86.6%		13,802,307	13,802,307	14,510,148	$217,652,220
Major Venture Capital				8.3%	7.4%			1,246,666	1,246,666	$18,699,990
OTHER				0.0%	0.0%			0	0	$0
VENTURE Total				8.3%	7.4%			1,246,666	1,246,666	$18,699,990
PRE-IPO: sum of all stock				100.0%	94.0%			15,048,973	15,756,814	$236,352,210
IPO shares					6.0%				1,000,000	$15,000,000
TOTAL OUTSTANDING					100.0%				16,756,814	$251,352,210

REVENUE $M	REVENUE $M
Last 12 mos	Prior Quarter
$23.1	$11.4
Growth/Year	Growth/Year
82.1%	103.4%
	Nr of employes: 425

(7) Vesting for Stock Option Plans is usually 4 years, with one year waiting period, 1/4 per year thereafter and fair market value at time of grant.
Lead Underwriters: Merrill Lynch + Alex. Brown

1,000,000	nr shares sold by company	$31,500,000	IPO TOTAL CASH RAISED BEFORE FEES AND EXPENSES
1,100,000	nr shares sold by selling shareholders	$2,205,000	7.00% IPO fee for underwriters
2,100,000	IPO TOTAL	$545,000	1.73% Estimated expenses of IPO
		$28,750,000	91.27% NET TO COMPANY

SARATOGA VENTURE FINANCE EQUITY TABLE ™
WAGES AND STOCK OWNERSHIP AT INITIAL PUBLIC OFFERING (IPO)

Sigma Designs, Inc.

IPO DATE: 15 May 1986
$17.00 Price per Share

DOS microcomputer boards and add-on hardware
Inception: 7 January 1982
Fremont, California

TITLE f = Founder	(4) COMPENSATION	(3B) OFFICERS OWNERSHIP	(3),(6),(7) MGT & EMPS OWNERSHIP	(1) PRE IPO OWNERSHIP	(2) POST IPO OWNERSHIP	(3B) OFFICERS OWNERSHIP	(3),(6),(7) MGT & EMPS OWNERSHIP	(1) PRE IPO OWNERSHIP	(2) POST IPO OWNERSHIP	IPO VALUE $17.00 Per Share
f Chair,CEO,Pres	$77,000	23.3%	7.4%	7.4%	6.4%	424,634	424,634	424,634	424,634	$7,218,778
f VP Mfg	$67,000	23.3%	7.4%	7.4%	6.4%	425,634	425,634	425,634	425,634	$7,235,778
f VP Prod Devl	$67,000	22.5%	7.1%	7.1%	6.2%	409,962	409,962	409,962	409,962	$6,969,354
f VP Engineering	$72,000	21.7%	6.9%	6.9%	6.0%	305,634	395,634	395,634	395,634	$6,725,778
VP Fin, CFO	$73,886	4.3%	1.3%	1.3%	1.2%	77,726	77,726	77,726	77,726	$1,321,342
VP Marketing	$58,199	3.4%	1.1%	1.1%	0.9%	61,262	61,262	61,262	61,262	$1,041,454
VP Sales	$69,000	1.6%	0.5%	0.5%	0.5%	29,844	29,844	29,844	29,844	$507,348
OFFICERS & EXECUTIVES		100.0%	31.7%	31.7%	27.6%	1,824,696	1,824,696	1,824,696	1,824,696	$31,019,832
ALL OTHER			49.1%	49.1%	42.8%		2,826,701	2,826,701	2,826,701	$48,053,917
TOTAL COMMON BEFORE OPTIONS			80.8%	80.8%	70.4%		4,651,397	4,651,397	4,651,397	$79,073,749
OPTIONS-Outstanding			11.9%	11.9%	10.4%		686,461	686,461	686,461	$11,669,837
OPTIONS-Available			7.3%	7.3%	6.4%		421,001	421,001	421,001	$7,157,017
OPTIONS-Total			19.2%	19.2%	16.8%		1,107,462	1,107,462	1,107,462	$18,826,854
COMMON-Total			100.0%	100.0%	87.1%		5,758,859	5,758,859	5,758,859	$97,900,603
Major Venture Capital				0.0%	0.0%			0	0	$0
OTHER				0.0%	0.0%			0	0	$0
VENTURE Total				0.0%	0.0%			0	0	$0
PRE-IPO: sum of all stock				100.0%	87.1%			5,758,859	5,758,859	$97,900,603
IPO shares					12.9%				850,000	$14,450,000
TOTAL OUTSTANDING					100.0%				6,608,859	$112,350,603

(7) Vesting for Stock Option Plans is usually 5 years at 20% per year and fair market value at time of grant.
Lead Underwriters: Laidlaw Adams & Peck Inc.

850,000	nr shares sold by company	$17,000,000	IPO TOTAL CASH RAISED BEFORE FEES AND EXPENSES
150,000	nr shares sold by selling shareholders	$940,000	5.53% IPO fee for underwriters
1,000,000	IPO TOTAL	$300,000	1.76% Estimated expenses of IPO
		$15,760,000	92.71% NET TO COMPANY

REVENUE $M	REVENUE $M
Last 12 mos	Prior Quarter
$10.1	NA
Growth/Year	Growth/Year
57.9%	NA
Nr of employes: 120	

SARATOGA VENTURE FINANCE EQUITY TABLE ™
WAGES AND STOCK OWNERSHIP AT INITIAL PUBLIC OFFERING (IPO)

Silicon Graphics, Inc.

IPO DATE: 29 October 1986
$11.25 Price per Share

3D computer systems
Inception: 9 November 1981
San Jose, California

TITLE f = Founder	(4) COMPENSATION	(3B) OFFICERS OWNERSHIP	(3),(6),(7) MGT & EMPS OWNERSHIP	(1) PRE IPO OWNERSHIP	(2) POST IPO OWNERSHIP	(3B) OFFICERS OWNERSHIP	(3),(6),(7) MGT & EMPS OWNERSHIP	(1) PRE IPO OWNERSHIP	(2) POST IPO OWNERSHIP	IPO VALUE $11.25 Per Share
Pres,CEO,Dir	$156,057	26.6%	11.9%	3.9%	3.1%	400,050	400,050	400,050	400,050	$4,500,563
f CHAIR+CTO	$138,077	39.4%	17.6%	5.7%	4.6%	592,133	592,133	592,133	592,133	$6,661,496
VP-ENG	$108,655	0.0%	0.0%	0.0%	0.0%		0	0	0	$0 *
VP-NA Sales	$104,705	0.0%	0.0%	0.0%	0.0%		0	0	0	$0 *
VP-Fin&Admin	$125,000	0.0%	0.0%	0.0%	0.0%		0	0	0	$0 *
VP-R&D		0.0%	0.0%	0.0%	0.0%		0	0	0	$0 *
VP-MKTG;VP-OEM;Pres. Int'l		0.0%	0.0%	0.0%	0.0%		0	0	0	$0 *
VP-HR VP-OPS VP-SLS		0.0%	0.0%	0.0%	0.0%		0	0	0	$0 *
OTHER EMPS Avg of 4 = $60,316		33.9%	15.1%	4.9%	3.9%	509,662	509,662	509,662	509,662	$5,733,698
OFFICERS & EXECUTIVES		100.0%	44.6%	14.5%	11.6%	1,501,845	1,501,845	1,501,845	1,501,845	$16,895,756
ALL OTHER			50.2%	16.3%	13.1%		1,692,225	1,692,225	1,692,225	$19,037,531
TOTAL COMMON BEFORE OPTIONS			94.8%	30.8%	24.7%		3,194,070	3,194,070	3,194,070	$35,933,288
OPTIONS-Outstanding			5.2%	1.7%	1.3%		174,400	174,400	174,400	$1,962,000
OPTIONS-Available			0.0%	0.0%	7.9%			0	1,025,600	$11,538,000
OPTIONS-Total			5.2%	1.7%	9.3%		174,400	174,400	1,200,000	$13,500,000
COMMON-Total			100.0%	32.5%	34.0%		3,368,470	3,368,470	4,394,070	$49,433,288
Major Venture Capital				41.0%	32.9%			4,246,151	4,246,151	$47,769,199
OTHER				26.5%	21.3%			2,749,763	2,749,763	$30,934,834
VENTURE Total				67.5%	54.1%			6,995,914	6,995,914	$78,704,033
PRE-IPO: sum of all stock				100.0%	88.2%			10,364,384	11,389,984	$128,137,320
IPO shares					11.8%				1,530,000	$17,212,500
TOTAL OUTSTANDING					100.0%				12,919,984	$145,349,820

(7) Vesting for Stock Option Plans is usually 5 years, with ten month waiting period, 2% per mo thereafter and fair market value at time of grant.

Lead Underwriters: Morgan Stanley + Alex. Brown

1,530,000 nr shares sold by company	$20,250,000		IPO TOTAL CASH RAISED BEFORE FEES AND EXPENSES
270,000 nr shares sold by selling shareholders	$1,422,000	7.02%	IPO fee for underwriters
1,800,000 IPO TOTAL	$460,000	2.27%	Estimated expenses of IPO
	$18,368,000	90.71%	NET TO COMPANY

Avg. of 7=$819K *

REVENUE $M	REVENUE $M
Last 12 mos	Prior Quarter
$41.5	$14.2
Growth/Year	Growth/Year
92.6%	106.0%
Nr of employes: 331	

SARATOGA VENTURE FINANCE EQUITY TABLE ™
WAGES AND STOCK OWNERSHIP AT INITIAL PUBLIC OFFERING (IPO)

Software Publishing Corporation

IPO DATE: 15 November 1984
$7.00 Price per Share

Software for microcomputers
Inception: 18 April 1980
Mountain View, California

TITLE f = Founder	(4) COMPENSATION	(3B) OFFICERS OWNERSHIP	(3),(6),(7) MGT & EMPS OWNERSHIP	(1) PRE IPO OWNERSHIP	(2) POST IPO OWNERSHIP	(3B) OFFICERS OWNERSHIP	(3),(6),(7) MGT & EMPS OWNERSHIP	(1) PRE IPO OWNERSHIP	(2) POST IPO OWNERSHIP	IPO VALUE $7.00 Per Share
f Pres,CEO	$119,286	31.9%	25.1%	17.0%	13.4%	925,000	925,000	925,000	925,000	$6,475,000
f VP,Gen Mgr.	$107,094	32.8%	25.7%	17.5%	13.8%	950,000	950,000	950,000	950,000	$6,650,000
f VP R&D	$107,094	32.8%	25.7%	17.5%	13.8%	950,000	950,000	950,000	950,000	$6,650,000
VP F&A,CFO	$75,361	2.6%	2.0%	1.4%	1.1%	75,000	75,000	75,000	75,000	$525,000
OTHER		0.0%	0.0%	0.0%	0.0%		0	0	0	$0
OFFICERS & EXECUTIVES		100.0%	78.6%	53.3%	42.1%	2,900,000	2,900,000	2,900,000	2,900,000	$20,300,000
ALL OTHER			12.1%	8.2%	6.5%		444,947	444,947	444,947	$3,114,629
TOTAL COMMON BEFORE OPTIONS			90.7%	61.5%	48.5%		3,344,947	3,344,947	3,344,947	$23,414,629
OPTIONS-Outstanding			9.3%	6.3%	5.0%		344,617	344,617	344,617	$2,412,319
OPTIONS-Available			0.0%	0.0%	2.0%		0	0	139,063	$973,441
OPTIONS-Total			9.3%	6.3%	7.0%		344,617	344,617	483,680	$3,385,760
COMMON-Total			100.0%	67.8%	55.5%		3,689,564	3,689,564	3,828,627	$26,800,389
Major Venture Capital				29.7%	23.4%			1,616,000	1,616,000	$11,312,000
OTHER				2.5%	1.9%			134,000	134,000	$938,000
VENTURE Total				32.2%	25.4%			1,750,000	1,750,000	$12,250,000
PRE-IPO: sum of all stock				100.0%	80.9%			5,439,564	5,578,627	$39,050,389
IPO shares					19.1%				1,315,000	$9,205,000
TOTAL OUTSTANDING					100.0%				6,893,627	$48,255,389

(7) Vesting for Stock Option Plans is usually 4 years, with 25% at end of a one year waiting period, 1/48th per month thereafter and fair market value at time of grant.

Lead Underwriters: Robertson + Rothschild

1,315,000	nr shares sold by company	$11,200,000	IPO TOTAL CASH RAISED BEFORE FEES AND EXPENSES
285,000	nr shares sold by selling shareholders	$800,000 7.14%	IPO fee for underwriters
1,600,000	IPO TOTAL	$375,000 3.35%	Estimated expenses of IPO
		$10,025,000 89.51%	NET TO COMPANY

REVENUE $M	REVENUE $M
Last 12 mos	Prior Quarter
$23.5	$7.4
Growth/Year	Growth/Year
131.9%	104.5%
	Nr of employes: 130

SOURCE: Saratoga Venture Finance © All rights reserved. See prospectus for data. The above contain certain estimates.

SARATOGA VENTURE FINANCE EQUITY TABLE ™
WAGES AND STOCK OWNERSHIP AT INITIAL PUBLIC OFFERING (IPO)

Sun Microsystems, Inc.

IPO DATE: 4 March 1986
$16.00 Price per Share

UNIX workstations
Inception: 24 February 1982
Mountain View., California

TITLE f = Founder	(4) COMPENSATION	(3B) OFFICERS OWNERSHIP	(3),(6),(7) MGT & EMPS OWNERSHIP	(1) PRE IPO OWNERSHIP	(2) POST IPO OWNERSHIP	(3B) OFFICERS OWNERSHIP	(3),(6),(7) MGT & EMPS OWNERSHIP	(1) PRE IPO OWNERSHIP	(2) POST IPO OWNERSHIP	IPO VALUE $16.00 Per Share
f CEO	$239,748	18.3%	9.2%	4.4%	3.9%	1,147,263	1,147,263	1,147,263	1,147,263	$18,356,208
f VP-TECH		25.1%	12.6%	6.1%	5.3%	1,571,093	1,571,093	1,571,093	1,571,093	$25,137,488
f Board Director		18.4%	9.2%	4.4%	3.9%	1,149,011	1,149,011	1,149,011	1,149,011	$18,384,176
VP R&D		14.1%	7.1%	3.4%	3.0%	884,077	884,077	884,077	884,077	$14,145,232
EVP	$122,987	5.4%	2.7%	1.3%	1.1%	336,875	336,875	336,875	336,875	$5,390,000
VP-SLS	$117,812	0.0%	0.0%	0.0%	0.0%	0	0	0	0	$0 *
VP-FIN	$128,700	0.0%	0.0%	0.0%	0.0%	0	0	0	0	$0 *
VP-EUR	$104,000	0.0%	0.0%	0.0%	0.0%	0	0	0	0	$0 *
OTHER	Avg. of 8 = $60,554	18.7%	9.4%	4.5%	4.0%	1,170,248	1,170,248	1,170,248	1,170,248	$18,723,968 *
OFFICERS & EXECUTIVES		100.0%	50.2%	24.2%	21.2%	6,258,567	6,258,567	6,258,567	6,258,567	$100,137,072
ALL OTHER			34.1%	16.4%	14.4%		4,254,338	4,254,338	4,254,338	$68,069,408
TOTAL COMMON BEFORE OPTIONS			84.4%	40.6%	35.6%		10,512,905	10,512,905	10,512,905	$168,206,480
OPTIONS-Outstanding			15.6%	7.5%	6.6%		1,948,956	1,948,956	1,948,956	$31,183,296
OPTIONS-Available			0.0%	0.0%	2.2%		0		660,383	$10,566,128
OPTIONS-Total			15.6%	7.5%	8.8%		1,948,956	1,948,956	2,609,339	$41,749,424
COMMON-Total			100.0%	48.1%	44.4%		12,461,861	12,461,861	13,122,244	$209,955,904
Major Venture Capital				41.1%	36.0%			10,654,885	10,654,885	$170,478,160
OTHER				10.8%	9.4%			2,786,514	2,786,514	$44,584,224
VENTURE Total				51.9%	45.5%			13,441,399	13,441,399	$215,062,384
PRE-IPO: sum of all stock				100.0%	89.9%			25,903,260	26,563,643	$425,018,288
IPO shares					10.1%				3,000,000	$48,000,000
TOTAL OUTSTANDING					100.0%				29,563,643	$473,018,288

(7) Vesting for Stock Option Plans is usually 4 years, with six month waiting period, 1/48 per mo thereafter and fair market value at time of grant.
Lead Underwriters: Robertson + Alex. Brown

3,000,000	nr shares sold by company	$64,000,000	IPO TOTAL CASH RAISED BEFORE FEES AND EXPENSES
1,000,000	nr shares sold by selling shareholders	$3,920,000	IPO fee for underwriters 6.13%
4,000,000	IPO TOTAL	$600,000	Estimated expenses of IPO 0.94%
		$59,480,000	NET TO COMPANY 92.94%

REVENUE $M	REVENUE $M
Last 12 mos	Prior Quarter
$115.2	$42.2
Growth/Year	Growth/Year
196.6%	73.5%
Nr of employes: 1,223	

Avg. of 11 = $1.7M *

SARATOGA VENTURE FINANCE EQUITY TABLE ™
WAGES AND STOCK OWNERSHIP AT INITIAL PUBLIC OFFERING (IPO)

Vertex Pharmaceuticals Incorporated

IPO DATE: 24 July 1991
$9.00   Price per Share

Drug designer
Inception: 4 January 1989
Cambridge, Massachusetts

TITLE f = Founder	(4) COMPENSATION	(3B) OFFICERS OWNERSHIP	(3),(6),(7) MGT & EMPS OWNERSHIP	(1) PRE IPO OWNERSHIP	(2) POST IPO OWNERSHIP	(3B) OFFICERS OWNERSHIP	(3),(6),(7) MGT & EMPS OWNERSHIP	(1) PRE IPO OWNERSHIP	(2) POST IPO OWNERSHIP	IPO VALUE $9.00 Per Share
f Pres,CSO	$162,880	80.4%	33.3%	7.8%	4.9%	520,000	520,000	520,000	520,000	$4,680,000
VP-BusDev	$83,807	0.0%	0.0%	0.0%	0.0%	0	0	0	0	$0 *
Sr. Scientist	$92,054	0.0%	0.0%	0.0%	0.0%	0	0	0	0	$0 *
OTHER		19.6%	8.1%	1.9%	1.2%	126,999	126,999	126,999	126,999	$1,142,991
OFFICERS & EXECUTIVES		100.0%	41.4%	9.7%	6.1%	646,999	646,999	646,999	646,999	$5,822,991
ALL OTHER			58.6%	13.8%	8.6%		915,343	915,343	915,343	$8,238,087
TOTAL COMMON BEFORE OPTIONS			100.0%	23.5%	14.7%		1,562,342	1,562,342	1,562,342	$14,061,078
OPTIONS-Outstanding			0.0%	0.0%	0.0%		0	0	0	$0
OPTIONS-Available			0.0%	0.0%	9.4%		0	0	1,000,000	$9,000,000
OPTIONS-Total			0.0%	0.0%	9.4%		0	0	1,000,000	$9,000,000
COMMON-Total			100.0%	23.5%	24.1%		1,562,342	1,562,342	2,562,342	$23,061,078
Major Venture Capital				73.5%	45.8%			4,875,742	4,875,742	$43,881,678
OTHER				3.0%	1.9%			200,000	200,000	$1,800,000
VENTURE Total				76.5%	47.7%			5,075,742	5,075,742	$45,681,678
PRE-IPO: sum of all stock				100.0%	71.8%			6,638,084	7,638,084	$68,742,756
IPO shares					28.2%				3,000,000	$27,000,000
TOTAL OUTSTANDING					100.0%				10,638,084	$95,742,756

Avg. of 4=$286K *

(7) Vesting determined by board of directors.
Lead Underwriters: Kidder + Cowen + BT Securities

3,000,000 nr shares sold by company	$27,000,000		IPO TOTAL CASH RAISED BEFORE FEES AND EXPENSES
0 nr shares sold by selling shareholders	$1,732,500	6.42%	IPO fee for underwriters
3,000,000 IPO TOTAL	$600,000	2.22%	Estimated expenses of IPO
	$24,667,500	91.36%	NET TO COMPANY

REVENUE $M	REVENUE $M
Last 12 mos	Prior Quarter
$0.8	$0.0
Growth/Year	Growth/Year
Not meaningful	Not meaningful
Nr of employes: 53	

SARATOGA VENTURE FINANCE EQUITY TABLE™
WAGES AND STOCK OWNERSHIP AT INITIAL PUBLIC OFFERING (IPO)

Worlds of Wonder

IPO DATE: 20 June 1986
$18.00 Price per Share

Electronic toys
Inception: March 1985
Fremont, California

TITLE f = Founder	(4) COMPENSATION	(3B) OFFICERS OWNERSHIP	(3),(6),(7) MGT & EMPS OWNERSHIP	(1) PRE IPO OWNERSHIP	(2) POST IPO OWNERSHIP	(3B) OFFICERS OWNERSHIP	(3),(6),(7) MGT & EMPS OWNERSHIP	(1) PRE IPO OWNERSHIP	(2) POST IPO OWNERSHIP	IPO VALUE $18.00 Per Share
f CEO	$332,641	71.5%	51.2%	25.6%	20.5%	4,918,356	4,918,356	4,918,356	4,918,356	$88,530,408
EVP-COO	$203,591	8.9%	6.4%	3.2%	2.5%	610,715	610,715	610,715	610,715	$10,992,870
EVP-DEV		2.7%	2.0%	1.0%	0.8%	187,500	187,500	187,500	187,500	$3,375,000
EVP-MKTG		0.0%	0.0%	0.0%	0.0%	0	0	0	0	$0
EVP-SLS	$199,096	4.4%	3.1%	1.6%	1.2%	300,000	300,000	300,000	300,000	$5,400,000
EVP-MFG/ENG	$199,096	5.4%	3.9%	2.0%	1.6%	375,000	375,000	375,000	375,000	$6,750,000
EVP-ADMIN	$167,243	3.2%	2.3%	1.1%	0.9%	217,500	217,500	217,500	217,500	$3,915,000
EVP-FIN/CFO		2.7%	2.0%	1.0%	0.8%	187,500	187,500	187,500	187,500	$3,375,000
EVP		0.0%	0.0%	0.0%	0.0%	0	0	0	0	$0
OTHER Avg. of 3=$115,186		7.1%	5.1%	2.6%	2.0%	491,875	491,875	491,875	491,875	$8,853,750 *
OFFICERS & EXECUTIVES		100.0%	75.8%	38.0%	30.4%	6,883,446	7,288,446	7,288,446	7,288,446	$131,192,028
ALL OTHER			12.0%	6.0%	4.8%		1,151,639	1,151,639	1,151,639	$20,729,502
TOTAL COMMON BEFORE OPTIONS			87.8%	44.0%	35.2%		8,440,085	8,440,085	8,440,085	$151,921,530
OPTIONS-Outstanding			12.2%	6.1%	4.9%		1,174,750	1,174,750	1,174,750	$21,145,500
OPTIONS-Available			0.0%	0.0%	3.4%		0	0	810,250	$14,584,500
OPTIONS-Total			12.2%	6.1%	8.3%		1,174,750	1,174,750	1,985,000	$35,730,000
COMMON-Total			100.0%	50.1%	43.4%		9,614,835	9,614,835	10,425,085	$187,651,530
Major Venture Capital				0.0%	0.0%			0	0	$0
OTHER				49.9%	39.9%			9,577,350	9,577,350	$172,392,300
VENTURE Total				49.9%	39.9%			9,577,350	9,577,350	$172,392,300
PRE-IPO: sum of all stock				100.0%	83.3%			19,192,185	20,002,435	$360,043,830
IPO shares					16.7%				4,000,000	$72,000,000
TOTAL OUTSTANDING					100.0%				24,002,435	$432,043,830

Avg. of 3= $2.9M *

REVENUE $M	REVENUE $M
Last 12 mos	Prior Quarter
$93.1	$44.6
Growth/Year	Growth/Year
Not meaningful	Not meaningful
	Nr of employes: 134

(7) Vesting for Stock Option Plans is usually 4 years, with a three month waiting period, 1/48 per mo thereafter and fair market value at time of grant.
Lead Underwriters: Smith Barney + Dean Witter

4,000,000	nr shares sold by company	$108,000,000	IPO TOTAL CASH RAISED BEFORE FEES AND EXPENSES
2,000,000	nr shares sold by selling shareholders	$6,780,000 6.28%	IPO fee for underwriters
6,000,000	IPO TOTAL	$755,000 0.70%	Estimated expenses of IPO
		$100,465,000 93.02%	NET TO COMPANY

B: Resources for the Entrepreneur

Sources of Venture Capitalists

National Venture Capital
  Association
1655 North Fort Meyer Drive,
  Suite 700
Arlington, VA 22209
703-528-4370
Publishes an up-to-date directory
of their members.

Western Association of Venture
  Capitalists
3000 Sand Hill Road
Building 2, Suite 260
Menlo Park, CA 94025
415-854-1322
Sells a detailed annual directory
of member firms in eleven
western states.

Venture Economics, Inc.
75 2nd Avenue
Needham, MA 02194
617-449-2100
Guide to Venture Capital Sources
A combination of directory and
articles written by experienced
venture capital people.
Venture Capital Journal
Monthly publication about
venture firms, company
financings, and trends affecting
venture capitalists.

General Legal Counsel

Bruce Jenrette
  Fenwick Davis & West
  2 Palo Alto Square, Suite 800
  Palo Alto, CA 94306
  415-494-0600

Mike Phillips
  Morrison and Foerster
  755 Hanson Way
  Palo Alto, CA 94304-1003
  415-345-1500

Allan Abravanel
  Perkins Coi, Suite 2500
  U.S. Bancorp Tower
  Portland, OR 97204
  503-295-4400

Chuck Katz
  Perkins Coi
  12001 3rd Avenue, 40th Floor
  Seattle, WA 98101-3099
  206-583-8888

Dick Riordon
  Riordon & McKinzie
  300 S. Grand Avenue
  Los Angeles, CA 90070
  213-629-4824

James W. Loss
  Riordon & McKinzie
  611 Anton Blvd., Suite 1160
  Costa Mesa, CA 92626
  714-433-2900

Richard Testa
  Testa, Hurwitz & Thibeault
  53 State Street, 17th Floor
  Boston, MA 02104
  617-371-7500

Paul Kreutz
  Ware & Friedenrich
  400 Hamilton Avenue
  Palo Alto, CA 94311
  415-328-6561

(Continued)

General Legal Counsel

(continued)

Larry Sonsini
  Wilson Sonsini Goodrich and
    Rosati
  2 Palo Alto Square
  Palo Alto, CA 94306
  415-493-9300

Sources of Information About Writing a Business Plan

Ask the local offices for a copy.

Ernst & Young
  Outline for a High Technology,
  New Venture Business Plan

Peat Marwick, Private Business
    Advisory Service
  Business Planning

Deloitte Ross Tohmatsu
  Writing an Effective Business Plan

Intellectual Property Attorneys

Lois Abraham
  Brown & Bain
  600 Hansen Way, Suite 100
  Palo Alto, CA 94306
  415-856-9411

Alan MacPherson
  Skjerven, Morrill, MacPherson,
    Franklin & Freil
  25 Metro Drive, Suite 700
  San Jose, CA 95110
  408-283-1222

Attorney Referral Desk
  Townsend & Townsend
  379 Lyton Avenue
  Palo Alto, CA 94301
  415-326-2400

Accounting Firms

To request assistance, call up the nearest office listed in the white pages of the telephone book and ask for the managing partner.

  Arthur Anderson

  Coopers and Lybrand

  Deloitte Ross Tohmatsu

  Ernst & Young

  KPMG

  Price Waterhouse

Investment Bankers

Dick Franyo
  Alex Brown
  135 E. Baltimore Street
  Baltimore, MD 21202
  301-727-1700

Jim Furno
  Cowen
  Exchange Place, 26th Floor
  Boston, MA 02109
  617-523-3221

Eff Martin
  Goldman Sachs
  555 California Street,
    Suite 3120
  San Francisco, CA 94104
  415-393-7607

Dan Case
  Hambrecht & Quist
  One Bush Street
  San Francisco, CA 94104
  415-576-3631

(Continued)

Investment Bankers

(continued)

Ken Kannappan
 Kidder Peabody
 555 California Street, Suite 3200
 San Francisco, CA 94104
 415-398-6400

Barry Frieberg
 Merrill Lynch
 250 Vessy Street
 World Trade Center
 New York, NY 10281
 212-449-8500

Carter McClelland
 Morgan Stanley
 1251 Avenue of the Americas
 New York, NY 10020
 212-703-8545

Sandy Robertson
 Robertson, Colman & Stephens
 1 Embarcadero Center,
  Suite 3100
 San Francisco, CA 94111
 415-781-9700

Sources of Information About Going Public

Going Public
 Bowne
 190 9th Street
 San Francisco, CA 94103
 415-864-2300
 This is one of the companies
 specializing in printing
 prospectuses.

Strategies for Going Public
 Deloitte Ross Tohmatsu
 Ask the local partner to get
 you a copy.

The Going Public Decision
 Ernst & Young
 Ask the local partner to get
 you a copy.

Equipment Leasing Companies

Lee Meier
 Meier Mitchell & Company
 4 Orinda Way, Suite 200B
 Orinda, CA 94563
 510-254-9520

Ron Swanson
 Western Technology
  Investment
 20109 1st Street, Suite 202
 San Jose, CA 95131
 408-436-8577

Ron Lapin
 John Hancock Leasing
 2230 Foothill Boulevard
 Plaza Center, Suite 600
 Hayward, CA 94541
 510-886-2556

Norman Nelson
 Phoenix Leasing
 2401 Kerner Boulevard
 San Rafael, CA 94901
 415-485-4500

Public Relations Firms

Steve Benjamin
 The Benjamin Group Inc.
 3945 Freedom Circle
 Santa Clara, CA 95054
 408-988-8933

(Continued)

Public Relations Firms

(continued)

Paul Franson
  Franson & Associates
  181 Metro Drive, Suite 300
  San Jose, CA 95110
  408-453-5221

Frank Rich
  MRT
  51 Yale Street, Box 362
  Winchester, MA 01890
  617-721-0589

Regis McKenna
  Regis McKenna Inc.
  1755 Embarcadero Road
  Palo Alto, CA 94303
  415-494-2030

Other Resources

National Investor Relations
  Institute
1730 M Street NW
Washington, DC 20036
202-861-0630
For advice on post-IPO investor
relations. They have local
chapters meeting across America
in most metropolitan areas.

American Electronics Association
5201 Great America Parkway
P.O. Box 54900
Santa Clara, CA 95056-0990
408-987-4200
There is a regular circuit of meetings at which CEOs of a new
company can speak to investors.
AEA holds several forums each
year on both coasts of the U.S. as
well as in Europe.

Financial Modeling Software: StartUp™

StartUp is a software tool for forecasting financial statements quickly
and easily. It runs on either IBM-compatible PCs with Lotus 1-2-3™
spreadsheet software, or on Apple Macintoshes with Excel™ spreadsheet
software. If you know the basics of spreadsheeting, StartUp is simple to use.

When you input the required information, StartUp produces an income
statement, balance sheet, and cash flow statement. The income statement
is in either the standard format or given as percentage of revenue—the
format most commonly used by venture capitalists. The income statement automatically feeds its profit to the balance sheet in the retained
earnings section, and the cash flow statement automatically changes
every time the balance sheet changes.

Input drives output. The formulas linking the input (such as
headcount) to the output (such as expenses) can be changed if you
choose. You can add or subtract lines or relable them as you would in
any spreadsheet model. Each recalculation of the model will tell you how
much capital your business will require each year.

StartUp will help you develop your business plan faster and keep your
financial projections current with your plan. Most important, StartUp
enables you to immediately test the assumptions of your business plan.

Ordering information is on the last page of this book.

C: Three Venture Capital Firms Describe Themselves

Kleiner Perkins Caufield & Byers
San Francisco and Palo Alto, California

Kleiner Perkins Caufield & Byers is an active Bay Area venture capital partnership with a large capital base for future investment. Over the past decade we have backed nearly 100 companies, which have accrued market valuations of many billions of dollars. In this process we have been privileged to work with some of America's outstanding entrepreneurs, and have been pleased to see that among this group are several hundred individuals who have achieved their visions and have become millionaires in the process. The partnership's funds are contributed by a group of very large and sophisticated institutions that additionally from time to time invest directly with us; thus, there is virtually no limit to the size of the financial commitment we can make. We are interested in a variety of products, markets, and technologies and in ventures ranging from startups to more mature situations. We seek opportunities to invest in companies that will grow rapidly and become profitable. It is essential that these companies be managed by entrepreneurs who are innovative, ambitious, and success-oriented. We focus particularly on the caliber of management, their character and experience, and on well-thought-out plans.

We enjoy taking the role of lead investor and working closely with the management groups of our portfolio companies. Further, we attempt to be sure that our venture groups work with each other to accelerate success and reduce risk. This network is epitomized by the constant networking of our companies for mutual benefit, and is a major advantage that we have shown we can offer.

We seek opportunities with the potential to achieve significant shares of high-growth markets. Examples of the fields in which we have investment experience include: computers and computer peripherals, software, office equipment, medical products and instruments, microbiology, genetic engineering, telecommunications, instrumentation, semiconductors and their capital equipment, lasers and optics, and unique consumer products and services.

We provide the entrepreneurial team with resources beyond financial backing through contacts, recruiting assistance, and our business experiences. As entrepreneurs ourselves, we have founded and operated our own successful companies; carried profit and loss responsibility for very large organizations; been partners of important investment banking houses; and negotiated major contracts, mergers, and public underwritings. Further, we have direct experience in manufacturing, engineering, marketing and financial control, as well as backgrounds in a variety of technologies. This qualifies us to understand and support entrepreneurs in their efforts to create and build new businesses.

We are one of the few groups to have consistently funded successful new ventures through all phases of the business cycle. Our partnership is looking for new investment opportunities.

Sutter Hill Ventures
Palo Alto, California

Sutter Hill Ventures has been financing technology-based companies since 1962. We believe strongly that Sutter Hill brings more than investment dollars to a business. We are interested in becoming a partner with management to face together the financial, managerial, and other opportunities that confront a company during its early growth. With that partnership relationship, we believe that entrepreneurs backed by Sutter Hill have launched more successful startups and grown more $100 million revenue companies than any other venture capital firm in the United States during the past 25 years.

Sutter Hill Ventures is actively looking for equity investments in privately held companies throughout the United States. Our interests lie primarily with companies that produce products with some degree of technology and whose markets are potentially worldwide. Our dollar participation may initially range from $100,000 up to $2,000,000 per investment; larger equity needs can easily be put together by us with other leading venture capital firms. Our ultimate objective is to have the company in which we invest either go public or get acquired so we can recycle these dollars into new investments. This cycle typically may take five to seven years; therefore, we are long-term investors.

We are primarily interested in financing startups, and we expect to continue to be a leader among venture capital firms in starting new companies. Measurex, Integrated Genetics, Dionex, Qume, Biomation, Diablo Systems, and Xidex all got their starts at Sutter Hill. More recently, we have been the founding investor of companies such as Apollo Computer, Priam, Quantum, LSI Logic, Mentor Graphics, LifeScan, Relational Technology, and Cohesive Network. We understand startups and find them to be both exciting and rewarding.

Additionally, we are interested in making new equity investments in existing high technology companies as well as buying stock from existing stockholders. The latter approach could provide liquidity for some stockholders and give the company its first institutional investor to help promote its future success.

We do desire a seat on the board when the dollar investment becomes large. As emphasized earlier, we wish to become a partner with management to help assure the future success of the company and are prepared to assist management in any way. We invite you to call the companies where Sutter Hill has been a significant partner with management. In addition to the companies previously mentioned, we have played an important partnership role at Masscomp, Prime Computer, Hybritech, Tellabs, Weitek, Linear Technology, VMX, and Gemini Research.

Sierra Ventures Management Company
Menlo Park, California

Considerations in Evaluating Potential Investments

Management Team.   Who are the key members of the management team, particularly the president, chief operating officer, or chief executive officer? Have they had prior profit and loss responsibility? What organizations have they managed in the past and what results were achieved? Are they likely to attract a strong group of managers and employees to their venture? What is their reputation within their industry? How relevant and substantial is their past experience? If the founding team needs management strengthening, are the founders willing to accept necessary changes?

Nature of Product or Service.   What product or service is the company offering? How is it unique? How can its uniqueness be protected over time? Who are current and potential competitors and what is the proposed venture's competitive advantage? What size market share is projected and how quickly can it be obtained? Does the industry have attractive growth prospects and profit margins? What are the marketing risks? Is the venture likely to become a technical and/or marketing leader? Are there any conflicts with current Sierra interests?

Financial Outlook.   How large and profitable can the company become . . . and how quickly? What are the chances of the venture generating at least $25 million in annual revenue with a profitable operating history within five to seven years? How soon after startup does the venture turn profitable? How large are projected profit margins? Does industry experience suggest these margins are attainable? Is management's financial plan realistic? Are the true financing needs of the business understood from the outset? How capital intensive is the investment and what are the likely sources for this capital? Longer term, is the business likely to be attractive for a private purchase, public offering, or some other type of eventual liquidity?

Initial Investors. Who are the other investors and what type of future support, both financial and managerial, are they likely to provide? Are the other investors' goals, objectives, and timetables likely to be consistent with Sierra's?

Size, Timing, and Cost of Investment. How big of an investment is required? (Sierra normally seeks to invest at least $1,000,000 in a company during the first year of our relationship.) How soon is the venture likely to require additional capital and what is Sierra's expected participation? Is the valuation being put on the company consistent with market conditions and Sierra's return objectives?

Bibliography

Sylvester, David. "The Ghosts of a Bull Market." In "Business Monday," *San Jose Mercury News*, August 10, 1987.

Maran, Meredith. "How to Shrink an Engineer." *West* magazine, *San Jose Mercury News*, July 27, 1986.

Bennett Jr., Thomas E. "What Do Bankers Want?" *Inc.*, June, 1987, pp. 149-150.

Clifford, Donald K., and Cavanaugh, Richard E. *The Winning Performance*. New York: Bantam Books, 1985.

Coyne, Kevin. "Sustainable Competitive Advantage—What It Is, What It Isn't." *Business Horizons*, January/February, pp. 27-34.

Drucker, Peter. *Innovation and Entrepreneurship*. New York: Harper & Row, 1985.

Engstrom, Ted W., and David J. Juroe. *The Work Trap*. Old Tappan, NJ: Fleming H. Revell, 1979.

Freudenberger, Herbert J. *Burnout: How to Beat the High Cost of Success*. New York: Bantam Books, 1980.

Harrell, Wilson. "Entrepreneurial Terror," *Inc.*, February 1987, pp. 74-76.

Kaufman, Steve. "High-tech Survivalists." *San Jose Mercury News*, September 29, 1986.

Mamis, Robert A. "Great Companies That Were Started with $1,000 or Less: The Secrets of Bootstrapping." *Inc.*, September 1991, pp. 52-70.

Peters, Tom. "On Excellence." *San Jose Mercury News*, March 27, 1986.

Porter, Michael. "How to Get a Competitive Edge." *The Economist*, January 15, 1987, p. 57.

Porter, Michael. "The State of Strategic Thinking." *The Economist*, May 23, 1987, pp. 17-22.

Ries, Al, and Jack Trout. *Marketing Warfare*. New York: Penguin Books, 1986.

Ries, Al, and Jack Trout. *Positioning*. New York: Warner Books, 1981.

Uttal, Bro. "Inside the Deal That Made Bill Gates $350,000,000." *Fortune*, July 21, 1986, pp. 23-31.

INDEX